MYTH, MAGIC, AND MYSTERY

One Hundred Years of American Children's Book Illustration

Introductory Essay by Michael Patrick Hearn

Essays by
Trinkett Clark and H. Nichols B. Clark

6 Febury 1997
For Tom,
with best wishes,
Nil and TRinkett Clark
and
Michael Patrick Hearn

ROBERTS RINEHART PUBLISHERS
in cooperation with
THE CHRYSLER MUSEUM OF ART

W9-AVK-853

IN MEMORY
OF
JAMES MARSHALL
AND
MARGOT TOMES
MPH

FOR CHARLOTTE ALLEGRA RICE CLARK
AND
HER GRANDPARENTS
DOROTHY BLAKE CLARK AND CHARLES ARTHUR CLARK, JR.
ROSEMAE SAIBEN CLARK AND CLINTON RICE CLARK
WHO OPENED SO MANY DOORS AND MINDS

TC AND HNBC

Copyright © 1996 by The Chrysler Museum of Art
International Standard Book Numbers 1-57098-079-9 (paper)
and 1-57098-080-2 (cloth)
Library of Congress Catalog Card Number 96-67396

Published by Roberts Rinehart Publishers
5455 Spine Road, Mezzanine West, Boulder, Colorado 80301

Published in the UK and Ireland by Roberts Rinehart Publishers
Trinity House, Charleston Road, Dublin 6, Ireland

Distributed in the U.S. and Canada by Publishers Group West

Book design by Frederick R. Rinehart and E. Jack Van Zandt

Printed in Hong Kong

Exhibition schedule for *Myth, Magic, and Mystery: One Hundred Years
of American Children's Book Illustration:*

The Chrysler Museum of Art, Norfolk, Virginia: June 2, 1996-September 8, 1996
The Memphis Brooks Museum of Art, Memphis, Tennessee:
November 3, 1996-January 6, 1997
The Delaware Art Museum, Wilmington, Delaware: February 7, 1997-April 6, 1997

TABLE OF CONTENTS

FOREWORD

We are pleased to present *Myth, Magic, and Mystery: One Hundred Years of American Children's Book Illustration,* the first comprehensive exhibition to survey this important subject. Considerable attention has been paid to the early practitioners of this genre, notably Howard Pyle, N. C. Wyeth, and their followers, but no one has attempted to explore the evolution of illustration with its connections and divergences over the past century. The task has proved formidable, especially since in recent years upwards of 5,500 children's books are published annually. Equally significant, people of all ages have expressed very strong opinions about their favorite illustrators, and most of the time we have included sanctioned examples. The selection process does, however, leave lots of room for discussion, and we hope that visitors will see old friends and make new ones. Since the material crosses several generations, we also encourage parents and grandparents to introduce special parts of their own childhoods to their children and grandchildren. Finally, we hope by removing the illustration from its accustomed context as part of a book, to be seen as artwork on its own, that visitors will come to appreciate the high level of quality and seriousness of purpose that these artists bring to their task.

We are deeply indebted to the many public and private owners who have so willingly lent to the exhibition. All of the artists who were approached responded with great enthusiasm and generosity, and we were especially gratified that they recognized the merit of the project. Indeed, nearly every loan request found a positive response, and we express our heartfelt thanks to our museum colleagues and to the private collectors whose wonderful loans make this a very special exhibition.

This project and its catalogue received generous support from The Henry Luce Foundation, Inc., and additional funding has been provided by the Ezra Jack Keats Foundation. We encountered the unusual challenge of securing publication permissions from artists and publishing houses for nearly 250 works, and should like to recognize the generosity of both the artists and their publishers. We are extremely grateful to HarperCollins, Simon & Schuster, Houghton Mifflin, The Putnam & Grosset Group, Dr. Seuss Enterprises, L. P., Western Publishing Company, Inc. and Harcourt Brace and Company for their exceptional generosity. Our thanks go to Penguin USA, Little, Brown and Company, William Morrow, Random House, Doubleday Bantam Dell, Farrar, Straus, and Giroux, and J. F. Schreiber Verlag, for their cooperation.

We are also indebted to E. A. Carmean and his staff at the Memphis Brooks Museum of Art, and to Steve Bruni and his staff, especially Jenine Culligan and Mary Holahan, of the Delaware Art Museum, for their enthusiasm in hosting the exhibition at their respective institutions.

The exhibition has been organized by guest curator and independent scholar Michael Patrick Hearn, H. Nichols B. Clark, Curator of American Art at the Chrysler Museum of Art, and Trinkett Clark, former Curator of Twentieth-century Art at the Chrysler Museum of Art. We owe special thanks to them, although they did admit that it was, in the words of one of the artists, William Joyce, "like being paid to go to recess." In their preface they thank the many people who have contributed to the realization of this exhibition. I will not repeat their names here but do wish to add my thanks to theirs, especially to the many members of the Museum's staff whose dedication ensured the success of this project. Finally, we all express special thanks to Rick Rinehart and Jack Van Zandt of Roberts Rinehart Publishers for the excellent design and publication of this book, and to Liliane McCarthy who elegantly edited the manuscripts and provided a sensitive sounding–board for ideas.

Catherine H. Jordan
Acting Director

PREFACE

Anyone who has participated in the experience of a child learning to read knows what an exciting and liberating rite of passage it is. Reading not only opens up vast new realms of information and imagination, it also fosters an independence that is crucial to maturity. From the middle of the seventeenth century, ideas about treating children as individuals and new approaches to education began to take shape. Jan Amos Comenius' *Orbis sensualium pictus* (1658) laid the groundwork for some of these attitudes, especially the role of pictures in the teaching process, and John Locke in his *Some Thoughts Concerning Education* (1693) stated his belief that if children were stimulated by pictures in books, they would be more inclined to read. The enjoyment of pictures, which utilizes sight, is a concrete experience rather than an abstract phenomenon of sound. As a result, the visual encounter generates greater understanding.

Ellen Key, in her prophetic book *The Century of the Child*, which appeared in 1900, argued that our century was going to endow child development with its rightful emphasis and introduce children to the educational process at a much earlier stage of life than had been standard. Within this framework, books and particularly pictures books would assume a significant role.

The central motivation for this exhibition and accompanying book emanates from a reflection of Howard Pyle, one of the founders of the American tradition in illustration, about the rewards of his career:

> We forget the books we read as grown-ups, but the stories of childhood leave an indelible impression, and their author always has a niche in the temple of memory from which the image is never cast out to be thrown into the rubbish-heap of things that are outgrown and out lived.

Although Pyle here honors the text, he was equally devoted to the artistic interpretation. Recognizing the symbiosis of text and illustration, this project focuses on the art to explore a truth that continues to have a profound resonance and provides the first comprehensive survey of American children's book illustration from the turn of the century down to the present. We hope to explore an aspect of American art that has not received the attention it merits and to acknowledge its foundations in the rich British and continental tradition. In identifying universal as well as specifically American themes found in stories such as "Little Red Riding Hood" and "Cinderella" or "Rip Van Winkle" and *Uncle Remus: His Songs and His Sayings*, the authors will articulate why these narratives achieved the impact and longevity that they have enjoyed.

The exhibit covers the past century and surveys what the authors consider among the best children's book illustration of the period. It commences with the florescence of illustration in America and culminates in the present, a period of tremendous energy and zeal for picture making despite formidable competition from electronic media. The exhibit and book will be divided into four major categories: "And the Dish Ran Away with the Spoon: A First Look at the World of Words, from Mother Goose to Dr. Seuss,"; "Here and Now, Then and There: Stories for Young Readers"; "High Adventure and Fantasy: Art for All Ages"; "Happily Ever After: Fairy Tales, Fables and Myths." The twenty-six letters of the alphabet will be represented by different artists to offer a rich range of style and variation, and certain classic stories will be shown through several examples done from periods to reflect the vagaries of aesthetic taste.

Among those aspects of the exhibit central to American ideas and culture, works included will provide numerous insights into distinctly American art and attitudes, as well as probe their identification with an American spirit. For example, Ingri and Edgar Parin d'Aulaire won the Caldecott Medal, the premier artistic award, for their illustrations of *Abraham Lincoln* in 1940, and James Daugherty won the Newbery Medal, the corresponding literary award, for *Daniel Boone* (which he also illustrated) in the same year. Without doubt, these paradigms of American justice and right were embraced at a time when such noble concepts were being shattered by the unfolding events in Europe. Artistically, the illustrations in these two books reflect Social Realist and Art Deco aesthetics. Consequently, an artistic and social pulse can be felt through children's book illustration, and we hope to explore these phenomena throughout.

As a result, this undertaking explores the art of illustration in a broader and more meaningful art-historical and sociological context. The extended time line enables the reader to understand the changing role of children's book illustration in America. Tied to a pragmatic, worldly attitude that has informed American artistic expression since Colonial times, there exists a certain continuity. Despite the allegiance to a prosaic expression that deemphasized fantasy, the earlier artistic traditions conveyed a sheltered almost patronizing attitude towards children and their existence.

The wide range of material will enable children, parents, and grandparents to "connect" with some of their favorite books and through this experience participate in a shared educational and cultural moment. Both image and word constitute an important form of communication between generations. In an era plagued by the dissolution of the nuclear family, such cooperative undertakings are crucial, and children's literature performs a vital sociological function. The exhibit and book, we hope, provides limitless opportunity for active response to what is on view, and in this way makes its own "indelible impression."

This project evolved out of a love of reading to our daughter Charlotte, but we quickly realized how vast and complex the undertaking was. Fortunately, through the good graces of Karl Michael Emrys, we stumbled upon Michael Patrick Hearn, who was the right person to give the exhibit and book the shape and focus it required. It has been a pleasure to work with Michael and to draw from his vast wealth of knowledge and insight. While it has been a collaborative effort, to him must go the not-cowardly lion's share of credit.

Many people have assisted immeasurably in making this project a reality. First, we would like to thank Catherine H. Jordan, acting director of The Chrysler Museum of

Art, who provided unwavering support in the realization of our objectives. Most of the Museum's staff helped in innumerable ways, and we would like to express our gratitude to them. Foremost, Georgia Lasko, who took care of so many details and kept so many different logistical components on the right track. The Registrar's office, Catherine Jordan and Irene Roughton, handled many complex shipping arrangements, and the art handlers, Willis Potter, Sue Christian, Carol Cody, and Richard Hovorka, matted and framed many works and installed the show in the handsome space designed by Jim Armbruster and prepared by Stewart Howard, Ricardo Lawrence, William Hooten, and James Hopkins. Scott Wolff photographed many of the works, and to him we are deeply grateful. The library staff, Rena Hudgins, Susan Midland, Julia Burgess, and Peter Dubeau, attended to incessant requests with cheerful efficiency. Allen Wallace, Mary Howell, and Lita Liwag-Sutcliffe worked diligently to prepare grant applications for the catalogue and exhibition, and Steve Kazansky, Sandy Rech and Catherine Johnson made sure we spent the largesse wisely. Finally, to Ann Vernon, Lynne Priest, Ruth Sanchez, and Chioke Murray of the Education Department, our thanks for developing creative programming during the run of the exhibit, and to Donna Drew Sawyer of the Marketing and Communications Department and Steve Leickert our gratitude for making these programs a success. Just beyond our walls, we would like especially to thank the staff of the Children's Department of the Norfolk Public Library: Terri Raymond, Terry Wanser, Eunice Jones, and Patricia Talley.

In addition to the lenders and artists without whose cooperation this exhibition could not have been possible, many individuals assisted in the success of this project. To Rita Dove we are extremely grateful for her permission in allowing us to quote "The First Book" in full and to her assistant, Leslie Williams, for making the necessary arrangements. We would like to thank: Anne Anninger and Margaret Smith, The Houghton Library, Harvard University; Anna Lou Ashby, Cara Dennison, Charles E. Pierce, Jr., Stephanie Wiles, and David Wright, The Pierpont Morgan Library; Christopher Beetles; Mary E. Bogan and Alicia Ahlvers, The May Massee Collection, Emporia State University; Andreas Brown; Victoria Clark, Genë Harris, Virginia O'Hara, and Christine Podmaniczky, Brandywine River Museum; Andrew Cosentino, Sybille Jagusch, Tambra Johnson, Harry Katz, and Margaret Coughlan, Library of Congress; James Cummins and Ingrid Turner; Rodolphe d'Erlanger; Dennis M. V. David; Allan Daniel and Kendra Krienke-Daniel; Mr. and Mrs. Walter A. Eberstadt. Katie Dunkelman; Caitlyn Dlouhy, Holly McGhee, and William Morris, HarperCollins; Cindi DiMarzo, Putnam & Grosset Group; Rodney Engen; Stephen Ferguson, Firestone Library, Princeton University; Frances Foster, Farrar, Straus and Giroux; Andrea V. Grimes, San Francisco Public Library; Paul Goldman, Department of Prints and Drawings, The British Museum; Duffy Goble, Victoria Jones, and Bernard McTigue, The Library, University of Oregon; Vincent Giroud and Sandra Markham, Beinecke Library, Yale University; Gregory Gilbert; Mr. and Mrs. Peter E. Gilbert; Anne Hobbs, Victoria and Albert Museum; Trudy Hansen and Barbara Trelstad, Jane Voorhees Zimmerli Art Museum, Rutgers

University; Sinclair Hitchings and Karen Shafts, Boston Public Library; Maryl D. Hosking, Margaret Glover, Robert Rainwater and Roberta Waddell, The New York Public Library; Karen Hoyle, Carolyn Davis, Andrew Kluess, and Melissa Pauna, The Kerlan Collection, University of Minnesota; Sally Hartman; Constance Kimmerle, Karol Schmiegel and Stephen Urice, Rosenbach Museum and Library; Thomas Jalkut and Andree Saulnier, Nutter, McClennen & Fish; Dee Jones and Pat Peterson, The de Grummond Collection, University of Southern Mississippi; Mr. and Mrs. Parker Jayne; Nina Kooij; Mr. and Mrs. Frederic R. Kellogg; Karen Lightner and Martha Repman, The Free Library of Philadelphia; Billie M. Levy; Judy Larson, The High Museum; Jerry J. Mallett, The Mazza Collection Galleria, The University of Findlay; Patrick Maund; Richard Michelson; Angeline Moscatt and Despina Croussouloudis, Central Children's Room, Donnell Library, The New York Public Library; Charles Price; Paula Quint, The Children's Book Council; Sue Reed and Carol Troyen, Museum of Fine Arts, Boston; Ellen Embardo, Richard Fyffe, and Heather Tebbs, Homer Babbidge Library, The University of Connecticut; Charles Ritchie and Lynn Russell, National Gallery of Art; Walt and Roger Reed; David Russell; Lois Sarkisian; Justin G. Schiller; Charles Scribner III; Mr. and Mrs. Carl Shirley; Nicholas Smith; Mary Stevens; Elizabeth Stone; Mr. and Mrs. W. B. Dixon Stroud; Anne Elisabeth Suter; Wendy Watson; and Ann White.

M.P.H.
H.N.B.C.
T.C.
June 1996

I

Michael Patrick Hearn

DISCOVER, EXPLORE, ENJOY

125. Hans Augusto Rey (1898-1977). Born in Hamburg, Germany; came to the U.S. in 1940. "George Sees Yellow Hat," from *Curious George* [Boston: Houghton Mifflin Company, 1940]. © Margret E. Rey, 1940; Reprinted with the permission of Houghton Mifflin Company. de Grummond Children's Literature Collection, University of Southern Mississippi

A book has an obligation to build taste, to cultivate a sense of lasting values. It should be a work of art and beauty, created with love and produced with care. It should convey a sense of quality, inside and out, through the harmonious blend of type and image, through fine art work and attractive colors, through the use of good print on the right paper. What an object lesson in esthetics this could be to a child, painlessly and easily absorbed by him. Add to this a theme handled with a dash of imagination, of meaningful sense and nonsense, and you have all the elements of a book the child would cherish.

Fritz Eichenberg[1]

I have been asked: "Don't you find it limiting to draw for children?" Children are people. People are people. To children even animals are people. As soon as you remove the *false distinction*, drawing is a limitless endeavor. I believe, furthermore, that there is an *artificial distinction* between "art" and other human activities. Art is not something special, but only an extension, one more manifestation, of life. . . . There is no real distinction between "art" and illustration, between old art and new art. There is only good art and bad art.

Uri Shulevitz[2]

Illustration has long been treated as the poor relation of the arts. It is humored, even secretly enjoyed and admired, but rarely given any serious critical attention. The prevalent attitude towards illustration is that the artist ultimately compromises his or her vision to meet the constraints of commerce. Perhaps this is true, but many have mastered these restrictions to produce some extraordinary images. As the history of art proves, restraint and repression can produce great art just as readily as freedom may. "The illustrator has to guard the integrity of the manuscript he is illustrating," Fritz Eichenberg warned. "He has to keep in mind that his art is going to be reproduced, printed, locked up with type between the covers of a book. That takes a lot of self-discipline, to which not many artists like to be submitted."[3] Illustration also requires that an artist not only be faithful to the text, but express the designer's unique character. The common complaint is that the illustrator does not invent—he merely follows the writer. Of course that prejudice is meaningless when the artist is also the author, but in that case the illustrator is criticized for producing narrative rather than pure art, whatever "pure art" may mean.

One must also recognize that those who have given any serious thought to this issue are usually of literary rather than artistic training. They are primarily book people, readers. Their principle concern is how well an illustration depicts the text, art as companion rather than art as itself. They have no visual vocabulary with which to discuss the aesthetics of an illustration, what it requires as a work of art. Illustration is indeed a hybrid form, but once that is recognized it can be appreciated for what it is. "Too much distinction is made today between 'fine art' and 'applied art,' between 'fine art' and 'commercial art,'" Barbara Cooney has complained. "Somewhere between these terms hovers the word 'illustration.' Yet all these terms are of comparatively recent vintage in the history of art. In ancient Greece all art was covered by one word: *tekhne*. The classical artist used his skill whence the need arose. The artist today whose pictures lie within book covers should work with as much care, skill, and understanding as the artist whose pictures hang on the wall in gold frames."[4] Indeed the importance is the work itself. Illustration is an art with its own history that is just as worthy of attention as any of the "fine" arts.

Artists, unlike critics and curators, do not always worry about such distinctions. Nearly every major painter from Manet to Matisse did *livres d'artist*. And some of these were actually children's books. Marie Laurencin, Salvador Dali, and Max Ernst all illustrated Lewis Carroll. The very first book Joan Miró ever did was Lise Hirtz's collection of children's verse *Il etait une petite pie* (1920). Pierre Bonnard provided the pictures for Léopold Chauveau's fables *Histoire du poisson-scie et du poisson-marteau* (1923) and *Les Histoires du pétit Renaud* (1927). Jules Pascin produced an elegant edition of Charles Perrault's *Cendrillon* (1930), and Maurice Denis drew a limited edition coloring book, *Premiers paysages* (1926). El Lissitsky designed the first abstract picture book, *Pro dva kvadrata* (1922). This Suprematist parable then inspired Kurt Schwitters, Kate Steinmetz, and Theo Van Doesburg to collaborate on the Dada children's book *Die Scheuche* (1925). Likewise Oskar Kokoschka, Alexandre Benois, George Grosz, John Heartfield, Karl Hofer, Marc Chagall, Jean Cocteau, Andy Warhol, and so many others have all at one time appeared between the covers of a children's book.

The English artist Walter Crane once observed that children's illustration appeals "to designers of an imaginative tendency, for in a sober and matter-of-fact age they afford perhaps the only outlet for unrestricted flights of fancy open to the modern illustrator, who likes to revolt against 'the despotism of facts.' "[5] Apparently some artists actually do *like* illustrating children's books. "I wanted to paint purely that which gave me pleasure, scenes that interested me," Ludwig Bemelmans admitted, "and one day I found that the audience for that kind of painting was a vast reservoir of impressionists who did very good work themselves, who were very clear-eyed and capable of enthusiasm. I addressed myself to children."[6] However, Robert McCloskey confessed when he won the Caldecott Medal for *Make Way for Ducklings* (1941), "I'm not a children's illustrator. I'm just an artist who, among other things, does children's books." He later said, that as an art student in Boston, "It never would have occurred to me to *draw* those things [ducks] or to paint them unless they were in a deep forest pool with a nude, perhaps, and a droopy tree and a gazelle or two, just to improve the composition."[7] By contrast *New Yorker* cartoonist William Steig humbly said, "Books for children are something I take very seriously. I am hopeful that more and more the work I do for children, as well as the work I do for adults, will approach the condition of art."[8]

The low regard towards illustration and children's book illustration in particular that persisted for years even now makes it difficult to appraise the art in any depth. So much is now lost or destroyed. Except in a few remarkable instances, galleries generally did not exhibit original art for children's books until fairly recently. Most of those who did trade in it have been book dealers with no background in art. Museums have rarely bothered to collect it. Libraries have been more receptive to preserving it, but still only sporadically. Publishers, too, have shown little respect for illustrations. Until recently, they retained the work, as a rule, and treated it atrociously when they did not discard it. If it was returned at all, it was often not in the condition in which it was first submitted. Drawings and paintings have been scratched and smeared and stained and mangled and heavily marked up with pencil, ink, tape, glue, coffee, or greasy finger prints. Some have actually come back soiled with foot prints or tire tracks. Also, the illustrators themselves have not always respected their own work. The purpose of an illustration is to be reproduced, not displayed, and artists have employed certain shortcuts that have not always added to the life of the art. They often scrimp on materials. Papers discolor or disintegrate, colors fade, glues dry out, and Chinese white, often used to make corrections, tends to oxidize and turn grey.

Sometimes it is easier to appreciate all the art that goes into an illustration when it is divorced from the book in which it appears. It is remarkable how different the printed version looks next to the original, not just in scale but also in color and texture. There are certain drawbacks, of course, in exhibiting art from books. An illustration is often only a fragment of a larger work. The perfect picture book is a distinctive art form in which every element of design from cover to cover contributes to the whole. Lynd Ward described the book as "a unique physical and emotional phenomenon," "an integrated production in which [the artist's] work as a maker of pictures based on the subject matter of the text dovetailed with his function as over-all designer, manipulating details of typography, pictures, layout, endpaper design and binding materials into a single orchestral combination calculated to produce an effect on the reader in tonal harmony with the verbal impact of the text."[9] It is a sequential work, and therefore the placement and pacing of the pictures are important principles of the form. Ward noted that for the illustrator, "the turning of the page is the thing he has that no other worker in the visual arts has: the power to control a succession of images in time, so that the cumulative effect upon the viewer is the result of not only what images are thrown at him, but the order in which they come. Thus the significance of those coming late in the sequence is built up by what comes earlier."[10] A single illustration on exhibit cannot suggest its relationship to the rest of the pictures and therefore cannot fully suggest the work of art as originally conceived and executed by the artist. The same problem exists in a book exhibit in a library unless the leaves are somehow turned for the viewer. Also many people are disconcerted by the "windows" through the picture, white spaces left for the placement of type. It makes the artwork appear incomplete even though it is only a utilitarian device.

The technology does put enormous constraints on designers. While full-color photoreproduction affords them the luxury of employing almost any medium possible, other cheaper processes generally require preseparated art with paper or acetate overlays for each of the tones to be printed on top of the key drawing. Often to get a cleaner, crisper black line even in full-color work, the artist will have the underlying drawing photographed and printed in blue (which the camera does not pick up) on watercolor paper so that each color may be applied one at a time. Then the drawing and the painting can be shot separately to get sharper definition of line and tone. Consequently the original art may be unimpressive when it is shown broken down into its basic components. The printed version is the final work of art.

Of course, even once illustration is accepted as art, one must get past the prejudices against children's book illustration. How can all those bunnies and fairies be taken seriously? Perhaps no more seriously than all the mutilated martyrs and overripe goddesses of Renaissance painting or than the big blotches, bad drawing, broken crockery, and political cant of contemporary art. Theme is not the final issue, but the manner in which it is presented. The best artists transcend subject matter, however banal or puerile. James Johnson Sweeney, former director of the Museum of Modern Art, argued that being "essentially a work of visual art—something that speaks directly to the eye and through the eye," children's book illustration should never serve as "merely a vessel for the conveyance of information. Its real role is that played by a Gothic stained glass window in the Middle Ages, or a mosaic in the apse of a Romanesque church. It should be aimed primarily to stimulate the imagination through the eye—to educate in the true sense, by drawing something out of the observer—to mature the observer through stimulation, to exercise the imagination and develop the power for creating images. It is a work of visual art and should be approached, in the making, as one, and weighed on its completion by the same standards."[11] Robert Lawson said that there is no such thing as a children's illustrator, just an illustrator. "The moment anyone's work looks as though it were obviously done for children," he argued, "then we are talking down to children, we are talking baby talk with illustrations which I think is low and stupid. I think that to *rise* to the levels demanded by the clear ideals of children is a far greater task and a much more satisfying accomplishment than meeting the muddle-headed demands of their elders."[12] Perhaps it is best to approach children's book illustration with a smile rather than a straight face. Then there is much to admire there. The ability to delight requires as much art as that required to outrage or offend. After a while, "serious" art can get terribly tiresome as the Whitney Biennial proves. The one thing it cannot and dare not do is bore.

The children's book illustrator has an enormous responsibility. No one can deny that what is read and seen in childhood has inestimable power on the formation of a mind. Often one's earliest introduction to art does not take place in a gallery or museum, but through a picture book; and first impressions may indeed be the most profound and lasting. The artist has enormous power. One sees the pictures before one reads the text, leaving immediate impressions long before the authors have a chance to speak. It is John Tenniel's Alice whom most people remember, not Lewis Carroll's. The most vivid and lasting impression of Winnie-the-Pooh is probably how E. H. Shepard chose to draw him and not how A. A. Milne describes this bear of little brain. Yes, illustrators bear an enormous responsibility. Characters and images encountered in childhood are rarely forgotten. Ludwig Bemelman's Madeline, Maurice Sendak's Wild Things, Garth Williams' Charlotte and Wilbur, H. A. Rey's Curious George, and James Marshall's George and Martha may become friends for life to be passed on from one generation to the next. And Hilary Knight's Eloise will surely survive long after the Plaza has been torn down.

THE PIONEERS

Of course there could be no children's book illustration if there was no children's literature, and books designed specifically for young readers were generally neglected until relatively late in human history. Prior to the Romantic age, childhood seemed to be something to be overcome like the measles rather than enjoyed. The literary pabulum fed unruly boys and girls in those dark ages of the nursery were books of courtesy, grammar, natural history, and religious instruction. Most were not illustrated, and if they were it was with abominable cuts. When the majority of the people were illiterate, books were luxuries. Princes sometimes received sumptuous volumes, usually fable books, filled with elegant plates, but these were few and far between. Literature of distinction written specifically for the young began to emerge at the court of Louis XIV with Jean de La Fontaine's *Fables choisies* (1668–1693) and Charles Perrault's *Histoires ou Contes du temps passé* (1697), but they did not immediately generate any school of juvenile illustration. Most children's books remained uninspired and uninspiring, and boys and girls desperately seized on the more imaginative and exciting adult lore such as *The Pilgrim's Progress* (1678), *Robinson Crusoe* (1719), and *Gulliver's Travels* (1726).

John Locke demanded in *Some Thoughts Concerning Education* (1693) that learning be a game rather than a chore, and one way to make reading more effective would be through the inclusion of pictures to spark the interest of the child. All books for boys and girls should be illustrated. "If his Aesop has pictures in it," Locke explained, "it will entertain [the child] much the better, and encourage him to read." Apparently the first one to practice Locke's principle of combining amusement with education and to profit by it was John Newbery, the first important publisher to specialize in children's books. Unfortunately, the quality of the anonymous cuts in his pretty little Dutch-papered picture books was poor. The only good thing that can be said in favor of Newbery's illustrations is that they were always there and there were plenty of them. No, children's book illustration did not really come of age until the publication of *German Popular Tales* (1823–1824), the first English translation of Grimm's fairy tales and the very first illustrated edition in any language of those famous stories. This classic collection of German folklore not only revolutionized the world's juvenile literature by providing amusement for its own sake, it was also the first masterpiece of children's book illustration due to George Cruikshank's delightful etchings. "Here," explained Charlotte M. Yonge in *Macmillan's Magazine* (August 1869), "was once again the true unadulterated fairy tale, and happy the child who was allowed to revel in it—perhaps

176a. (left) George Cruikshank (1792-1878). British. "Cinderella and the Glass Slipper," from *The Fairy Library* [London: David Bogue, 1854]. Museum of Fine Arts, Boston, Bequest of John T. Spaulding 1948. 760

176b. (right) George Cruikshank (1792-1878). British. "Cinderella and the Glass Slipper," from *The Fairy Library* [London: David Bogue, 1854]. Rare Books and Special Collections, Princeton University Library

happier if under protest, and only permitted a sweet daily taste." Perhaps even more important, as William Thackeray declared in *The Westminster Review* (June 1840), was that Cruikshank's plates constituted "the first real, kindly, agreeable, and infinitely amusing and charming illustrations in a child's book in England." John Ruskin with his usual hyperbole called them the greatest thing in etching since Rembrandt. That may be so, but they were also funny. "There must be no smiling with Cruikshank," declared Thackeray. "A man who does not laugh outright is a dullard, and has no heart."

Here lies one of the principle problems in appreciating early nineteenth-century book illustration. In a sense, the form of reproduction was nearly as crucial as the design itself. In preparing the Grimm plates there was no middleman, no craftsman to come between the conception and execution of the art. Cruikshank designed and etched his own plates. No final drawings for the illustrations survive—only preliminaries—because the print itself is the actual work of art. Cruikshank worked out the composition in pencil or ink and then transferred it to the plate, making final changes when he etched the picture. To fully understand his achievement as an illustrator, it is perhaps best to study the earlier sketch and the finished etching side by side [cat. nos. 176a and 176b].

158a. John Tenniel (1820-1914). British. "The Mad Hatter's Tea Party," from *Alice in Wonderland* [London: Macmillan and Co., 1865]. Purchase, A. H. Parker Fund, Manuscript Department, Houghton Library, Harvard University

Cruikshank never learned the craft of white line wood engraving, soon the most popular form used in the reproduction of book illustrations. Although he did know how to draw on wood for reproduction, he never prepared the blocks himself as he had his etchings. It was a technique, perfected by Thomas Bewick in the late eighteenth century, that spawned a whole industry of wood engravers, but it did not really come into its own as an art form until the Victorian age. The Pre-Raphaelites like Dante Gabriel Rossetti, John Everett Millais, and Edward Burne-Jones perfected this method of commercial illustration through their haunting designs, but they, like Cruikshank, did not prepare the cuts themselves. Surely the most famous wood engravings ever published are John Tenniel's illustrations for Lewis Carroll's *Alice's Adventures in Wonderland* (1865) and *Through the Looking-Glass and What Alice Found There* (1872). Here are the Mad Hatter, the March Hare, the Cheshire Cat, and all the others, maybe not exactly as Carroll imagined them, but as they are best known now [cat. no. 158a]. In a sense, Tenniel did for wood engraving what Cruikshank had done for copper etching. He brought new life to the form and created a masterpiece of children's book illustration. But unlike Cruikshank, Tenniel had to rely on the craftsman to complete the work for him.

Again there are no original drawings for the two Alice books, only preliminaries. Tenniel made a pencil study of an illustration, then traced the outline, and transferred the tracing to the block on which he made his final drawing, making any changes from the earlier sketch he wished. Tenniel drew with the hardest pencils directly on the wood and was left to the mercy of the craftsmen to "interpret" his picture. In this way all the actual "drawings" of the illustrations for the two books were destroyed when the blocks were engraved. The Dalziel Brothers, his engravers, perhaps should be considered co–designers of the illustrations for *Alice in Wonderland* and *Through the Looking-Glass*. Then metal plates were made of the engravings. No copy of the books was ever

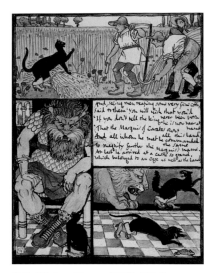

183. Walter Crane (1845-1915). British. "Puss Kills the Ogre," from *Puss in Boots* [London: George Routledge and Sons, 1873]. Museum of Fine Arts, Boston, Gift of Mrs. John L. Gardner 1892.2576

printed from the actual wood blocks. The fastidious Tenniel was a hard man to please. He persuaded Carroll to suppress the first edition of *Alice in Wonderland*, because he was unhappy with the printing. It may have been Carroll who had some cuts redesigned and reengraved. That of the White Rabbit as herald in *Alice in Wonderland* was scrapped and reworked for the final version. A completely new rendition of Hatta in prison in *Through the Looking-Glass* replaced the first even after it had been engraved and a proof pulled, and several of Alice as queen on the chessboard also were redone to give her dress less crinoline; "plugs," or little pieces of wood, were inserted in the blocks to make the corrections. The wood engraving, like the etching before, was the final work of art.

Carroll's Alice understood that pictures were just as important as conversations in children's stories, but the book itself did not become a work of art until Walter Crane began designing for the color printer Edmund Evans [cat. no. 183]. This was the era of the toybook, a cheaply printed pamphlet of eight pages of gaudy color pictures printed on one side of the leaf, but the inventive and eclectic Crane elevated this flimsy form to an art. While other printers employed chromolithography for their pictures, Evans specialized in a fairly new method of color wood engraving, which he perfected with Crane in this series. Crane made a drawing on the woodblock, and Evans engraved it and had a proof pulled for the artist to color. Then the printers tried to duplicate the tones with as few plates as possible. They began with black, red, yellow, blue, and a flesh tint; a remarkable variety of hue and texture was achieved through gradations with the engraver's burin and the overlapping of the colors. Later on, photography was introduced for the keyblocks, which saved Crane's original ink drawings, but again the artist colored the proofs as a guide to the engravers on the finished prints.

The young Crane's earliest toybooks were no better and no worse than many others on the market; but once he converted to the Arts and Crafts movement, he was determined to make them as artistically designed as any other decorative art. A friend in the navy happened to pass on to him some curious Japanese color prints, which gave Crane "the real impulse to that treatment in strong outlines, flat tints and solid blacks, which I adopted with variations in books of this kind from that time (about 1870) onwards."[13] He grew "accustomed to introduce into these children's book designs not only pictorial ideas which influenced one at the time, but any passing impression, or whim of fancy and form, as in details of dress, furniture, and decoration."[14] Whatever caught his eye— asian art, classical design, Venetian painting, and Persian miniatures—all found expression in his humble picture books. His vast erudition and careful execution of these illustrations earned him the title "Academician of the Nursery." Perhaps nowhere were the eclectic standards of the English Arts and Crafts movement better defined than in these toybooks. Contemporary decorators cribbed ideas from the illustrations; and mothers lined their nurseries with prints clipped from these picture books so their children might be weaned on tasteful design almost from birth.

When the publishers refused to give him a royalty on the toybooks, Crane quit and worked with Evans on another kind of children's book. In his selection of traditional nursery songs, *The Baby's Opera* (1877), Crane perfected his concept of the art of the book. Here he decorated every part of the book's makeup, covers, title page, contents page, and every other page in the book; and every design contributed to a single, unified artistic statement. In the sequel, *The Baby's Bouquet* (1878), Crane extended this design even further by adding decorative endpapers. Here finally was the modern artistic picture book, and every illustrator in the field owes much to Crane's legacy. It should also be noted that Crane was as much a master of black and white as of color, and his exquisite edition of *Household Stories from the Collection of the Bros. Grimm* (1882) remains one of the most beautifully illustrated and designed interpretations of the classic German folktales [cat. no. 151].

When at first Crane refused to follow *The Baby's Opera* with a sequel, Evans looked elsewhere for another picture book and discovered Kate Greenaway's *Under the Window* (1878). This pretty little collection of original verse, embellished with dainty color wood engravings, proved even more popular than Crane's efforts and inspired a Greenaway craze for baleful babes in old-fashioned dress both in Britain and abroad that has yet to fully subside. It is clear that Crane always resented Greenaway's success at what he thought was his expense. She was clearly a follower of his, but Greenaway brought a delicacy, grace, and innocence to her lovely editions of *Mother Goose* (1881) and Robert Browning's *The Pied Piper of Hamelin* (1888) that were lacking in Crane's more robust and sophisticated books [cat. no. 55a]. She was one of the first women to earn her living as an illustrator and was shrewd at business. She demanded and received a royalty, and her originals were returned to her for future sale in galleries.

151. Walter Crane (1845-1915). British. Cover from *Household Stories from the Collection of the Bros. Grimm* [London: Macmillan and Company, 1882]. Justin G. Schiller (Personal Collection)

55a. Kate Greenaway (1846-1901). British. "Where the waters rushed and fruit trees grew," Frontispiece for *The Pied Piper of Hamelin* [London: George Routledge and Sons, 1888]. The Pierpont Morgan Library, New York. Gift of Mrs. George Nichols, 1957.14. Norfolk only [Illust.]

54b. Randolph Caldecott (1846-1886). British. "The youth did ride, and soon did meet/John coming back amain," from William Cowper, *The Diverting History of John Gilpin* [London: George Routledge and Sons, 1878]. Private Collection

When Crane refused to illustrate any more toybooks, Evans hired Randolph Caldecott to continue the highly lucrative series. And he got a royalty. Evans was now able to print on both sides of a leaf and thus extended Caldecott's potential as a picture book illustrator with sixteen instead of eight pages. Crane may have been a master of compression, but Caldecott was a genius at expansion. He took the slimmest texts, only a few verses of some traditional nursery rhyme, and wove a whole engaging story in pictures around them. He literally filled in the blanks with all sorts of supplemental scenes that did not so much illustrate as extend the narrative possibilities. Except for some similarities in archaic subject matter, Caldecott's style, too, differed from Crane's. While Crane's figures seem static, Caldecott's jump all over the page [cat. nos. 54a and 54b]. While Crane tried to cram as much as he could into a composition, Caldecott followed in what he called "the art of leaving out as a science." He argued that "the fewer the lines the less error committed."[15] In contrast to Crane's cramped, stylized, and complex compositions, Caldecott's drawings looked lithe and spontaneous. "To this desolate field," noted Robert Lawson, "Randolph Caldecott brought the manna of a mature talent, gayety, spirited action, a universal and, in many cases, a sophisticated humor. These drawings are no shoddy hand-me-downs, tossed off at low cost for children. They were the product of one of the best illustrators of the day, excellently printed, artistically far superior to much of the adult fare of the time."[16]

In these toybooks, Evans and Caldecott were clinging to a declining craft. Photoreproduction was now the rage, but Caldecott much preferred the way color wood engraving reproduced his work to the new method. Crane declared in *Of the Decorative Illustration of Books Old and New* that "the photograph, with all its allied discoveries and its application to the service of the printing press, may be said to be as important a discovery in its effects on art and books as was the discovery of printing itself. It has already largely transformed the system of the production of illustrations and designs for books, magazines, and newspapers, and has certainly been the means of securing to the artist the advantage of possession of his original, while its fidelity, in the best processes, is, of course very valuable." But Caldecott demanded the old method. He tried process reproduction once and hated it. Yet Caldecott's drawings, like Crane's and Greenaway's, were photographed and then engraved on wood, so he could retain the originals or tart them up with color for exhibitions. He even avoided a black keyblock, preferring sepia, which gave a pleasant, almost faded antique finish to his eighteenth-century-inspired pictures. He sloshed the proofs with watercolor and achieved surprisingly attractive results from Evans' engravers. The old process provided him with the opportunity of making little changes in his illustrations before turning them over to Evans. "My method of going at once at the design on the very piece of paper which is to be needed," he explained, "frequently results in the necessity of slight modifications of proportion or expression in the figures. I feel bolder if I know that a knife or some Chinese white will clear away too wild a line or too clumsy a touch."[17]

54a. Randolph Caldecott (1846-1886). British. "His neighbour in such trim,/Laid down his pipe, flew to the gate,/And thus accosted him," from William Cowper, *The Diverting History of John Gilpin* [London: George Routledge and Sons, 1878]. Private Collection

While Crane was by nature a progressive, being one of the most visible members of the socialist Fabian Society, Greenaway and Caldecott traded in nostalgia. Their children's books celebrated a preindustrial Britain, where there were no railroads and certainly no factories to pollute the English landscape. "I thus had two formidable rivals in children's books," Crane admitted. "I do not know whether the children were more interested, but I think their elders were, in the work of Caldecott and Kate Greenaway, who seemed to suit the English taste more exactly perhaps than I did."[18] He was not far off. While much of Greenaway's and Caldecott's work is still in print, that by Crane, the true father of the picture book, is generally forgotten.

These three established a standard of fine book design that has often been emulated but rarely equalled. "Walter Crane and Caldecott were the pioneers," declared Beatrix Potter. "Their successors were imitators only."[19] Perhaps the artist most worthy of inclusion with Crane, Greenaway, and Caldecott was L. Leslie Brooke. His charming picture book designs encompass the refinement of Crane, the grace of Greenaway, and the humor of Caldecott. No one, not even Caldecott himself, drew more expressive animals than did Brooke in his classic *Johnny Crow's Garden* (1903). The English influence on the picture book also spread far beyond Britain's shore. In France, Louis-Maurice Boutet de Monvel further refined the principles of the art of the picture book in perhaps the most beautiful example ever published, *Jeanne d'Arc* (1896) [cat. no. 57a]. His color lithographs have never been duplicated in their delicacy of drawing and subtlety of color. This Frenchman was almost as well known in America

57a. (top) Louis-Maurice Boutet de Monvel (1851-1913). French. "Jeanne before the Dauphin, from *Jeanne d'Arc* [Paris: Plon, Nourrit & Co., 1896]. Memorial Art Gallery of the University of Rochester, gift of Simon N. Stein

177a. (left) Felix O. C. Darley, (1822-1888). American. "Cinderella with Fairy Godmother" from *Grandfather Lovechild's Nursery Stories. Fred Fearnought* [Philadelphia: George B. Zieber, 1847]. Rare Books and Special Collections, Princeton University Library

32a. (right) Henry Louis Stephens (1824-1882). American. "Froggie Dressing," from *Froggie Would A-Wooing Go* [New York: Hurd & Houghton, 1865]. Department of Printing and Graphic Arts, The Houghton Library, Harvard University

as he was in his homeland and profoundly influenced its artists, for he came to the United States to paint children's portraits as well as a suite of panels based upon his Joan of Arc illustrations now housed in the Corcoran Gallery of Art. The publication of *Jeanne d'Arc* in a multinational edition was a fitting way to end the first century of distinguished children's book illustration.

THE AMERICAN SPIRIT

While the art was flourishing in England and elsewhere, American illustration lagged far behind. The young republic had a finite literate public, and without a strong international copyright law, there was no real motivation for local designers to do better work. Publishers did not even have to hire them. If a person wanted to pirate a cut from a foreign publication, he was fully within his rights to take it without compensation. Also the formidable persistence of Puritanism in American education generally discouraged the use of any entertaining cuts in juvenile reading. The first important professional American illustrator is often said to be Alexander Anderson, the New York doctor turned artist; but his vocation was really wood engraving. More an artisan than an artist, he copied any Bewick cuts he could find for use in the books he was hired to illustrate.

Perhaps the true father of American illustration was F. O. C. Darley. This American-born artist's conventional but still charming American pictures graced American books by American-born authors like Washington Irving, James Fenimore Cooper, and Henry Wadsworth Longfellow. He was also Edgar Allan Poe's very first illustrator. Although not a prolific children's book artist, Darley was perhaps the earliest artist of note to depict such quintessential American heroes as Santa Claus and Yankee Doodle along with Cinderella, Tom Thumb, Robin Hood, Beauty and the Beast, and other celebrities of the European nursery [cat. no. 177a]. Arguably the finest picture book artist of the day was not Darley but the political cartoonist H. L. Stephens. He was a brilliant draughtsman and clever illustrator who is now unjustly ignored [cat. no. 32a]. Perhaps Stephens has been overlooked because there was nothing self-consciously American about his style or subject matter. He worked in the anthropomorphic manner of the famous French satirist J.–J. Grandville. Although Stephens is neglected today, right after the Civil War he produced a long series of remarkable toybooks as fine as any other published in the United States during the nineteenth century.

Reconstruction brought with it the first wave of truly American illustration through the numerous periodicals that suddenly sprang up in that expansive period. This unprecedented growth in the illustrated magazine trade carried over into the juvenile market as well. The principle children's magazines of the time were *The Riverside Magazine, Our Young Folks, Wide Awake, Harper's Young People*, and, most important of all, *St. Nicholas*. They kept the publishers well stocked with material for books, and all of them were chock–full of pictures by some of the best contemporary artists. They were rather haphazardly used in the magazines, and rarely did art directors consider the pictures' placement on the page. Crane noted how they were "often daringly driven through the text, scattering it right and left, like the effect of a coach and four upon a flock of sheep."[20] Nevertheless, these periodicals helped nurture the careers of a new generation of illustrators.

Specialization had not yet made a distinction between the careers of the adult and juvenile designers. Illustrators were interchangeable between the two markets, between the two audiences. Nearly everyone who contributed to *Harper's Magazine* likely showed up in *Harper's Young People;* an artist for *The Century* also found a place in *St. Nicholas.* Consequently, A. B. Frost was probably as well known and beloved by young readers for his regional humor as by their parents. After a brief stay in London where he worked on books by Charles Dickens and Lewis Carroll, Frost returned to the United States to become *the* American illustrator through new editions of *Uncle Remus: His Songs and His Sayings* (1895) and Thomas Bailey Aldrich's *The Story of A Bad Boy* (1894) as well as his extensive magazine work [cat. no. 208]. Never fond of the initial Uncle Remus illustrations by Frederick S. Church and James H. Moser, Joel Chandler Harris could not have been happier with Frost's pictures. He so admired them, he said, "because you have breathed the breath of life into these amiable brethren of wood and field, because, by a stroke here and touch there, you have conveyed into their quaint antics the illumination of your own inimitable humor, which is as true to our sun and soil as it is to the spirit and essence of the matter set forth. The book was mine, but now you have made it yours, both in span and pitch."[21] None can doubt his enthusiasm, for Frost brought Brer Rabbit and Brer Fox and all the other characters of these African-American folktales vividly to life. Howard Pyle likewise assured Frost "that you are the one and only real artistic humorist in the country, and that your humor is of a sort that is as broad and as deep as the great American heart. It has always been my opinion that long after the great raft of American painters and illustrators have passed away into oblivion, your work will remain as typifying the great American sense of humor which stands rooted in our humane American heart, and blossoms in a wit that is to be found nowhere else."[22]

Frost was only one of the many American artists who so effortlessly went from magazine to children's book illustration. Mark Twain hand-picked E. W. Kemble to illustrate *Adventures of Huckleberry Finn* (1884) after seeing a cartoon of his in the old *Life* [cat. no. 139]. Kemble, with his spidery line and backcountry subject matter, was an obvious disciple of Frost's.[23] Reginald Birch's reputation was secure when Frances Hodgson Burnett's *Little Lord Fauntleroy* (1886) made its debut in the pages of *St. Nicholas.* His racy line really belonged to the Caldecott school, but his best work was done for the American juvenile trade. He did not always think his was an enviable task. "Illustrations for children are difficult," he explained, "because the stories invariably introduce so many different things—animals, flowers, birds—and you have to get them right; to say nothing of the exercise of imagination necessary to picture gnomes, fairies and other fanciful creatures."[24] But he kept at it for sixty years.

Perhaps the most inventive American children's book illustrator of the period was Peter Newell. Like Frost, Kemble, and Birch, he made his way through the magazines.

139. E. W. Kemble (1861-1933). American. Frontispiece, *Adventures of Huckleberry Finn* [New York: Charles L. Webster & Co., 1884]. The Mark Twain House, Hartford, Ct.

MYTH, MAGIC, AND MYSTERY

97a. Peter Newell (1862-1924). American. "Pet Shop with Mice Escaping," from *The Hole Book* [New York: Harper Brothers, 1908]. Department of Printing and Graphic Arts, The Houghton Library, Harvard University

119a. Palmer Cox (1840-1924). Born in Granby, Quebec, Canada; Came to the U.S. in 1863. "The Brownies in Automobiles," n.d. Rare Book Department, The Free Library of Philadelphia

He also worked primarily in black and white but, unlike these colleagues, Newell relied on tone rather than line. He was one of the few artists of his generation who took full advantage of the new half-tone process with his rich velvety grays. Newell possessed a sweet, gentle, childlike sense of humor. He was also one of the first artists to recognize the picture book as a unique object. He designed *Topsys & Turvies* (1893–1894) as a book that children could "read" both rightside-up and upside-down. *The Slant Book* (1910) was printed on an angle, and holes were actually punched through both *The Hole Book* (1908) [cat. no. 97a] and its sequel, *The Rocket Book* (1912). These novelty picture books had to be trademarked as well as copyrighted. Although largely and unfairly forgotten by critics and scholars today, Newell was so admired in his day that he was the American illustrator chosen by Lewis Carroll's publishers out of all others to make new

120a. (left) Gelett Burgess (1866-1951). American. "Patience," from *Goops and How to Be Them* [New York: Frederick A. Stokes, 1900]. Betsy B. Shirley Collection of American Children's Literature, The Beinecke Library of Yale University

147a. (middle) Howard Pyle (1853-1911). American. "Untitled (Yankee Doodle by the Cannon)," from *Yankee Doodle, an Old Friend in a New Dress. Illustrated by Howard Pyle* [New York: Dodd, Mead and Company, 1881]. Delaware Art Museum, Bequest of Joseph Bancroft

147b. (right) Howard Pyle (1853-1911). American. "Untitled (Washington Reviewing the Citizenry)," from *Yankee Doodle, an Old Friend in a New Dress. Illustrated by Howard Pyle* [New York: Dodd, Mead and Company, 1881]. Delaware Art Museum, Bequest of Joseph Bancroft

pictures for *Alice in Wonderland* (1901), *Through the Looking-Glass* (1902), and *The Hunting of the Snark* (1903). Of course, he was soundly trounced by the press for daring to replace John Tenniel in the Alice books, and yet Newell produced quite a different and still admirable edition of these children's classics in his inimitable style.

But perhaps no other American picture book of the late nineteenth century was more beloved by young readers than Palmer Cox's *The Brownies, Their Book* (1887). From their initial appearance in *St. Nicholas* in 1883 until their last in 1914, the Brownies grew into an even greater fad than Kate Greenaway [cat. no. 119a]. Cox was a brilliant merchandiser and turned the Brownies into the Smurfs of their era. He put out book after book and licensed the characters for everything from dolls to china to chocolate to a Broadway extravaganza. Cox was not much of an artist, but he gave every little character its own distinct dress and character. Far too much was going on in every picture for one to notice the careless, clumsy execution. Their frantic energy saved them. Nearly as well known as Palmer Cox's Brownies were Gelett Burgess' Goops, a silly parody of the excesses of the Art Nouveau style, which appeared in *St. Nicholas* and then in the mock book of manners *The Goops and How to Be Them* (1900) [cat. no. 120a]. The name has stuck, but the witty pictures have unfortunately been forgotten.

The most important artist to emerge from the American children's periodicals was surely Howard Pyle. He started out with *St. Nicholas*, but soon switched to *Harper's Young People*, where most of his great children's books were first serialized. Oddly, although now considered the most representative of American illustrators, Pyle depicted surprisingly few purely American subjects. Except for the uncharacteristic color picture book of *Yankee Doodle* (1881) [cat. nos. 147a and 147b], he produced *The Merry Adventures of Robin Hood* (1883), the legends of the knights of the Round Table, and collections of traditional fairy tales. It is no surprise then that he was one of the first American illustrators to be recognized abroad and one of the few American artists "of considerable invention and decorative ability" that Crane mentioned by name in *Of the Decorative Illustration of Books Old and New* (1896). In his studio in Wilmington, Delaware, Pyle drew a continent he did not know, recreated times he had only read about. He had almost no interest in contemporary American life. But he obviously studied what Crane, Greenaway, and Caldecott were doing just as much as he studied Albrecht Dürer's work. Pyle was nearly as eclectic as Crane and was likewise a merchant in nostalgia. Although he did not fully embrace the Englishman's art ("Too many draperies, too many draperies,"[25] he complained), Pyle obviously based the design of *The Merry Adventures of Robin Hood* on Crane's *Household Stories*. However, in his book, Pyle was more concerned with depicting action than decoration.

That was what he tried to pass on to his students. Pyle had his own ideas of what illustration should be and was determined to create a new generation of American illustrators. But when he offered to give such a course at the Pennsylvania Academy of the Fine Arts in Philadelphia, he was curtly told that illustration was not a *fine* art. He therefore joined the faculty of Drexel Institute and later took in students at his studio in Delaware. His classes were so successful that when the Pennsylvania Academy came back to him, he now turned them down. He also admitted women to his classes (but resented how they knitted in the front row while he tried to inspire them). He told his students to not just paint pictures, but to put down life itself. His favorite advice was, "Throw your heart into the picture and jump in after it."[26] He was less interested in technical accuracy than in the emotion conveyed in pictures. He was not one to hold back his opinions. (He informed one pupil that he must be either color blind or a genius.) Pyle was an inspiration to generations of artists. "No illustrator worthy of the name can look on the work of Howard Pyle," said Robert Lawson, "and then do careless or insincere work himself without feeling a sense of personal reproach, a sense of shame that he has failed this good and honest master. His presence is in every decent studio; inspiring, encouraging, helpful, corrective or justly wrathful."[27]

THE GOLDEN AGE

Pyle and his colleagues excelled in drawing in black and white, but printing technology progressed so swiftly in the United States that by 1902 Pyle was telling his students that they had to learn to paint in color. That would be the only thing wanted within ten years, he said. He was understandably optimistic. Advancements in color printing both in the United States and abroad ushered in a golden age of children's book illustration. The Arts and Crafts movement had spread from London to St. Petersburg, from New York to San Francisco; and nowhere were its principles more obviously fulfilled than in the production of opulent nursery books. Everyone seemed to be doing them. For example, in the United States, Will H. Bradley, perhaps the most important American practitioner of Art Nouveau, not only wrote and illustrated his own children's story, *Peter Poodle, Toymaker to the King* (1906), he also designed a special typeface for use in the book [cat. no. 115].

The Banquet

115. (left) Will H. Bradley (1868-1962). American. "Peter Poodle," Frontispiece for *Peter Poodle, Toy Maker to the King* [New York: Dodd, Mead & Company, 1906]. Lent by The Metropolitan Museum of Art, Gift of Fern Bradley Dufner, 1952. © Metropolitan Museum of Art, 1995

163. (right) W. W. Denslow (1865-1915). American. "The soldier with the green whiskers led them through the streets," from *The Wonderful Wizard of Oz* [Chicago: George M. Hill Company, 1900]. Print Collection, Miriam and Ira D. Wallach Division of Art, Prints and Photographs; The New York Public Library, Astor, Lenox and Tilden Foundations

Color was now crucial for a children's book to succeed, but the relatively expensive three-color process was not the only method available to inventive designers. The first edition of *The Wonderful Wizard of Oz* (1900) proved what could be achieved with just a little imagination and effort [cat. no. 163]. Both the author L. Frank Baum and the illustrator W. W. Denslow knew that children preferred color to black and white, and they filled this American fairy tale with over one hundred two-color textual illustrations and twenty-four color plates. Thus it was both a decorated and illustrated book. But because they paid all the printing costs to get it published, Baum and Denslow had to economize somewhere in the reproduction. With his extensive background in designing art posters, Denslow knew what could and could not be done. He drew all the pictures in black and white and then worked closely with the printers to break them up into different colors. There is no black at all in the full-page plates, for Denslow chose a simple scheme of pale blue, yellow, and red plus a dark blue for the key block. Through the overlapping and different gradations of the plates, he secured an extraordinary range of tone. *The Wonderful Wizard of Oz* is still a remarkable example of the art of the book and one of the most lavishly illustrated children's books ever published.

Perhaps the most dramatic change in the juvenile book market was the illustrated gift book made possible by the introduction of fine color photoreproduction. Most of these titles were standard literature or "classics," not requiring payment to any author. The English preferred fairy tales, the Americans adventure stories; and there was an absurd degree of duplication in subject. (For example, when *Alice in Wonderland* went out of copyright in 1907, at least seven newly illustrated editions came out immediately in England.) While these gift books were not always well made or even well designed, the art was often stunning and as beautifully executed as any contemporary painting. When one thinks of the classic children's book illustrators, one immediately recalls this period. Arthur Rackham, Edmund Dulac, Kay Nielsen, N. C. Wyeth, Maxfield Parrish, and Jessie Willcox Smith were just a few of the many whose extraordinary work graced these volumes. Unlike earlier children's book illustrators, many of these artists were highly trained. Pyle himself insisted that the aim of his teaching was "not essentially the production of illustrators of books but rather the production of pictures."[28]

As always, there was some resistance to change. Purists refused to take seriously any book illustrated completely by mechanical means: What sophisticated bibliophile could tolerate them? It seemed more science than art. Where was the hand of man in their production? Of course the hand of the artist rarely touched a plate once a picture was turned over to that whole industry of professional etchers and engravers that emerged in the nineteenth century to meet the demand for cheap illustrated publications. Objections to the process block on aesthetic grounds gave rise to private presses which employed a multiplicity of printing techniques that avoided camera reproduction. They issued precious volumes in extremely limited and expensive editions for the connoisseur. The English designer William Nicholson was pivotal in reviving the woodcut as a form of illustration with *An Alphabet* (1898) [cat. no. 21]. He issued this book of bold, flat, economically colored designs in a limited edition actually printed from the original blocks. The trade edition, however, required some changes to make it more appropriate for children. Consequently "E for Executioner" became "E is for Earl" and "T for Topers" became "T for Trumpeter."

New processes always produce new artists, and again England took the lead. Of course not all of those working in London at the time were English-born. Edmund Dulac came from France and Kay Nielsen from Denmark, but above them all stood Arthur Rackham the Cockney. His lush romanticism in opulent productions from *Rip Van Winkle* (1905) and *Peter Pan in Kensington Gardens* (1907) through *The Wind in the Willows* (1940) set the standard by which all other illustrated books at the time were judged [cat. no. 160]. He was primarily a line man, the color often just a second thought; but his richness of invention and particular way of drawing fairies and enchanted groves inspired several generations of illustrators. Dulac was by nature a painter whose exquisite watercolors are among the finest pictures of the classic tales of Perrault,

160. Arthur Rackham (1867-1939). British. "A Hundred flew off with the String and Peter clung to the tail," from *Peter Pan in Kensington Gardens* [London: Hodder & Stoughton, 1906]. Collection of Kendra Krienke and Allan Daniel, New York City

81a. Beatrix Potter (1866-1943). British. "Mice tailoring with cat looking through window," 1901, from first version of *The Tailor of Gloucester*. Rare Book Department, The Free Library, Philadelphia

Andersen, and the Arabian Nights ever published. Nielsen was originally a stage designer, and his stylized fairy tale renderings are among the most haunting pictures in children's literature. An illustrator could now be considered a serious artist. Rackham was the first of the color plate designers to arrange to have his work for books exhibited and sold in an art gallery. It was also the dealer's responsibility to arrange with the publishers to have the pictures issued in books. In this way illustration was briefly elevated to the status of fine art.

Although in spirit she really belonged to the Crane and Caldecott school of illustration, Beatrix Potter was another English artist who came into her own with the introduction of the three-color process. Her little volumes, the size of a child's hand, were picture books rather than gift books in the Rackham tradition [cat. no. 81a]. She was not much of a draughtsman, but she painted exquisite watercolors with a naturalist's precision of the animals and landscape of her beloved Lake District. She may have dressed up Peter Rabbit and all her other pets in clothes to illustrate her fanciful tales about them, but Potter painted only what she knew. "If you ever want to make a picture book," she declared, "remember that you have to see everything very clearly yourself before you can make other people see."[29] Her Peter Rabbit titles are still among the most popular children's books ever published and are today an industry all their own.

In America, the illustrated gift book market was dominated by alumni of Howard Pyle's classes. Through his vast connections in the publishing trade, Pyle often found them their first book assignments. He wanted his students to produce American books with American themes for American children. One of his very first pupils was also the most famous of his many female pupils, Jessie Willcox Smith. She had also studied with Thomas Eakins and became an exceptional illustrator of nursery rhymes and fairy tales, usually executed in oil. She was best known for tender portraits of berouged babies and their doting mothers in the spirit of Mary Cassatt that adorned the covers of women's magazines for years; she established as prevalent a style in American illustration as did Kate Greenaway in England. Maxfield Parrish applied to Pyle to take his course at Drexel; but on viewing the young man's portfolio, Pyle informed Parrish that there was nothing he could teach him. Parrish did audit a few classes but dropped out when he realized that Pyle was right. Parrish became the highest paid illustrator in America, famous for his languid nudes in bosky settings beneath what became known as Parrish blue skies. Most of his brilliantly colored illustrations were commissioned by magazines before they appeared in books.

Pyle's prize pupil was N. C. Wyeth. He, perhaps more than anyone else, most dramatically epitomized the Brandywine tradition in American art established by Pyle and his disciples. Like Pyle, Wyeth felt as much at home on Treasure Island or in King Arthur's Court or Robin Hood's Sherwood Forest as he did in his house in Chadds Ford, Pennsylvania [cat. no. 153]. Like Pyle, Wyeth never visited Europe before painting its legends and literature. He did not have to. "In every illustrative problem," he explained, "I must first find something that echoes within me. In my research for the picture I look for those things that have come within the range of my experience. Scholarly research and the marshaling of correct details in a picture are of little avail without such a procreative basis. This does not necessarily mean that the artist needs to visit China in order to illustrate a Chinese story. But he will be wise to search the narrative for a common denominator in his own experience and that of his oriental subject theme."[30]

Wyeth's attitude to illustration was perhaps best summarized by the slogan of the 1928 Book Week poster he designed, "Books: Romance, History, Travel." Action lay at the center of his rugged compositions, but there was also a psychological depth to his work. He often depicted not only battles but epiphanies as well, moments of heightened awareness within a story. After Pyle, Wyeth perhaps has left the most lasting contribution to American children's classics. Wyeth too became an eminent teacher, his most famous pupil being his son Andrew. But he eventually came to resent what Pyle had taught him. Yes, his students were successful illustrators, but not one became a distinguished painter. Wyeth felt that Pyle had merely passed on tricks of the trade, shortcuts to immediate commercial ends. His students were merely journalists in paint. They sought out the dramatic, the picturesque, the novel in the world around them rather than studying the eternal and immediate beauty of nature. But no one can look on his rugged canvases and deny that N. C. Wyeth *was* a skillful painter.

153. N. C. Wyeth (1882-1945). American. "One more step, Mr. Hands," said I, "and I'll blow your brains out!," from *Treasure Island* [New York: Charles Scribner's Sons, 1911]. Reprinted with the permission of Atheneum Books for Young Readers, an imprint of Simon & Schuster Children's Publishing Division. Lent by the New Britain Museum of American Art, Harriet Russell Stanley Fund

Other exceptional American illustrators never passed through Pyle's classes. While Pyle, Frost, and Kemble learned their craft in the magazines, many of the new generation learned theirs in the newspapers. Harrison Cady, John R. Neill, and Johnny Gruelle graduated from the newsroom to children's books. Some of them found a steady income in illustrating various juvenile series. Cady made his name with *The Happychaps* (1908), Carolyn Wells' imitation of Palmer Cox's *Brownies*, and his fortune with Thornton W. Burgess' Bedtime Story-Books [cat. no. 84]. Neill succeeded Denslow as the illustrator of the Oz books, and Gruelle produced a steady stream of

MYTH, MAGIC, AND MYSTERY

121. (left) Johnny Gruelle (1880-1938). American. Cover for *Raggedy Ann in Cookie Land* [Chicago: P. F. Volland & Co., 1931]. Kendra Krienke and Allan Daniel, New York City

84. (right) Harrison Cady (1877-1970). American. "Peter Rabbit with Uncle Billy Possum," from *The Adventures of Peter Cottontail* [Boston: Little, Brown & Company, 1914]. Kendra Krienke and Allan Daniel, New York City

Raggedy Ann stories [cat. no. 121]. Academically trained illustrators sometimes turned to American children's books. The Canadian-born artist E. Boyd Smith returned from his studies in Paris to produce several handsome albums worthy of comparison with Boutet de Monvel's work. Carl Larsson's Swedish influence, too, may be detected in Smith's studies of New England farm life. Frederick Richardson also trained abroad and emulated the contemporary French style in his translucent watercolors for Frank R. Stockton's *The Queen's Museum and Other Fanciful Tales* (1906) and *Mother Goose* (1915).

The camera had eliminated the middleman, the craftsman, the artisan. It reproduced directly from the art and generally with surprising fidelity. Artists could use whatever method they desired. Arthur Rackham preferred watercolor and ink, N. C. Wyeth oil; but there was also considerable mixing of media. The camera could also reduce and enlarge, so the artist did not have to be concerned with scale, just style. And style was everything. Novelty was desired as much as skill, and never before or since did children have a wider variety of interpretations to choose from. There was a raft of Rackham imitators, but on the whole, illustrators sought individual, distinctive renditions. The same classics were done over and over and over again, and yet no two looked exactly alike.

The color process did have its disadvantages. A picture could be printed on only one side of a certain kind of expensive coated stock, so the plates were on different paper than the rest of the book. Consequently they were either bound or stuck in the book without regard to the rest of its design; and pictures did not always appear concurrently with the specific passages in the texts they depicted. And some seemed inappropriate. There was some distortion between the original and printed versions, but the wiser artists made the best of the method's flaws. Rackham, for example, said that he had to learn to intensify his colors, because he knew some of their quality would be lost between being photographed and published.

Parrish, perhaps more than any of his contemporaries, adapted his working methods to the scientific principles of photoreproduction. His work in black and white was often a form of collage in which he drew the outlines and other details in india ink, modeled the forms (sometimes cut out of paper for sharpness) with lithographic crayon, and pasted on different prepared patterned cardboard for texture and contrast. For his brilliant color effects, Parrish applied flat, thin, transparent oil glazes of pure color that could easily be broken down into its basic components within the camera. Consequently, almost none of his clear, brilliant hues were lost in reproduction. Sometimes the results were a bit too mechanical, and he tended to rely on the same truckload of pictorial clichés; but at his best, Parrish had no peer as a master of beguiling composition and piercing color. He was a modest man and seems to have finished his illustrations without regard for any future use for them. "Unfortunately," noted the gallery director Martin Birnbaum, "he did not study the chemistry of his pigments with sufficient care, and many of the beautiful colors—except an azure he made of precious powdered lapis lazuli—have faded or turned black. However, future generations will always delight in the color reproductions of his works which do not fade."[31]

Color plates were generally supplemental to the text and did not always integrate with it. Some volumes seemed less illustrated books than sumptuous albums of pretty pictures. A plate could be plucked from a copy without damage to the integrity of the whole. And because they were usually pasted in, they often fell out without anyone being the wiser. At times they were even reprinted in books for which they were never intended. Obviously some pictures were painted specifically with gallery sale in mind. Because they might end up on someone's wall, they could not be too tied down to the printed page. They had to stand as individual paintings.

These ambitiously illustrated gift books generally abandoned Walter Crane's concept of the art of the book. The "ornamental" tendency had given way to the "epic." It constituted a narrative rather than a decorative school of art. "This very perfection of reproduction led to the artist's abuse of it," insisted Elizabeth MacKinstry, "and at best these illustrations, things of delight as they were, were only pictures reduced for a book page, far too confused and crowded, when reduced, for the space occupied. At the worst they were dreary things, insipid and neither easel pictures nor book decorations. Gradually the breaking down of old plates, and the haste which is an absolute commercial necessity of today, reduced this once delightful school to a sort of brownish mist, which cries out for description by the good old term of a *gruzzle*."[32] But she was being unfair. Whatever their limitations and compromises, these illustrated gift books contained some of the most stunning pictures ever to grace children's literature.

BETWEEN THE WARS

World War I put an immediate end to the opulent era of book illustration. Rackham and Wyeth continued to illustrate the classics nearly up to their deaths, but the illustrated gift book market never really recovered. There were new ideas of how books should be produced and illustrated. With peace came an economic boom, and the children's book trade quickly developed into its own unique industry in America. It was a commercial phenomenon unequalled anywhere else in the world. Several important events made that possible. Macmillan's children's line was selling so well by 1919 that the company set up under Louise Seaman (later Bechtel) the very first independent children's division of any major American publishing house. She was soon joined by May Massee at Doubleday (and later Viking), Helen Dean Fish at Frederick A. Stokes, and many other remarkable women editors who established a separate and lucrative industry within the industry. "The year 1919, we cannot forget, marked a release from war," explained Bechtel. "It brought a general increase in book production, a new prosperity, new techniques in printing, and the inspiration of many beautiful books from Europe. All this flowered into children's bookmaking of the twenties and thirties such as the world never before had seen."[33]

With sales soaring, Frederic G. Melcher of *Publishers Weekly* and the American Booksellers Association revived the Boy Scouts' idea of an annual celebration of children's books. In 1919, under the slogan "More Books in the Home," he and a consortium of editors, librarians, teachers, and booksellers established the annual Children's Book Week for the promotion and purchase of the latest titles. Also through *Publishers Weekly*, Melcher pushed for children's bookselling year round rather than just at Christmastime or for birthdays. There were already some booksellers specializing in juvenile literature. Bertha Mahony (later Miller) opened the first Bookshop for Boys and Girls in Boston in 1916; in 1919 Marion Cutter followed her lead in New York City with another children's bookstore. In 1924 Mahony expanded her catalogues into *The Horn Book*, the first journal devoted exclusively to reviewing juvenile literature.

Of course none of this could have happened without the growth and support of the modern children's library movement. Progressives demanded universal literacy and more libraries to help keep the public informed. Boys and girls were no longer told to shush in the public libraries but given their own rooms filled with their own books. As a result, the single most important market for children's books became the libraries. Anne Carroll Moore, the first director of Work with Children at the New York Public Library, was the most powerful of the new breed of children's librarian. They were not just custodians or civil servants, but social activists. Moore set up the Children's Room at the public library when it opened in 1911; it quickly became the model for libraries all over the country. Coincidentally, the same year that Bechtel was appointed children's book editor at Macmillan and that of Children's Book Week was initiated, Moore became the first regular children's book reviewer in the pages of *The Bookman*.

Children's books had become one of the few industries in the United States that was produced by, run by, reviewed by, sold by, and sold to women. It became so segregated that Melcher pleaded in an editorial in *Publishers Weekly* (1 July 1939) for "Men Wanted?" By that time two thirds of the titles on recommended reading lists prepared by Moore and others were written by women. It should not be misconstrued that there was anything inherently feminist in the profession's day-to-day business operations; but children's books nevertheless provided an opportunity denied women in most other fields, including the publishing trade. Ruth Hill Viguers argued in an editorial in *The Horn Book* (April 1967), that the reasons for this prevalence of ladies as "both plowers of the field and keepers of the hearth" were "economic, many may be attributed to temperament, and many to women's age-old inheritance of responsibility for the nurture and care of children."

Many of them were on a noble crusade. May Massee believed, "Cultural redemption of America is through children's books. The first ideas of a nation when it is just beginning to read, must be ideas that are worth something."[34] While Anne Carroll Moore followed the slogan "the right book for the right child at the right time," Massee had carved in the wall of her Viking office *Ne quid nimium, etiam moderatio* ("Nothing too much, not even moderation"). Not everyone in America was a convert to the cause, so it is no surprise that some children's book editors were at times justifiably defensive about their work. Ursula Nordstrom of Harper and Row sniffed that some men in her own company thought picture books "look easy to do. Why, there's nothing to it, really, you just tell about a bunny and what happened, and your cousin can do the pictures. It is hard to keep a loving and patient tone when all you want to do is point out coldly that the creation of a picture book in thirty-two pages, where every word counts, and the pacing, the turning of the pages, is tremendously important, is as precise and beautiful as the writing of a good sonnet."[35] Massee insisted that "it takes more trouble to make good children's books than adult books, as it takes more trouble to care for a child than a man."[36] This same sense of mission was shared by many of their illustrators. Henry C. Pitz found them "a special breed of human being. They are not always greatly gifted; but, as a whole, they are the most devoted and dedicated group I know. Most of them give all they can."[37]

Progressives all, these pioneering librarians were dedicated to the edification of the young. They had no interest in coddling or catering to childish whims. It was an era when there was such a thing called "good taste." And it was something that had to be taught. Artists shared this philosophy. "Now, is there any vocation that could be richer and more fulfilling than work for children?" asked Ingri Parin d'Aulaire. "The little book we have just finished, we always hope, is going to help build up taste and artistic feeling in thousands of children who own this book, not only for the moment, but for the rest of their lives."[38] A large number of these publications were obviously tailored to suit the interests of librarians rather than the capacities of those who were supposed to most benefit from them. Many were indeed more for adults than children. In 1922 Melcher, whom Bechtel called "the fairy-godfather of children's books," came up with another effective way of bringing attention to the field. He established the Newbery Medal (named for the London bookseller John Newbery) to be given annually to honor "the most distinguished contribution to American literature for children" published in the United States in the previous year.

The British illustrator Charles Keeping may have indeed been correct when he observed that in the juvenile book industry "artists have been the poor children and yet they have been contributing half the strength of children's books."[39] Although picture books were eligible for the Newbery (Wanda Gág's *Millions of Cats* was a runner-up in 1929), it was not until 1937 that Melcher recognized children's book illustration with the Caldecott Medal, given annually to "the most distinguished American picture book." As with the Newbery, he turned over the responsibility of choosing the Caldecott to a committee of prominent librarians. These professionals may indeed have been experienced in social as well as literary matters, but generally they had little or no training in art. Consequently there have been some peculiar choices and odd omissions over the years. How else can one explain why Thomas Handforth's *Mei Li* (1938) beat out James Daugherty's *Andy and the Lion* (1938) or Ingri and Edgar Parin d'Aulaire's *Abraham Lincoln* (1939) was honored over Ludwig Bemelmans' *Madeline* (1939)? However, on occasion the award has recognized some remarkable work.

The new children's book trade needed illustrators; and, instead of waiting for them to stop by, the more creative editors went out and found them. They pressed into service for children such "adult" designers as Peggy Bacon, Boris Artzybasheff, and James Daugherty. Massee met Ludwig Bemelmans at a dinner in his home and recruited him for her list. Margaret Wise Brown preferred to work with fine artists like Clement Hurd and Esphyr Slobodkina [cat. no. 89a]. Perhaps the most important of these graphic designers was the young printmaker Wanda Gág. She had to prove herself in the art galleries before anyone in the children's book trade would take her seriously as an illustrator. Ever since childhood back in New Ulm, Minnesota, Gág had wanted to do children's books. Then art school prejudices steered her in other directions. She had tried to break into publishing when she moved to Greenwich Village, but no one was interested in her stories and pictures. Then Ernestine Evans, the head of the newly founded juvenile division of Coward

100. Wanda Gág (1893-1946). American. "Old Man Confronted by Cats in a Landscape," from *Millions of Cats* [New York: Coward, McCann & Geohegan, 1928]. The Kerlan Collection, University of Minnesota

89a. Clement Hurd (1908-1988). American. "Bedtime," from *Goodnight Moon* [New York: Harper & Row Publishers, 1947]. The Kerlan Collection, University of Minnesota

McCann, happened to see a show of her prints and drawings, and she asked Gág if she might be interested in illustrating a book for her. So the artist brought in the manuscript and preliminary drawings for a story of her own, and Evans signed up *Millions of Cats* (1928) [cat. no. 100]. "If the history of the art of the picture book is ever written," declared Lynd Ward, "the name of this artist will undoubtedly be graven there in large letters, for she, writing her story as well as drawing it, has discovered the richest potentialities of each factor, and to the process of integration has brought a wealth of originality. No other books have quite that feeling of the artistic whole."[40] Unfortunately, Gág inspired other artists, far less gifted with words than she, to insist on writing their own texts.

As Bechtel noted, the American picture book market was still largely dominated by imported goods. Moore and her colleagues recognized that the United States was a nation of immigrants, and to serve the growing populations in the cities, they encouraged librarians traveling abroad to look for picture books for children who as yet had not mastered English. Mahony Miller's Bookshop for Boys and Girls was well stocked with British, French, Swedish, German, Russian, and other foreign publications. It is no surprise that to compete with imported picture books, editors actively sought foreign-born artists. This preference for European rather than what Bechtel called "the banal, 'sappy'" American illustration was no doubt due as much to snob appeal as to artistic taste: real artists came from Paris, not Cleveland. Artzybasheff and Slobodkina emigrated from Russia, Miska Petersham and Willy Pogány from Hungary, Gustaf Tenggren from Sweden, and Bemelmans was Austrian. Ingri and Edgar Parin d'Aulaire were truly an international couple. She was Norwegian, and he was born in Munich to an Italian father and a French-American mother but was a Swiss citizen; and they made their reputation in children's books with picture biographies of famous Americans. Even the woodcuts in C. B. Falls' *A B C Book* (1923), one of the first modern American picture books, seemed slightly foreign due to their obvious debt to William Nicholson's *An Alphabet* and *The Square Book of Animals* (1899), and to Falls' Art Deco colors. Its sequel, *The Modern A B C Book* (1930), was more self-consciously "American" with "J is for Jazz" and "K is for Kodak."

Artists were encouraged to do picture books about other peoples in other lands. "We believe," declared Massee in Viking's first juvenile catalogue in 1932, "that when children's books reflect the best influences from the peoples who make this country what it is, they will be most truly American books. . . . We want them to be clear-minded and beautiful, books that will make young Americans think and feel more vividly, make them more aware of the world around them and more at home in the world within, more able to give something to their generation and thoroughly to enjoy the giving." Unfortunately, many of these seemed designed merely to meet a need. "We can all remember the period a few years ago," noted Robert Lawson, "when the Better Minds decided that American children should learn all about the children of other countries. It would broaden their horizons and make for international good will and understanding. So for a couple of seasons we had a flood of Little Pedro and his donkey in

168. Feodor Rojankovsky (1891-1970). Born in Mitava, Russia; Came to the U.S. in 1941. "By the campfire at night he talked with a trader named Finley . . . ," from *Daniel Boone: Historic Adventure of an American Hunter among the Indians* [Paris: Domino Press, 1931]. The Kerlan Collection, University of Minnesota

Mexico, Little Kookoo the Esquimaux and his pet narwhal, Little Kong of Hong Kong and his pet duck, and so forth, until every children's book list read like morning call at Ellis Island."[41]

They may have expressed an interest in what was going on in Europe, but most editors were still relatively conservative in their tastes in illustration. Cubism, Fauvism, Expressionism, and all the other radical strains in modern art were largely missing from American picture books until the Swiss designer Roger Duvoisin introduced the principles of the School of Paris to American children's books in the thirties. Leonard Weisgard in his picture books likewise absorbed what he had learned from contemporary French and Russian design. "The success of an illustration lies in the instinctive transference of an idea from one medium to another," he explained. "And so the more spontaneous it be and the less labored in application, the better."[42] There was resistance to what must have been considered "leftist" tendencies in this work, but Margaret Wise Brown immediately took Weisgard on seeing his portfolio. In Paris the American Esther Averill set up her own Domino Press to publish the picture book *Daniel Boone* (1931) in both French and English editions and recruited the Russian émigré artist Feodor Rojankovsky to illustrate it for the French, American, and British markets [cat. no. 168]. Rojankovsky then emigrated to the United States to work for Little Golden Books.

Another current trend were tales of contemporary America. Progressive education demanded a new kind of literature, modern books for modern children that reflected the city and street. Lucy Sprague Mitchell, one of the founders of the Bank Street School, set off a heated debate over the value of the fairy tale when she offered her dull little parables *The Here and Now Story Book* (1925) as a replacement for the old nursery stories. Carl Sandburg compromised by combining both schools of thought in the modern fairy tales of *Rootabaga Stories* (1922) that were illustrated in magazines by Robert Lawson and in books by Maud and Miska Petersham and Peggy Bacon [cat. no. 215b]. To the "here and now" school of juvenile literature belonged Mitchell's star pupil Margaret Wise Brown, both an author and editor at Young Scott Books; but "Brownie" was blessed with a touch of the poet, a quality that Mitchell and her many disciples so sorely lacked. Robert Lawson complained that the trend produced a "dreary flood of books in which the principal character was a vacuum cleaner, or a steam shovel or a carpet sweeper."[43] There was of course Virginia Lee Burton's *Mike Mulligan and His Steam Shovel* (1939) [cat. no. 62], and Hardie Gramatky came up with a talking tugboat in *Little Toot* (1939) [cat. no. 61]. But Burton expressed her doubts about the values of the modern industrial world in *The Little House* (1942) in which a charming cottage is barely saved from encroaching urbanization [cat. no. 63]. Of course one is left at the end with the niggling suspicion that it is just a matter of time before the little house has to be moved again or finally torn down.

The twenties was a period of remarkable experimentation and individual expression. Editors and artists tested techniques, sizes, shapes, bindings, type, paper, prices, and various markets. The more astute editors were rarely intrusive, knowing best when to trust their illustrators and leave them alone. Many believed, as Margaret McElderry

MYTH, MAGIC, AND MYSTERY

215b. (upper left) Peggy Bacon (1895-1987). American. "Hot Balloons Used to Open the Window in the Morning," from *Rootabaga Country: Selections from 'Rootabaga Stories' and Rootabaga Pigeons* [New York: Harcourt, Brace and Company, 1922; 1929 edition]. © Peggy Bacon, 1929, ren. 1957; Reprinted with the permission of Harcourt, Brace and Company Private Collection

61. (upper right) Hardie Gramatky (1907-1979). American. "Little Toot with Reflection in the Water," from *Little Toot* [New York: G. P. Putnam's Sons, 1939]. Reprinted with the permission of G.P. Putnam's, and imprint of the Putnam & Grosset Group Spencer Collection; The New York Public Library Astor, Lenox and Tilden Foundations

63. (left) Virginia Lee Burton (1909-1968). American. "Country," "Growing Suburbia," "City," and "Moving out to the Country," from *The Little House* [Boston: Houghton Mifflin Company, 1942]. © Virginia Lee Burton, 1942; Reprinted with the permission of Houghton Mifflin Company. The Kerlan Collection, University of Minnesota

70. Robert McCloskey (born 1914). American. "Policeman Stopping Traffic," from *Make Way for Ducklings* [New York: The Viking Press, 1941]. © Robert McCloskey, 1941; Reprinted with the permission of May Massee Collection, William Allen White Library, Emporia State University

123a. Robert Lawson (1892-1957). American. "Ferdinand Sitting in the Bull Ring," from *Ferdinand* [New York: The Viking Press, 1936]. © Robert Lawson, 1936; renewed 1964 by John W. Boyd. Reprinted with the permission of The Pierpont Morgan Library, Gift of Mary F. Cary Charitable Trust, 1970.16:33

of Harcourt Brace once argued, that "the best work comes when the artist is left as free as possible to make his own individual statement, not forced to conform to a concept established arbitrarily, but—within certain bounds of color and printing technique imposed by economic realities—left to interpret the text in his own way for the quick and appreciative eyes of a child, who is often less conservative in taste than his parents."[44] If these editors possessed any failings, Pitz thought it might lie in sometimes succumbing "to the temptation to be chic. I can think of some children's books that were lauded in the past. When they are five years old, they are like last year's hats—beginning to be repulsive. The weakness here comes from excess of virtue. These editors are looking for lively, expressive, eloquent work, and they are sometimes overeager."[45]

Publishers had to be economical at times. Increasing printing costs made extensive color impractical in most picture books. And some artists actually excelled in line only. Surely nothing would have been gained had *Millions of Cats*, Robert Lawson's *The Story of Ferdinand* (1936) [cat. no. 123a] or Robert McCloskey's sepia drawings in *Make Way for Ducklings* [cat. no.70] been published in full color. Occasionally one or more colors might be added to liven up a book, but making separations then was far more difficult than it is today. (Gág, for example, had to draw in pencil on ground glass.) As in America, some of the best English children's book illustration was done in black and white. The British publishers were relatively late in setting up juvenile literature divisions, and their children's book illustration had grown stagnant. They could not shake the Caldecott legacy. It was just more of the same, line drawings perhaps more appropriate for *Punch* than a picture book. William Nicholson briefly reemerged as a major children's book illustrator with *Clever Bill* (1926) and *The Pirate Twins* (1929), which he had drawn for his new family, as well as his famous pictures for Margery Williams's *The Velveteen Rabbit* (1922), but no British publisher was interested in subsequent children's books he proposed. Otherwise, it was much of the same except for E. H. Shepard's classic drawings for *Winnie-the-Pooh* (1926) and his daughter Mary Shepard's pictures for *Mary Poppins* (1934) and its sequels.

When the Depression hit, the very first branch of publishing forced to economize was the juvenile department, with severe reduction in staff, prices, and production. Some divisions were actually disbanded. Slowly the children's book trade began its recovery under Franklin D. Roosevelt's programs, but the experimentation of the twenties gave in to the social responsibility of the thirties. Patriotism pushed internationalism aside. Lynd Ward believed that American artists under the WPA finally "cut loose from the constricting traditions of European prestige and found in American subject matter both excitement and stimulation."[46] But it also smacked a bit of isolationism. The same spirit was carried over into children's books. "One development of the thirties was the increase in books of tall-tale American folklore," recalled Bechtel, which "brought a refreshing new note in children's books. Paul Bunyan with his ox and his ax, Pecos Bill with his exaggerated western doings—they accomplished much for American children."[47]

169. Ingri Parin d'Aulaire (1904-1980). Born in Konigsberg, Norway; Came to the U.S. in 1929 and Edgar Parin d'Aulaire (1898-1986) Born in Munich, Germany; Came to the U.S. in 1929. "Abe Reading by the Fire," from *Abraham Lincoln* [Garden City, L.I.: Doubleday, Doran and Company, 1939]. The Kerlan Collection, University of Minnesota

As the United States emerged as a world power between the wars, it desperately sought to define the American myth in children's books as in any other area. The trade now provided American heroes for American children. Ingri and Edgar Parin d'Aulaire dropped their Scandinavian tales to do their pictorial biographies of prominent Americans like *Abraham Lincoln*, a Caldecott winner [cat. no. 169]. James Daugherty won the Newbery Medal for *Daniel Boone* (1939) and recast the Aesop fable of Androcles and the Lion as the folksy American tall tale *Andy and the Lion*. But his style was more Italian Mannerist than Grant Wood or Edward Hopper. He filled his pictures with big, muscular, larger-than-life figures. "These tough, swaggering big-talk giants stood for the American working man," Bechtel explained. "They fitted both the comic-book aspects of heroism and a changing concept of the fairy tale. They loosened up our use of a truly American prose. The same social trends led to the increase of regional books, and to more proletarian children in all story books." There were all sorts of stories about young pioneers, the most famous being Laura Ingalls Wilder's Little House books. "Every famous American hero (including Benjamin Franklin) has been snatched from his grave and dusted off for the kiddies," laughed Robert Lawson, "and enough little girls have gone West in covered wagons to populate a new state of Oregon."[48] Ironically, Lawson won the Caldecott Medal for his own exercise in family history, *They Were Strong and Good* (1940). It was hardly his best book, but it spoke for the times. Far better than *They Were Strong and Good* was Lawson's burlesque of the Ben Franklin cult in *Ben and Me* (1939).

Not all threats came from abroad. The children's book trade was particularly shocked by the rise of the comic book. These crude, robust adventures in pictures were the opposite of what the genteel ladies in juvenile literature were offering young readers.

They were also cheap. Instead of fighting them, German-born H. A. Rey offered an alternative to Superman and Popeye by updating Wilhelm Busch's *Der Affe und der Schusterjunge* (1864) as *Curious George* (1940) [cat. no. 125]. Later, Crockett Johnson, one of the best comic strip artists in the country, turned to children's books and produced the delightful *Harold and the Purple Crayon* (1955). But surely the greatest worry for the complacent world of children's books was Hollywood. Many in the field were sure that Walt Disney was the devil incarnate. Ironically, Disney may have indirectly made an important contribution to the picture book. Many artists who worked for him were also children's book illustrators and learned how to tell a story in pictures during story conferences and while working on storyboards for him. Hardie Gramatky was head animator at the Disney Studios before he did *Little Toot*, and Kay Nielsen designed "The Night on Bald Mountain" sequence of *Fantasia* (as well as an early unproduced version of *The Little Mermaid*). Martin Provensen learned his craft at Disney and Alice Provensen at Walter Lantz, the maker of "Woody Woodpecker." "Our work in the animation studios taught us the concept of flow, linking one picture to another," they admitted.[49] Gustaf Tenggren went from working on *Snow White and the Seven Dwarfs* and *Pinocchio* to Little Golden Books and *The Poky Little Puppy* (1942) [cat. no. 88]. Popular culture was seeping into children's books as the industry had to adapt to the changing times and tastes.

88. Gustaf Tenggren (1896-1970). Born in Magra, Sweden; Came to the U.S. in 1920. "There he was, running around with his nose to the ground," from *The Poky Little Puppy* [New York: Western Publishing Company, 1942]. © 1942 Western Publishing Company, Inc., renewed 1970. Used by permission. The Kerlan Collection, University of Minnesota

Baby Booms and Busts

World War II hit the children's book trade as hard as the Depression had, with rising prices, paper and other shortages, resulting in smaller print runs. Also, many artists entered the armed forces. But children's books was one of the few branches of the publishing industry that did *not* decline. It continued to thrive as it turned out tales about tanks and bombers as well as nostalgic picture books that gave no indication that there was a war on. There were stories of heroism and patriotism and others that promoted solidarity with America's comrades in Latin America and Soviet Russia.

During the postwar baby boom, children's books suddenly became big business. Books about warfare were replaced with ones about America's place as a world power. The building of new schools and libraries demanded information-crammed treatises. There were now dull little books with dull little pictures that described how everything from jet airplanes to atomic energy worked. The 1943 Book Week slogan "Build the Future with Books" gave way to "Make Friends with Books" in 1950. But it was hardly a friendly time. The children's book industry continued to expand but not to experiment during the McCarthy era. The Cold War demanded that little Johnny read just as well as Ivan Ivanovich did, but only certain things. After all it was the age of suspicion. Many of the old masters were still working, but there was little encouragement for innovation in children's book illustration.

The enormous social upheaval of the sixties rocked the children's book industry. Lyndon Johnson in his bid to provide for the country's poor and illiterate set up the Great Society, which provided seemingly limitless funds to schools and libraries. The juvenile book business never had it so good. With new prosperity, prestige, and power came fierce competition, so publishers encouraged new artists with new methods of expression. Novelty was necessary. One could afford to take risks and make mistakes. The Civil Rights movement opened up children's books to a new prospective on the responsibility of the publishing industry to reflect the society as a whole. Of course no one publishes anything solely out of the goodness of one's heart. Northern publishers had long been resistant to alienating the Southern buyer, but the times they were a–changin'. Some even thought that by just coloring in a few faces one was taking a radical stand in support of integration. Black books meant business. The growing Black middle class as well as the funneling of federal revenue into the schools and libraries for multicultural curriculums created a market for far more varied and inclusive lists. African-American authors and artists who had long been denied their fair slice of the American pie were now baking it. Their contribution to modern children's books is inestimable, and they opened the closed club to members of all races, creeds, colors, and genders. There was even room for a nineteen-year-old high school art student named John Steptoe to produce *Stevie* (1969), the very first contemporary urban picture book to accurately reflect the Black Experience [cat. no. 67]. Diversity was now desirable, and there seemed to be plenty of money to allow illustrators to be as self-indulgent as

67. (upper left) John Steptoe (1950-1989). American. "Naw, my momma said he can't go in the park cause the last time . . . ," from *Stevie* [New York: Harper & Row Publishers, 1969]. Copyright © 1969, JohnSteptoe; Reprinted with the approval of the Estate of John Steptoe and The John Steptoe Collection

95. (upper right) William Steig (born 1907). American. "Dr. De Soto fastened his extractor to the bad tooth," from *Dr. De Soto* [New York: Farrar, Straus & Giroux, Inc. 1982]. © William Steig, 1982; Collection of Melinda Franceschini

104. (below) Maurice Sendak (born 1928). American. "And they put that batter up to Bake a Delicious Mickey-cake," from *In the Night Kitchen* [New York: Harper & Row Publishers, 1970]. © Maurice Sendak, 1970. Courtesy, Maurice Sendak and The Rosenbach Museum & Library

190b. Nancy Ekholm Burkert (born 1933). American. ". . . a poisoned apple . . . ," from *Snow White and the Seven Dwarfs: A Tale from the Brothers Grimm.* Translated by Randall Jarrell [New York: Farrar, Straus & Giroux, Inc., 1972]. Collection of the Brandywine River Museum, Museum Volunteers' Purchase Fund, 1982. Copyright © 1972 by Nancy Ekholm Burkert. Reprinted by permission of Farrar, Straus & Giroux, Inc.

they wanted. Such remarkable and varied designers as Nancy Ekholm Burkert [cat. no. 190a and b], Arnold Lobel, William Steig [cat. no. 95], Margot Zemach, and Margot Tomes now found a welcome home in children's books. And it is unlikely that such self-absorbed artists as Maurice Sendak [cat. no. 104], Tomi Ungerer, and Edward Gorey would have flourished in a less economically friendly time. It seemed like the prosperity would never end.

But it did. The slow dismantling of the Great Society under Richard Nixon and his successors panicked the already jittery juvenile book industry. Decreased population through abortion, contraception, and other birth control methods encouraged budgetary cuts to libraries, schools, and various children's services. Some artists who might have made significant contributions to the picture book deserted it for more lucrative trades elsewhere. One would have expected that there would be no room now for the second-rate. Sadly, there were fewer but not necessarily better children's books. Editorial courage diminished. During the Vietnam debacle, publishers drew inward and grew increasingly provincial. Fewer and fewer picture books were imported from anywhere but England. There was a brief baby boom during the Reagan years, but the prosperity was as false in the book

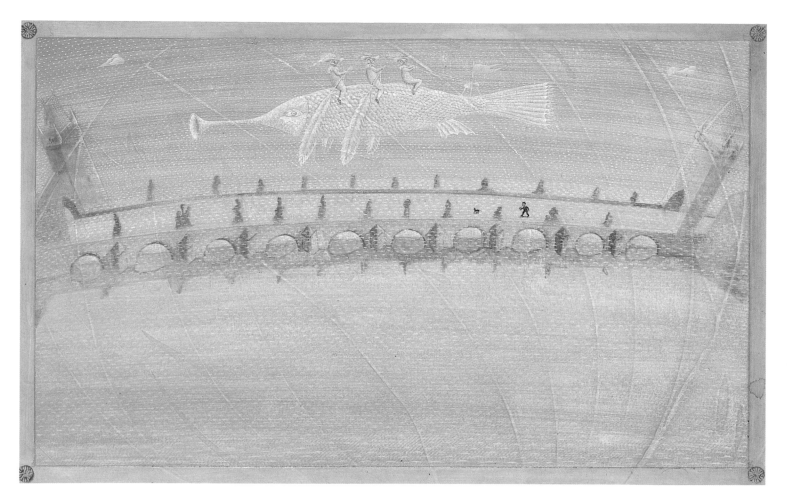

110. Peter Sís (born 1949). Born in Brünn, Czechoslovakia; Came to the U.S. in 1982 "I follow the determined cat back across the ancient bridge," from *The Three Golden Keys* [New York: Doubleday, 1994]. © Peter Sís, 1994; Collection of Peter Sís

industry as in every other aspect of American business. Conservatism and crass commerce have taken control of what people can and cannot read. Mass marketing, packagers, the chains, and political groups of various persuasions have done much to homogenize and sanitize the children's book trade. Children's book publishing resembles more and more just another branch of the toy industry. Its only hope lies in the courage of artists.

In surveying contemporary American children's book illustration, one is nevertheless dazzled by its variety in both material and manner. One can immediately see how far technology has advanced by comparing Charles Santore's interpretation of *The Wizard of Oz* (1991) to what W. W. Denslow had done ninety years before. The art of children's book illustration continues to grow in power and effect through an international core of artists. Ed Young from China, Allen Say from Japan, Antonio Frasconi from Uruguay, Uri Shulevitz and Anita Lobel from Poland, Peter Sís from Czechoslovakia [cat. no. 110], Vladimir Radunsky and Gennady Spirin from Russia, and Petra Mathers from Germany are just a few of the many remarkable designers who are now enriching contemporary American juvenile literature. The possibilities for expression now seem endless. Watercolor and pen and ink are no longer the only means to an end in contemporary children's books. Collage has been particularly well utilized by such masters as Leo Lionni [cat. no. 228], Ezra Jack Keats, and Eric Carle. Two generations of children's book illustrators are represented by Jerry Pinkney in watercolor and his son Brian with scratchboard.

In the half century he has been working in the juvenile trade, Maurice Sendak has frequently altered his style as he has grown in stature as an artist. He continues to test the picture book form and has the courage to vary his method to meet the message of the particular manuscript he has chosen to illustrate. It is no surprise then that one of his best students, Paul O. Zelinsky, has proven to be nearly as much an artistic chameleon as his teacher. Leo and Diane Dillon too have shown exceptional versatility through their long, distinguished career [cat. no. 196]. "To us every book we accept is different," they have explained, "and each provides us with a chance to do things we haven't done before, a chance to grow and expand as artists. Every manuscript presents a new challenge. We have looked for new solutions to different challenges, tried out new styles, experimented with different approaches."[50] Watercolor, india ink, color ink, woodcut, pastel, pencil, and oil are just a few of the many different materials they have mixed into their work for children. Each book is a new adventure. As ardent students of art, they have drawn on such varying sources as Japanese woodcuts, the Vienna Secession, and African design for a particular look for each book. No two look exactly alike, and yet each is immediately identifiable as a Leo and Diane Dillon book. No matter what the technique, their distinctive style always shines through.

228. Leo Lionni (born 1910). Born in Amsterdam, The Netherlands; Came to the U.S. in 1939. "Alexander and the Wind-up Mouse," from *Alexander and the Wind-up Mouse* [New York: Pantheon Books, 1969]. © Leo Lionni, 1970; Reprinted with the permission of Random House, Inc. Collection of Leo Lionni

MYTH, MAGIC, AND MYSTERY

196. Leo (born 1933) and Diane Dillon (born 1933). American. Cover for *The Porcelain Cat* [Boston: Little, Brown and Company, 1987]. © Leo and Diane Dillon, 1987. Private Collection

Others have handsomely profited from the study of the great illustrators of the past. One can trace the lingering influences of Arthur Rackham, Howard Pyle, and others in Trina Schart Hyman's dramatic designs. Hilary Knight has learned much from Boutet de Monvel, the Petershams, and Edmund Dulac as well as from both his parents, the popular magazine illustrators Katherine Sturges and Clayton Knight. Richard Egielski, another of Sendak's students, is an obvious fan of Peter Newell's work. *In the Night Kitchen* is Sendak's witty tribute to Winsor McCay's classic comic strip "Little Nemo in Slumberland." William Joyce honors McCay, Grant Wood, Edward Hopper, Busby Berkeley, King Kong, and so many other unlikely sources in his highly eclectic but still thoroughly individual and amusing art.

There is no single "school" of contemporary American children's book illustration.

133. James Marshall (1942-1992). American. "The Guests Arrive," from *The Stupids Have a Ball* [Boston: Houghton Mifflin Company, 1978]. © James Marshall, 1978; Reprinted with the permission of Houghton Mifflin Company. de Grummond Children's Literature Collection, University of Southern Mississippi

Variety in vision is apparent as one passes from Donald Crews' bold industrial art to Thomas Locker's lush Hudson River landscapes and on to the haunting dreamscapes of Chris Van Allsburg and David Wiesner. Perhaps no other modern American illustrator has created so many memorable comic characters than James Marshall, best known for his loyal and loving George and Martha and the incorrigible Stupids [cat. no. 133]. There is so much to discover, explore, and enjoy between the covers of a picture book. This exhibition does not pretend to be the definitive view of the last century of children's book illustration. After all, it can only reflect its three curators' eclectic and sometimes eccentric tastes. Instead it is offered as a sampling of some of the best, as merely an introduction that then may inspire further study and appreciation. It is also hoped that one may find here much art in the art of children's book illustration.

II

Trinkett Clark

AND THE DISH
RAN AWAY
WITH THE SPOON

*A First Look at the World of Words:
From Mother Goose to Dr. Seuss*

30. Richard Scarry (1919-1994). American. Cover from *Find Your ABCs* [New York: Random House, Inc., 1973]. Richard Scarry Estate. Copyright © 1973 by Richard Scarry. Reprinted with permission of Random House, Inc.

"The First Book" by Rita Dove

Open it.

Go ahead, it won't bite.
Well. . . maybe a little.

More a nip, like. A tingle.
It's pleasurable, really.

You see, it keeps on opening.
You may fall in.

Sure, it's hard to get started;
remember learning to use

knife and fork? Dig in:
you'll never reach bottom.

It's not like it's the end of the world—
just the world as you think

you know it.[1]

From the first breath, a baby absorbs the sounds of his or her environment like a sponge. For children (and adults) around the world, the earliest memories are most often happy ones that involve the experience of hearing the musical cadences of a nursery rhyme or lullaby while being rocked in the comforting arms of a parent or grandparent. Not only is this encounter warm and nurturing for both infant and adult, but it serves a fundamental purpose: Beyond sowing the seeds of a loving rapport between two beings, the actual experience of hearing these nursery rhymes awakens and nourishes the auditory senses. It is the lilting rhythm of the poetry and the repetitive, alliterative nature of these nonsense verses that first attract a baby's attention. Nonsense or not, these playful rhymes—both those handed down through the years and the more contemporary chantings of such authors as Edward Lear, Dr. Seuss, or Maurice Sendak—help to establish the linguistic foundations of a child.

Although the term nursery rhyme generally refers to the rhymes of Mother Goose, it also loosely encompasses those verses that are the natural offspring, specifically alphabet and counting poems. However, there is a distinction that needs to be elucidated: nursery rhymes are integral as an early introduction to the practical application of language. It is the oral tradition that first attracts the child and leads to the process of word association, which begins to occur towards the end of the infant's first year.[2] Frequent exposure to the singsong pattern of these rhymes eventually results in a child's familiarity with the alphabet, which then leads to reading. However, regardless of their individual goals, each category of books is important for another reason. Not only do the rhymes persist in one's subconscious through adulthood, but the art that accompanies these verses is something which lives on forever in the mind as well.

GREAT A, LITTLE a, BOUNCING B
ALPHABETS ABOUND

Throughout the years, the alphabet has been illustrated in many ways. The alphabet book usually has the most rudimentary text possible. Some just depict a letter, a single word, and one simple illustration [U, cat. no. 21]; others involve the reader in a search or game to look for all of the objects beginning with a certain letter [V, cat. no. 22]. Sometimes a character, such as Curious George [L, cat. no. 12] or Mary Poppins [N, cat. no.14] will serve as an intermediary, presenting a letter with particular flair. A specific theme may connect all of the alphabet together [A, cat. no. 1; H, cat. no. 8]. And often a simple story is told [D/E, cat. no. 4] or a rhyme or tongue twister may accompany the letter [G, cat. no. 7; M, cat. no. 13; O, cat. no. 15], actively involving the viewer in an entertaining experience. As the English philosopher John Locke so eloquently wrote in 1693:

> But then, as I said before, [learning] must never be imposed as a task, or made a trouble to [children]. There may be dice and playthings, with the letters on them to teach children the alphabet by playing; and twenty other ways may be found, suitable to their particular tempers, to make this kind of learning a sport to them.[3]

It is unrealistic to discuss in this essay the many different abecedarians that have been produced. The field is immense and the only continuity is that each book has the same goal: each alphabet serves to introduce visual literacy to children. It is important to note that the alphabet is a fertile forum that grants artists great liberties. As with all children's books, the words furnish the foundation of learning while the illustrations augment the process, opening doors onto unknown worlds. Locke was one of the first to acknowledge the need for illustrations, writing:

> If his Aesop has pictures in it, it will entertain him much the better, and encourage him to read, when it carries the increase of knowledge with it: For such visible objects children hear talked of in vain and without any satisfaction whilst they have no ideas of them; those ideas being not to be had from sounds, but from the things themselves or their pictures. And therefore I think as soon as he begins to spell, as many pictures of animals should be got him as can be found, with the printed names to them, which at the same time will invite him to read and afford him matter of inquiry and knowledge.[4]

As the images are not usually dependent on narrative, an alphabet allows the artist a broad range of aesthetic expression and inventive freedom. It opens up tremendous possibilities because of the quantity of work needed and the many techniques readily available—from woodcuts and lithographs to collage, from pen-and-ink drawings to watercolors and paintings.

As the earliest primers presented alphabets with imagery rendered from woodcuts, it seems natural that this medium would offer artists familiar with the process an opportunity for creative expression. In 1898, the English artist Sir William Nicholson illustrated *An Alphabet* with hand-colored woodcuts. In "U is for Urchin" [cat. no. 21], he ably demonstrated his craft; not only is there a sense of space and depth in this image,

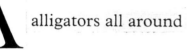

A alligators all around

B is for BASIL assaulted by bears

C for Crash!
D for Dash!

E for Elsewhere in a flash.

A   Maurice Sendak, "Alligators All Around," from the *Nutshell Library* series (New York: Harper & Row, 1962). © Maurice Sendak, 1962. Courtesy, Maurice Sendak and The Rosenbach Museum & Library. Used by permission of HarperCollins Publishers.   [cat. no. 1]

B   Edward Gorey, "B is for Basil assaulted by Bears," from *The Ghashlycrumb Tinies* (New York: Peter Weed Books, 1962). © Edward Gorey, 1962; Published with the permission of Edward Gorey. Collection of Edward Gorey. Courtesy of Gotham Book Mart Gallery, New York City.   [cat. no. 2]

C   Wanda Gág. "C is for Crash / D is for Dash," from *The ABC Bunny* (New York: Coward-McCann, 1933). Reprinted with permission of Coward-McCann, an imprint of the Putnam & Grosset Group. The Kerlan Collection, University of Minnesota.   [cat. no. 3]

D

"ABC—Now comes the D," called Noah.
"D for the Donkeys;
D for the Dogs;
D for the Doves;
D for the Ducks.
Hurry all the D's. The rain will soon fall."
But the Ducks dawdled a little.
"We like the rain!" they quacked.

"ABCD—Now for E," called Noah.
"E for the big Elephant;
E for the tall Elk;
E for the strong, broad Eagle.
The E's are the biggest of their kind."

E

F

is for Feet that won't fall asleep

D   Roger Duvoisin, "D" and "E," *A is for the Ark* (New York: Lothrop, Lee & Shepard Company, 1952). Jane Voorhees Zimmerli Art Museum, Rutgers, The State University of New Jersey, New Brunswick, New Jersey, Transfer from the Alexander Library. Photo by Jack Abraham. [cat. no. 4]

E   Stefano Vitale, "E," *The Folks in the Valley: A Pennsylvania Dutch ABC* (New York: HarperCollins Publishers, 1992). © Stefano Vitale, 1992; Used by permission of HarperCollins Publishers. Collection of Stefano Vitale. [cat. no. 5]

F   Esphyr Slobodkina, "F is for Feet that won't fall sleep," 1995, from *The Sleepy ABC* (New York: Lothrop, Lee & Shepard Company, 1953). © Esphyr Slobodkina, 1996; Reprinted with the permission of Lothrop, Lee & Shepard Company, an imprint of William Morrow. Collection of Esphyr Slobodkina. [cat. no. 6]

G Edmund Dulac, "'G' was a Giddy Young Girl," 1906, *Lyrics Pathetic & Humorous from A to Z* (London: Frederick Warne & Co., 1908). Collection of Ann Conolly Hughey. [cat. no. 7]

H Leo and Diane Dillon, "'H' is for Hausa," *Ashanti to Zulu: African Traditions* (New York: The Dial Press, 1976).© Leo and Diane Dillon, 1976; Dial Books. Collection of Leo and Diane Dillon. [cat. no. 8]

I Anita Lobel, "Ice Cream," *On Market Street* (New York: Greenwillow Books, 1981). © Anita Lobel, 1981; Reprinted with the permission of Greenwillow Books, an imprint of William Morrow. Collection of Anita Lobel. [cat. no. 9]

ice cream,

J   Charles B. Falls, "J is for Jazz," *The Modern ABC Book* (New York: John Day, 1930). Chapin Library of Rare Books, Williams College, Gift of Bedelia C. Falls. [cat. no. 10]

K   Charles B. Falls, "K is for Kangaroo," *ABC Book* (Garden City: Doubleday, Page and Company, 1923). © Doubleday 1923. Used by permission of Doubleday. May Massee Collection, William Allen White Library, Emporia State University. [cat. no. 11]

L   Hans Augusto Rey, "L = Lion Blows out the Candle," from *Look for the Letters: A Hide and Seek Alphabet* (New York: Harper & Row Publishers, 1942). © M. E. Rey, 1942. Lent by M. E. Rey. [cat. no. 12]

The Lion blows out the Candle, he will sleep, it is late

M Wendy Watson, "M for Magic," from *Applebet: An ABC* (New York: Farrar, Straus and Giroux, 1982). © Wendy Watson, 1982. Collection of Hubert A. Scoble & Margaret A. Gruszka. [cat. no. 13]

N Mary Shepard, "N is for Nursery," from *Mary Poppins from A to Z* (New York: Harcourt, Brace & World, 1962). © Mary Shepard, 1962; Reprinted with the permission of Harcourt Brace & Company. The New York Public Library, Central Children's Room, Donnell Library Center. [cat. no. 14]

O John O'Brien, "O," from *MacMillan Fairy Tale Alphabet Book* (New York: Macmillan Publishing Co., Inc., 1983). © John O'Brien, 1983; Reprinted with the permission of Simon & Schuster Books for Young Readers, an imprint of Simon & Schuster Children's Publishing Division. Collection of John O'Brien. [cat. no. 15]

P Chris Van Allsburg, "P was repeatedly Pecked," from *The 'Z' was Zapped* (Boston: Houghton Mifflin Company, 1987). © Chris Van Allsburg, 1987; Reprinted with the permission of Houghton Mifflin Company. Collection of Mr. and Mrs. David Lord Porter.   [cat. no. 16]

Q Cathi Hepworth, "Quarantine," from *ANTICS! An Alphabetical Anthology* (New York: G. P. Putnam's Sons, 1992). © Cathi Hepworth, 1992; Reprinted with the permission of G. P. Putnam's Sons, an imprint of the Putnam & Grosset Group. Collection of Cathi Hepworth.   [cat. no. 17]

R Anne Rockwell, "Rr," from *Albert B. Cub & Zebra: An Alphabet Storybook* (New York: Thomas Y. Crowell, 1977). © Anne Rockwell, 1977; The Kerlan Collection, University of Minnesota.   [cat. no. 18]

S Leonard Baskin, "S is for Self-Portrait," 1994, from (forthcoming alphabet book). © Leonard Baskin, 1996. Courtesy of R. Michelson Galleries, Northampton, Mass.   [cat. no. 19]

T Marcia Brown, "Tip-Toe Tommy
turned a Turk for Two-pence," from
Peter Piper's Alphabet (New York:
Charles Scribner's Sons, 1958).
© Marcia Brown, 1958. From the
Marcia J. Brown Papers, 1942–1994,
The M. E. Grenander Department of
Special Collections and Archives,
University Libraries, University at
Albany, State University of New
York.   [cat. no. 20]

U Sir William Nicholson, "U is for
Urchin," from *An Alphabet* (London:
William Heinemann, 1898). Courtesy
of the Fogg Art Museum, Harvard
University Art Museums, Anonymous
loan in honor of Daniel Bell.
[cat. no. 21]

V Richard Scarry, "Vinny
and Vicki," from *Richard
Scarry's Find Your ABCs*
(New York: Random
House, Inc., 1973).
© Richard Scarry, 1973;
Reprinted with the permis-
sion of Random House,
Inc. Estate of Richard
Scarry.   [cat. no. 22]

W William Steig, "Worry Wart," from *Alpha Beta
Chowder* (New York: HarperCollins
Publishers, 1992). © William Steig, 1992.
Collection of Jeanne Steig.   [cat. no. 23]

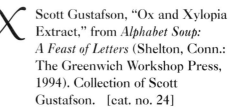 Scott Gustafson, "Ox and Xylopia Extract," from *Alphabet Soup: A Feast of Letters* (Shelton, Conn.: The Greenwich Workshop Press, 1994). Collection of Scott Gustafson.   [cat. no. 24]

Y Maud and Miska Petersham, "Y is for Yankee Doodle," from *An American ABC* (New York: Macmillan Publishing Co., Inc., 1941). Reprinted with the permission of Simon & Schuster Books for Young Readers, an imprint of Simon & Schuster Children's Publishing Division. Department of Special Collections, University of Oregon Library. [cat. no. 25]

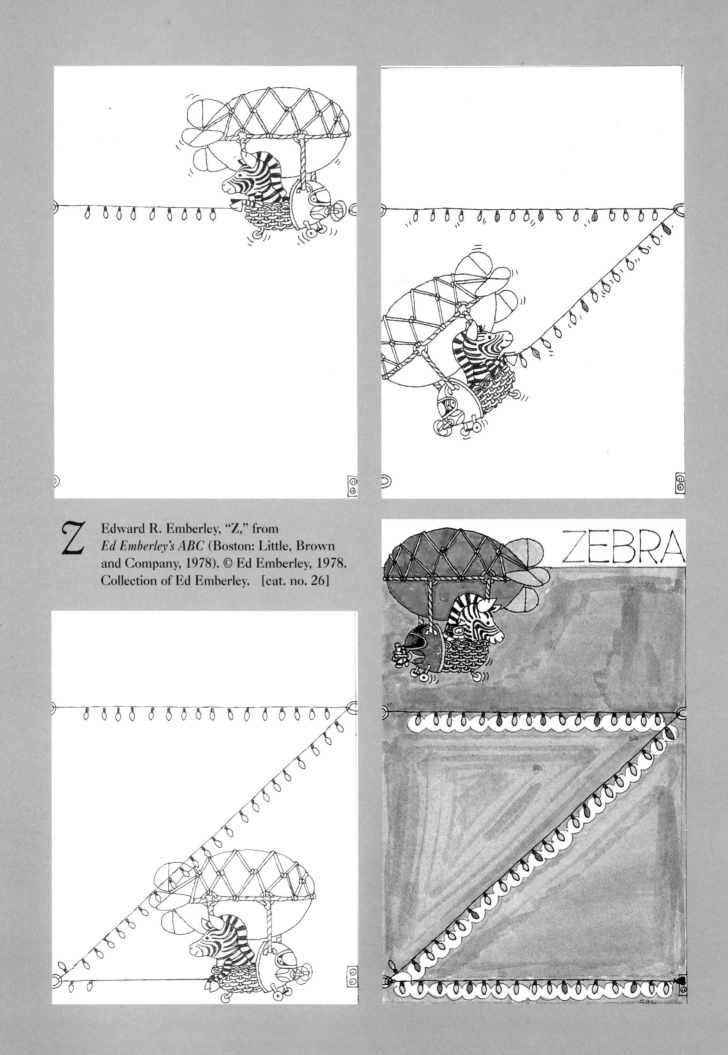

Z Edward R. Emberley, "Z," from
Ed Emberley's ABC (Boston: Little, Brown
and Company, 1978). © Ed Emberley, 1978.
Collection of Ed Emberley. [cat. no. 26]

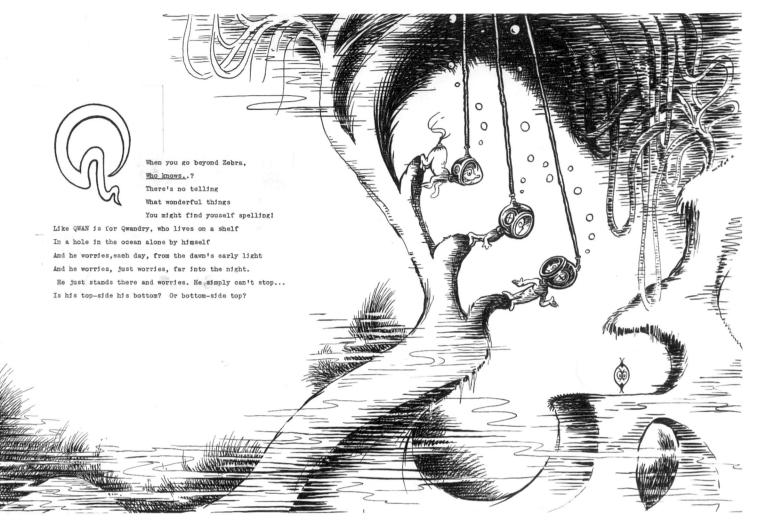

When you go beyond Zebra,
<u>Who knows</u>..?
There's no telling
What wonderful things
     You might find youself spelling!
Like QWAN is for Qwandry, who lives on a shelf
In a hole in the ocean alone by himself
And he worries,each day, from the dawn's early light
And he worries, just worries, far into the night.
 He just stands there and worries. He simply can't stop...
Is his top-side his bottom? Or bottom-side top?

27. Dr. Seuss (1904-1991). American. "When you go beyond Zebra *Who Knows?* . . . Like Quan is for quandary," from *On Beyond Zebra!* [New York: Random House, Inc., 1955]. Dr. Seuss Collection, Mandeville Special Collections Library, University of California, San Diego. Copyright © 1955 Dr. Seuss Enterprises, L.P., ren. 1983

but the artist has delineated the Urchin's shadow while conveying a feeling of the figure's loneliness.

Admiring Nicholson's skill, C. B. Falls employed the woodcut in his *ABC Book* of 1923. Although somewhat flat and stilted, Falls' "K is for Kangaroo" [cat. no. 11] is appealing because of its bold typography and bright palette of orange and blue. In this book, Falls demonstrates his skills in the fields of magazine illustration and advertising. His "J is for Jazz" from *The Modern ABC Book* (1930) [cat. no. 10], displays a much freer style, as the artist uses pen-and-ink with pencil, a less rigid medium. Expanding on Falls' lead, Wanda Gág tells an uncomplicated story with simple words and fluidly executed lithographs with *The ABC Bunny* (1934) [cat no. 3].

But it is Antonio Frasconi who uses the alphabet as an ingenious springboard for his woodcuts as he introduces other languages to young children in his groundbreaking

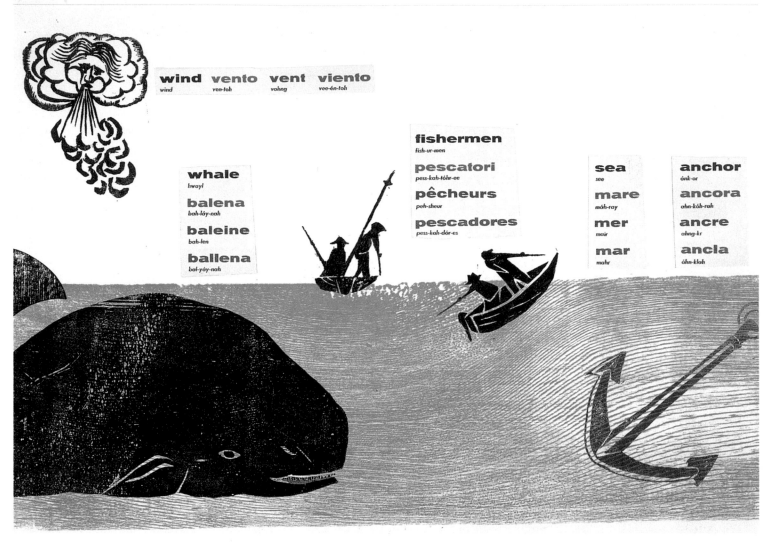

wind vento vent viento
wind   ven-toh   vahng   vee-én-toh

whale
hwayl

balena
bah-láy-nah

baleine
bah-len

ballena
bal-yáy-nah

fishermen
fish-ur-men

pescatori
pess-kah-tóhr-ee

pêcheurs
peh-sheur

pescadores
pess-kah-dór-es

sea
see

mare
máh-ray

mer
mair

mar
mahr

anchor
ánk-or

ancora
ahn-kóh-rah

ancre
ahng-kr

ancla
áhn-klah

28a. Antonio Frasconi (born 1919). Born in Uruguay; Came to the U.S. in 1945. "Wind, whale, fishermen, sea, anchor," from *See and Say* [New York: Harcourt, Brace & World, 1955]. Collection of Antonio Frasconi Copyright © 1955 by Antonio Frasconi

book, *See and Say,* of 1955 [cat. no. 28]. More like a dictionary than a simple alphabet book, this remarkable publication represents a culmination of the aim of the alphabet, teaching words, in this case in four languages—English, Italian, French, and Spanish— each designated by a different color. Each word is energized by Frasconi's inherent enthusiasm for the project, as well as his powerful imagery, use of color, and sense of composition. This book is a tribute to Frasconi's exceptional gift: In it he makes a technically laborious process seem effortless and vibrant.

And who could resist Maurice Sendak's lively *Alligators All Around* (1962) [cat. no. 1] where a family of alligators activate the alphabet. Alliteration plays a key role in the alligators' adventures, as the rollicking reptiles act out scenes associated with each letter. Illustrating the alphabet provided an intriguing challenge to the artist, who discussed it in the 1980 monograph by Selma G. Lanes:

31. Roger Duvoisin (1904-1980). Born in Geneva, Switzerland; Came to the U.S. in 1925. Endpapers from *A is for the Ark* [New York: Lothrop, Lee & Shepard Company, 1952]

> The least important aspect of *Alligators* is that it is an alphabet. I wanted to see how much I could get away with in a form that is so fixed and stilted. My alligators aren't teachers: they're like my later hero Max in *Where the Wild Things Are.* They stick their tongues out, stand upside down, and are very vain. They do the kind of things that all my children do.[5]

Certainly, Sendak succeeds in his mission with his usual spunk, but he has also produced (whether he likes it or not) an effective teaching tool.

It would be remiss to pass by *A is for the Ark* by Roger Duvoisin, published in 1952 [cat. nos. 4 and 31]. In this particular saga, the artist alphabetically chronicles the animals as they enter Noah's Ark under threatening skies. On the double-page spread depicting the letters D and E, the animals march into the vessel in order, but with haste. Noah is apprehensive about the looming storm and prods the ducks, who "dawdled a little. 'We like the rain!' they quacked." Behind them, the dogs, donkeys, elk, eagles, and elephants stride on board majestically. Eventually when Noah and the animals are safely stowed, the heavens open up and the real story begins. Then as the floodwaters recede, the animals disembark in reverse order and the story turns into a kind of memory game for the reader. This wonderful book offers bright, benevolent animals to the young child, while camouflaging the educational component.

An especially amusing alphabet book is Nancy Christensen Hall's *Macmillan Fairy Tale Alphabet Book* of 1983. Here artist John O'Brien illustrates the ABC's with the kind assistance of Mother Goose and her sidekicks. Together they provide a lively treasure hunt for words. The image of "O" [cat. no. 15] captures the "Old Woman Who Lived in a Shoe" in the midst of a major fracas, surrounded by a medley of famous personalities from fairyland including the Owl and the Pussycat, Orson from the medieval tale of *Valentine and Orson,* and the Walrus and oysters from Lewis Carroll's *Through the Looking Glass and What Alice Found There.* In O'Brien's image, the Old Lady is engaged in a futile chase, trying to catch a naughty boy who is racing off with her china. While recalling the fertile imagery of both Hieronymus Bosch and Pieter Brueghel, the artist visually recounts the text for the letter "O": "The ornery old lady was outnumbered by an outrageous number of offspring occupying her shoe." Humor and children run rampant: On the roof of the shoehouse stand three Wagnerian types—one, adorned in horned helmut, brandishes a spear. Mouths open, they are caught in mid-note and are defined by the word *opera.* Below, an "obese" child munches on "onions" and "oranges," while "Orville," "Olivia," "Omar," and "Oscar" slide down the shoe into an "octet of oboists" serenading under an "oak" tree. Set nearby is another, smaller shoe with a crescent moon on its door; of course! the "outhouse." And beneath the Old Lady is the word "outnumbered." Clearly this engaging watercolor overwhelms and enchants—O'Brien's witty attention to details provokes giggles and groans from both child and adult.

This sense of infectious joy triggered by an inventive alphabet is conveyed by many artists in a great variety of methods and media. From the colorful watercolors of Dulac, Duvoisin, and the Dillons, to the drawings of Edward Gorey, Marcia Brown, Ed Emberley, and Chris Van Allsburg (to mention a few), the constant link is an unabashed delight in exploring the many options that the alphabet—as a subject—represents. It generates an unleashing of the imagination and fosters myriad forms of self-expression. Ultimately, the teaching is done through the artist's vision. The image arrests the eye and lives on in the memory; therefore, each ABC book, embodying a magical power that is independent of any story, is truly a work of art.

GOOSEY, GOOSEY, GANDER
MOTHER GOOSE AND FRIENDS

By the time a baby is twelve months old, curiosity becomes a ruling force, thereby making it possible to capture its attention visually as well as orally. A child's inherent perception far surpasses any actual grasp of vocabulary at this point in the developmental process. As an infant grows into a toddler, the child begins to associate specific words and sound patterns with objects, activities, or emotions while learning how to express the self in a simple fashion. The educator Maria Montessori wrote about the extraordinarily sensitive aural functions of infants:

> First to become fixed in the little one's unconscious are the single sounds of language, and this is the basic part of the mother tongue: we might call it the alphabet. Syllables follow, and then words, but these are used without understanding . . . .[6]

Not only is this cognitive exercise repetitive and oral, it involves the visual and tactile senses as well, demonstrated by action verses such as "Pat-a-cake, pat-a-cake" and "This little piggy went to market." Soon the rhymes serve a definitive educational function as they incorporate the learning of letters and numbers, as well as songs, prayers, and games. Concurrently, the child delights not only in listening to nursery rhymes and lullabies, but also enjoys looking at the images that accompany the rhymes, cooing and crowing at both characters and content. With the introduction of picture books at an early age, the educational rudiments that trigger the imagination can be fostered while inspiring a thirst for knowledge: ultimately, the young child will realize that reading is instrumental in gaining knowledge. As Bruno Bettelheim has noted:

> Adults are usually unaware that learning to read, which they view as a rational under-taking and a typical ego achievement, can be mastered well only if the child initially, and for quite a while afterward, experiences reading both as fantasy satisfaction—as in his play—and as a very powerful magic. The child who greatly enjoys hearing stories that stimulate and satisfy his fantasies will also wish to know how to read these engross-ing tales to himself when no one is available to read them to him.[7]

Thus, through the early exposure of these volumes, unknown worlds and promises are offered. Much of this magic is due to the imagination of the artists making the illus-trations; given free rein, they are able to endow both animals and humans with all kinds of supernatural attributes. And, like magicians, the artists can suspend time: One intrin-sic characteristic in the illustrations that accompany nursery rhymes is that, in most cases, the image depicted suggests an undefinable bygone era. Usually the illustration is devoid of any chronological detail that would allow the viewer to pinpoint a partic-ular period in history. The architecture is often nonspecific and unrealistic; the vintage costumes are old-fashioned in a charming way; the landscape is bucolic. But in most cases these details harken an obscurely familiar, but imaginary past, simply known as "once upon a time." Perhaps the anachronistic references unearth faint memories, resuscitating a universal landscape called childhood. Memory is the special element that gives these illustrations their sense of enchantment and appeal.

Certainly, there are specific poetic jingles and images from those first books that are fondly etched in the minds of most individuals. The many scholars who have exam-ined the world of Mother Goose attest to the timelessness of her verses. Mother Goose herself is said to have remarked:

> Fudge! I tell you that all their [the critics] batterings can't deface my beauties, nor their wise pratings equal my wiser prattlings; and all imitators of my refreshing songs might as well write a new Billy Shakespeare as another Mother Goose—we two great poets were born together, and we shall go out of the world together.
>
> *No, no, my Melodies will never die,*
> *While nurses sing, or babies cry.*[8]

The origin of the Mother Goose songs (the familiar term in the United States) or nursery rhymes (as they are more commonly labeled in England) is unclear and has been the subject of much debate.[9] Many of these poems are centuries old and are endemic to the oral story-telling tradition, handed down in a manner similar to epic poems such as *Beowulf* and the *Chanson de Roland.* The fact that they have survived for so long is a testament to the remarkable power and magic that these verses convey to both children and adults.

It should be noted that nursery rhymes are not always lighthearted in nature or content; many of the rhymes created before 1800 originate from ancient proverbs, political lampoons, religious railleries, popular ballads, tongue twisters, chants of street vendors, and even bawdy drinking songs that were not initially intended for the nursery. Indeed, probably the only genuine nursery rhymes are lullabies and the rhyming alphabets and games for infants.[10]

In the seventeenth and eighteenth centuries, children were generally treated as miniature adults in society. Not only did they dress like grown-ups, but they were expected to behave like adults and therefore were exposed to both strong language and mature conversation. Certainly, there were few publications made specifically for children and these were didactic rather than entertaining. As the French literature professor Paul-Gustave-Marie-Camille Hazard commented:

> If, for centuries, grownups did not even think of giving children appropriate clothes, how would it even have occurred to them to provide children with suitable books?[11]

It is important to bear in mind that many nursery rhymes were known but not recorded or published; it is believed that some of these poems were already commonly recited in the sixteenth century, when William Shakespeare was a young man.[12] In 1697, Charles Perrault's *Histoires ou contes du temps passé; avec des moralités* (Histories or Tales of Past Times, with Morals) was published, subsequently appearing in English in 1729. It was subtitled *Contes de ma mère l'oye* (Tales of My Mother Goose) and actually included eight familiar, immortal classics such as "Little Red Riding Hood," "Sleeping Beauty," "Puss and Boots," and "Cinderella," but not any nursery rhymes per se.[13] Although Perrault's volume amused the French king Louis XIV and his court,[14] it did nothing to dispel the mystery surrounding the origins or identity of his "Mother Goose."

As legend would have it, a book of Mother Goose rhymes was supposedly published in Boston, Massachusetts, in 1719 by Thomas Fleet, a son-in-law of Mistress Elizabeth Vergoose (otherwise known as Mother Goose), a woman with a reputation for reciting nonsensical jingles to her brood of children and grandchildren.[15] If a book of rhymes was indeed produced, it did not survive. Although there are no facts to support the theory of Elizabeth Vergoose's claim, the tale serves as an example of the mythology surrounding "Mother Goose."

There is, however, one tiny volume now at the British Library known as *Tommy Thumb's Pretty Song Book*, which was published in England around 1744 by Mary Cooper.[16] Although only volume two survives, this collection originally comprised two volumes that included thirty-nine nursery rhymes and some woodcuts, and measured three by one and three-fourths inches.

Appearing in 1744, *A Little Pretty Pocket-Book* was published in London by John Newbery, a crucial figure who recognized that there was a market for publications composed specifically for children. Not only was this book intended to educate, but, it indicates that, like Locke, Newbery obviously recognized the need for an entertaining element, as evidenced by the title page:

A LITTLE PRETTY
POCKET-BOOK
Intended for the
Instruction and Amusement
of
Little Master Tommy,
and
Pretty Miss Polly.
With Two Letters from
Jack the Giant-Killer;
As also
A Ball and a Pincushion;
The Use of which will infallibly make Tommy
a good Boy and Polly a good Girl.
To which is added,
A Little Song-Book,
Being
A New Attempt to teach Children
the Use of the English Alphabet,
by Way of Diversion.[17]

Between 1765 and 1766, Newbery's successors published *Mother Goose's Melody*, or *Sonnets for the Cradle*.[18] An early edition of this volume made its way to the United States and in 1794, Isaiah Thomas (1750-1831), a publisher in Worcester, Massachusetts, pirated a facsimile of the British volume. Thus, Mother Goose had a presence on both sides of the Atlantic which has endured through modern times.

Among the children's books available in pre-Revolutionary America were hornbooks and primers that had been brought by the settlers from England. The aim of these was to teach basic reading skills, and to edify young children with spiritual and behavioral lessons. *The New-England Primer*, published in Massachusetts, first appeared at the end of the seventeenth century and became the most widely-used of these tracts. It contained a gloomy rhyming alphabet, prayers, poems, verses from the Bible, the Ten Commandments, and a few woodcuts. The overall effect was stiff and moralistic at best. Certainly, after so puritanical an experience, a child would not feel encouraged or impelled to explore other literature. Thus, the introduction of *Mother Goose's Melody* in America was a welcome and refreshing change for this audience, who, having fought a long and bitter war, were eager for entertaining material.

Mother Goose's Melody went through several printings and, although the first edition is no longer extant, there is one example of an edition published by Newbery's stepson, Thomas Carnan, in 1791.[19] This version included fifty-two rhymes with maxims, as well as sixteen songs by Shakespeare; each of these poems was accompanied by a tiny, crudely rendered woodcut.[20] The fact that this publication was fully illustrated proves how Newbery and his literary heirs believed in augmenting the resonance of nursery rhymes with images which would greatly appeal to children. It also reflected a shift in attitudes about child-rearing in that literature no longer had to be exclusively pedagogical.

Until the early part of the nineteenth century, many children's books boasted woodcuts. Featuring dense, cross-hatched lines, heavily shaded areas, and wooden forms, these stilted illustrations were often lackluster in spirit and primitive in character—and were in keeping with the stern Calvinist tenor of the times. However, around this time, educators in England and the United States began to reevaluate their theories regarding childraising and education, ultimately realizing that a protected but somewhat carefree upbringing was more psychologically nourishing. The old sociological and moral doctrines inevitably responded to a newly urbanized society, and this liberation of certain social constraints found a solid vehicle in children's literature. The pedantic tone evident in most of these books eased by the mid nineteenth century; the elements of humor, adventure, romance, and mystery emerged as salient and sometimes sanctioned ingredients. The world of fiction and fable was opened up, thus recasting children's books into an irresistible commodity.

Certainly the proliferation of books made expressly for children led to a burgeoning interest on the part of a handful of artists to enhance juvenile stories and nonsensical verses with their work. These artists were enticed not only by the new venue in which they could experiment freely, they were also attracted to the novel idea of reaching a mass audience through picture books. It is significant to remember that the growth of this market coincided with the Industrial Revolution and all of the residual ramifications—including more time for leisurely activities—that this milestone spawned in both Europe and the United States. The arena of children's book illustrations was furthered by the advent of increasingly sophisticated printing techniques in the nineteenth century. And also, in an ironic way, the very fact that traditional folk cultures were being jeopardized by industrial advances led to a rekindled interest in preserving the old fairy tales, folklore, and nursery rhymes. Thus, while fostering an inherent desire for literacy, the element of fantasy flourished in picture books, encouraging a child to be a child and not a tiny grown-up.

HEY, DIDDLE, DIDDLE!
THE GOLDEN AGE

Fairy tales and nursery rhymes now began to lure artists: the wealth of subject matter invited free interpretation. The publication of the first English translation of the Grimm brothers' *German Popular Stories* in 1823–26 signaled a landmark event for children's literature. The exuberant etchings of George Cruikshank graced the pages of these two volumes, capturing the imagination of both children and adults, while laying the cornerstone for the "Golden Age" of children's book illustration. Along with the expressive and inventive contributions of his successors, Richard Doyle and John Tenniel, as interpreted by the Dalziels, the enchanted visions of Cruikshank established the foundation of this movement. These black and white illustrations were drawn on a block of boxwood. The areas not intended to be printed would then be engraved or cut away. This technique allowed these artists to demonstrate their understanding of composition and line while imparting a sense of energy and whimsy not manifested in earlier children's books.

Although there were a few books illustrated in color in the early 1800s, the potential of children's book illustration was greatly expanded in the latter half of the nineteenth century through the efforts of Edmund Evans (1826–1905), who believed a book should be treated as a complete entity. Evans realized the importance of individual illustrations; he felt that each should be straightforward but key to the narrative sequence of the story. Using multiple blocks, he developed a complicated color printing process, enabling the picture book to be reproduced readily with pure, flat colors. Nursery rhymes provided much fodder for the artists who worked with Evans, as is apparent in the publications illustrated by Walter Crane, Randolph Caldecott, and Kate Greenaway. Through the efforts and encouragement of Evans, these artists were able to move away from the rigid, cross-hatched forms of the early wood engravings.

Crane began his career as an apprentice in wood engraving in London, where he studied under the tutelage of William James Linton, a colleague of Dante Gabriel Rossetti, John Tenniel, and John Everett Millais. In 1865, Crane's first color collaboration with Evans was realized in *The House That Jack Built*. This volume was the first in a series of nearly forty nursery rhymes which Crane illustrated for the printer. They were issued as Sixpenny Toy Books which, because of their low price, reached a broad market while maintaining a high quality due to Evans and Crane's dedication and love for the project. Among these titles was *Old Mother Hubbard*, published in 1874.

33. (above, left) Walter Crane (1845-1915). British. "Old Mother Hubbard went to the Cupboard," from *Old Mother Hubbard went to the Cupboard* [London: George Routledge and Sons, 1874]. Museum of Fine Arts, Boston, William A. Sargent Fund, 1964, 1556

37. (above, right) Peter Newell (1862-1924). American. "Old Mother Hubbard's Dog," from *Mother Goose's Menagerie* [Boston: Noyes, Platt and Co., 1901]. Courtesy of The Boston Public Library Print Department, John D. Merriam Collection

41. (left) Charles B. Falls (1874-1960). American. "Old Mother Hubbard," from *Mother Goose* [New York: Doubleday, 1924]. Chapin Library of Rare Books, Williams College

In the preparatory study for the image illustrating "Old Mother Hubbard went to the cupboard" [cat. no. 33], Crane depicts Mother Hubbard and her faithful companion in the delicate hues found in Japanese prints. There are wonderful details—the Canton platter in the cupboard, the Ionic column that graces the cupboard, the cross-stitched sampler on the wall, and pineapple wallpaper—that demonstrate Crane's remarkable facility for blending the mundane with the fanciful. Mother Hubbard sports fingerless gloves, a ruffled bonnet, granny glasses, and bustled overskirt. Her keys hang over her apron, signifying her domestic role. Over her long nose, Mother Hubbard peers at her forlorn pup. Sitting upright, paw outstretched, the loyal dog—a standard poodle of all things—emanates a human, almost regal, persona. It is not uncommon for a small child to regard an animal—whether alive, "stuffed," or pictured in a book—as a special friend or alter-ego, endowing it with human traits and a secret capacity for listening and understanding. And, although some grown-ups would not readily admit it, they do talk to their pets. Therefore, although he was certainly not the first to do so,[21] it seems perfectly reasonable that Crane—and other artists—would follow the lead taken by H. L. Stephens and anthropomorphize Mother Hubbard's hungry quadruped, fusing the realistic with the fantastic.

In each of these toybooks, Crane made it a priority to unify the imagery with the text. But, more importantly, the artist felt strongly about the impact of the illustration—it was not to be looked upon as a decorative supplement to the text. Rather, each stanza of the verse merited its own image. In turn, each illustration was regarded as a work of art that visually told the story. Undoubtedly, this approach was embraced by artists working after Crane as we shall see by bouncing forward briefly to examine other images of Mother Hubbard and her famous hound.

Another depiction of this saga, by Peter Newell, presents a humorous "Old Mother Hubbard's Dog" [cat. no. 37] in *Mother Goose's Menagerie* of 1901. Richly garbed from plumed hat and wig to his shoes, the mischievous mutt is perched on his hind legs—perhaps begging for a tasty morsel from the two children who watch with glee. Newell is known for the spunky, free-willed characters—who are often in "hot water"—which he depicts with such amusing veracity in *The Hole Book* (1908) and its popular successors. In the case of this earlier volume of nursery rhymes, the image of "Old Mother Hubbard's Dog" seems somewhat atypical. Although the children are not overly romanticized, there is a sweetness and innocence that resonates in this illustration—and yet there certainly looks like there is potential for some playful trouble.

Interestingly, C. B. Falls' 1924 ink and watercolor rendering of "Old Mother Hubbard" [cat. no. 41] from his book, *Mother Goose*, is much less sentimental in its attitude. In fact, it is almost stark in comparison with the earlier images discussed. Although attired in a pretty ruffled dress and bonnet—the decorative elements pictured—a stern Mother Hubbard dolefully contemplates her empty cupboard. Clearly, life in this household is tough and she works hard—her fire is neatly tended and a braid of garlic hangs overhead. Mother Hubbard's dour, emaciated face is downcast; her beloved pooch

49. Wendy Watson (born 1942). American. "Old Mother Hubbard," from *Wendy Watson's Mother Goose* [New York: Lothrop, Lee & Shepard Books, 1989]. © Wendy Watson, 1989; Reprinted with the permission of Lothrop, Lee & Shepard Books, an imprint of William Morrow Collection of Wendy Watson

watches her every move with ravenous anticipation. Falls' scene is a touching one, and he conveys a more somber presence than his predecessors.

In contrast to this sobering image, *Wendy Watson's Mother Goose* (1989) features a droll Mother Hubbard [cat. no. 49]. In the upper drawing, the faithful beast beckons his round mistress for his supper, while three feline friends devour a feast. The lower drawing shows the Widow Hubbard trying to console her dejected-looking pup as her kittens wash themselves contentedly. The illustrations portray the story in a simple, straightforward fashion, but still project the fanciful magic that forces a giggle from the reader. Watson uses bold outlines and flat, delicate colors. Although they are miles apart in terms of nationality, time, and aesthetics, Watson's and Crane's Mother Hubbards share the pure aim of telling a story with their art. That this goal has continued through the years says a great deal about the enduring legacy of Walter Crane.

34a. Randolph Caldecott (1846-1886). British. "And the Dish Ran Away with the Spoon," from *Hey Diddle Diddle, and Bye, Baby Bunting* London: George Routledge and Sons, 1882]. Gift of Mrs. Harcourt Amory, Manuscript Department, Houghton Library, Harvard University

Crane's colleague Randolph Caldecott also utilized this tactic of illustrating every nuance of a nursery rhyme, as evidenced in his book, *Hey Diddle Diddle and Baby Bunting* of 1882. In three charming images that mark the unlikely events described in the rhyme, "Hey Diddle, Diddle," the artist displays a freedom and whimsy not immediately elicited by earlier renditions of this verse. In the first scene "Hey diddle, diddle, The Cat and the Fiddle", a group of children dance blithely to the strains of a violin played by an orange tabby perched on a table. A reproving servant watches the revelry as she stands guard over a table laden with confections and cracker bonbons.[22]

For the second line, "The Cow jumped over the Moon, the little Dog laughed to see such fun,"[23] Caldecott has donned the cat in a red coat. Standing on a brick wall, he plays his instrument while his audience—two chickens, two pigs, the dog, and the frisky bovine—frolic to the merry tune. Above this lively tableau, a yellow crescent Moon winks sagely.

In the final vignette, "And the Dish ran away with the Spoon" [cat. no. 34a], Caldecott enchants his audience as he anthropomorphizes his subjects—the Dish and the

AND THE DISH RAN AWAY WITH THE SPOON

Spoon. The Dish, an oval platter, has flowers gracing his cheeks and forehead. Below two leafy stems which serve as eyebrows are two twinkling blue eyes, a nose, and a dimpled smile. Wearing black buckled shoes and a serviette knotted around his neck, the Dish strides off with an elegantly shod Spoon who sports a fringed skirt with flowing ribbons (perhaps made from a cracker seen on the table in the first scene). In the background, the cat still fiddles, while the decanter, a pitcher, and an assemblage of cracker-attired plates spring into a spirited reel. Although the animals are realistically rendered, Caldecott has endowed these characters with human attributes and irresistible personalities, liberating the imaginations of both children and adults.

Caldecott admired Crane's *The Baby's Opera: A Book of Old Rhymes with New Dresses* (1877). On the cover of this enchanting songbook, the artist depicts "Hey Diddle, Diddle" with a fiddling Cat and laughing Dog in evening dress, and a dancing Spoon and Dish. The Dish wears pointed slippers and a Chinese-style jacket, and his face is fashioned from a Canton platter. The traditional Blue Willow pattern in the center delineates his nose, mustache, and mouth. Certainly, this whimsical scene inspired Crane's colleague.

Throughout the years, Caldecott's particular image from "Hey Diddle Diddle" has been indelibly engraved in the minds of many young readers. It is reflected in the illustrations of "Hey Diddle Diddle" by Arthur Rackham (1913), where an impatient Dish is dragging a reluctant Spoon by the arm, and by that of Frederick Richardson (1915), with its promenading couple and a raucously laughing dog. Like the work of W. W. Denslow, Caldecott's imagery had a resonance that probably extended to the animators at the Walt Disney Studio, who have always endowed their animals with human qualities, but who have also breathed life into household objects—from the Queen's mirror in the movie *Snow White and the Seven Dwarfs* (1937), and the broom in the "Sorcerer's Apprentice," *Fantasia* (1940), to the candlesticks, clock, and teapot in *Beauty and the Beast* (1992). Caldecott's influence was far-reaching, not only in terms of his expressively and spontaneously rendered illustrations, his life-like drawings of animals, and his intuitive economy of line; he also cast open doors onto a boundless world of fantasy.

Another artist working during the Golden Age, Arthur Rackham amplified the capricious legacy of Caldecott, producing many marvelous books that have enraptured both children and adults for years. His *Mother Goose: The Old Nursery Rhymes* (1913), includes over 270 of the artist's favorite verses as well as pen and ink drawings, silhouettes, and full-color plates. One drawing, illustrating the rhyme "There was an old woman who lived in a shoe" [cat. no. 35] depicts a chaotic moment in the overwhelmed woman's life. In the foreground stands the forbidding old crone surrounded by some of her brood. While bowls of broth scatter the landscape, a young girl tattles on a brother, all the while holding him by the scruff of the neck. The old woman clutches a switch of twigs as she beckons the young rogue with a long bony finger. It is clear that the lad is terrified of this daunting harridan; it is also evident that the prolific character, under great stress, has momentarily lost control of her family. Behind her at least a dozen chil-

35. Arthur Rackham (1867-1939). British. "Old Woman who lived in a Shoe," from *Mother Goose. The Old Nursery Rhymes* [London: William Heinemann, 1913]. Courtesy of The Boston Public Library Print Department

MYTH, MAGIC, AND MYSTERY

dren caper and clamber around a giant, buckled, high-heeled shoe, complete with stitched toe and whimsically topped with roof and chimney.

Known for catching his subjects at a climactic moment, Rackham always leaves the ending up to his viewer's imagination and that is certainly the case here. Although this drawing may not have the twisting vegetation and bewitching characters so typical of Rackham, it does demonstrate the artist's remarkable facility for spatial compositions and expressive facial features, as well as his assiduous attention to detail.

At the turn of the century, these aesthetic concerns were manifested by many artists illustrating opulent children's books in both Europe and North America. Certainly, the books produced by Crane, Caldecott, Rackham, and other English artists had a reverberating presence in the United States. As the Americans were beginning to assimilate the ingenious vocabulary of the more established Europeans, the artist Howard Pyle provided the initial impetus for the movement in the United States. He began contributing drawings to the children's magazine *Harper's Young People* and *St. Nicholas* as early as 1873.[24] By 1894 he was teaching at the Drexel Institute of Arts and Sciences in Philadelphia, eventually opening his own school in Chadds Ford, Pennsylvania. Pyle passed on to his students a lasting legacy: many of them became luminaries in their own right.

Among Pyle's cadre was Maxfield Parrish, one of the first Americans to earn a reputation for his magazine covers, murals, and children's book illustrations. Known for his paintings with radiantly brilliant blue skies, Parrish first studied at the Pennsylvania Academy of the Fine Arts before attending a few of Pyle's classes at the Drexel Institute. In 1897 he was asked to create the illustrations for L. Frank Baum's book *Mother Goose in Prose*[25]—the first children's book for both artist and author. It was not a true collaboration, however, as the two men never met.[26] Baum reworked the nursery rhymes in prose, and Parrish produced fourteen pen-and-ink drawings—some with collage elements—and a color cover. "Humpty-Dumpty" [cat. no. 36] is a combination of drawing, collage, and Rossboard.[27] From a single sheet of drawing paper, Parrish cut the figure of Humpty-Dumpty, his ledge, and the cluster of castles. The artist attached this scene to two pieces of Rossboard having slightly different textures; the pattern of the sky is much denser than that of the infamous "wall." Then, using india ink, Parrish dotted the turreted hillside with feathery trees. The inventive technique of this illustration makes it particularly compelling.

It is the comical image of Humpty-Dumpty himself that beguiles the viewer. Living on the edge, as it were, he balances on the wall, a lock of hair pointing to his wide smile and ample girth below. In his sartorial ensemble, complete with collar and belted britches—albeit of an ambiguous nature with their double row of buttons and undefined cuffs—Humpty-Dumpty is someone not easily forgotten. Unaware of the definitive "eggs-istential" event that is impending, the illustrious egg seems overly confident as he gazes at us, poised on his precarious perch. With its humor and fastidious concern for details, "Humpty-Dumpty," and the other illustrations from *Mother Goose in Prose*, firmly established Parrish's reputation early on as a major force in the world of children's books.

At the same time that Parrish began enchanting his audience, another student of Pyle's began to prove herself as an able painter. Jessie Willcox Smith was an artist whose warmhearted illustrations indicate the true passion she held towards her subject matter and characters while reflecting the magic that emanates from each story. In 1885 Smith began to study art, eventually enrolling in Pyle's first illustration class at the Drexel Institute in 1894. Encouraged by her wise mentor, she developed her own style, which celebrated her genuine love for children. In a field dominated by men, she worked exceedingly hard to earn her reputation. And, despite struggles and disappointments, Smith eventually enjoyed a lucrative career, capturing in her romantic visions the innocence and joy of childhood.

36. Maxfield Parrish (1870-1966). American. "Humpty Dumpty," from *Mother Goose in Prose* [Chicago: Way and Williams, 1897]. Courtesy of the Syracuse University Art Collection

MYTH, MAGIC, AND MYSTERY

With a single image, Smith was able to relate an entire story, something that most artists could not begin to attempt. This rare gift was evident in many of her works and is demonstrated here with a delightful painting recounting the rhyme "Peter, Peter, pumpkin-eater" [cat. no. 38], which appeared in *Good Housekeeping* in 1913 (it subsequently appeared in the 1914 publication *The Jessie Willcox Smith Mother Goose*). This poignant painting shows Peter—a mere child as were all of Smith's characters—in the midst of a pumpkin patch filled with tendrils, orange blossoms, and, of course, the infamous pumpkin. It appears as though Peter has just ensconced his child bride in her new household and she is obviously unhappy. Arms raised, she implores her husband to reconsider his rash decision and not abandon her. It is a tender moment to witness, enhanced by the curling vines and cherubic characters that were in keeping with Smith's oeuvre.

Clearly, American illustrators were able to compete with the well-known European artists working during the Golden Age. In fact, it is illuminating to examine the way in

38. Jessie Willcox Smith (1863-1935). American. "Peter, Peter, Pumpkin Eater," from *Good Housekeeping*, November 1913; subsequently published in *The Jessie Willcox Smith Mother Goose* [New York: Dodd, Mead & Company, 1914]. Collection of Mr. and Mrs. Benjamin Eisenstat

39. L. Leslie Brooke (1862-1941).
British. "Little Bo-Beep," ca. 1904;
First appeared as *Little Bo-Peep*, one
of *Leslie's Little Books*, issued between
1904-1922; and in *Ring O' Roses: A
Nursery Rhyme Picture Book* [London:
Frederick Warne, 1922]. Courtesy of
Jo Ann Reisler, Ltd.

which the same rhyme was construed simultaneously by two artists working miles apart.
In the entrancing illustrations of the English artist, L. Leslie Brooke,[28] and the
American, Frederick Richardson,[29] we can examine the same episode from "Little Bo-
Peep," as both artists pay tribute to Caldecott and Crane. Although there are five verses
to this rhyme,[30] Brooke portrays the first three with four images—three drawings and
a delicately colored watercolor [cat. no. 39]. Richardson only illustrates the first and
best known stanza [cat. no. 40].

MYTH, MAGIC, AND MYSTERY

Little Bo-peep has lost her sheep,
And can't tell where to find them;
Leave them alone, and they'll come home,
And bring their tails behind them.

40. Frederick Richardson (1862-1937). American. "Little Bo-Peep," from *Mother Goose: The Classic Volland Edition* [Chicago: P.F. Volland & Company, 1915]. Collection of Kendra Krienke and Allan Daniel, New York City

Brooke first depicts Bo-Peep sitting in a tree, serenading her sheep, who gambol below her in a pastoral setting. In the next scene, Ms. Peep sleeps soundly in an empty meadow under her tree. The activity captured in the watercolor, obviously the most important episode to Brooke, shows the young girl embarked on her search mission. In the last drawing, the three truant lambs return, looking somewhat "sheepish." And rightly so—where are their tails? Beneath these animals, Brooke has resolved the puzzle—the tails can be found hanging from a branch.

In terms of their interpretation and style, these two artists could not be further apart; Brooke's protagonist, seen here in the watercolor, is easy to recognize. A young girl, Bo-Peep emotes perplexed consternation as well as determination. Dressed in a simple short dress and solid walking shoes, she is contemplating the sobering reality of her sheep's escape. Searching for her flock on a path in the verdant countryside, Little Bo-Peep, beribboned crook in hand, deliberates on her route. Pausing, she encounters an elderly, bearded gentleman with trusty dog in tow. Bo-Peep questions the fellow shepherd, but, judging by his blank stare, her inquiry goes unanswered. The serious countenance of both Bo-Peep and the shepherd show the artist's thoughtful regard for his subject matter. In Brooke's use of flat planes of color, his attention to details, and his supple lines that delineate the forms, his genuine understanding of Crane and Caldecott's oeuvre is obvious.

Richardson also displays these characteristics, but in a looser manner. His Bo-Peep, an adolescent beauty, forlornly roams the wild woods as if in a trance. Her costume and hair are meticulously rendered, although her shoes are probably not practical footwear for the average shepherdess. At first glance, it seems as if Richardson executed this vignette of Little Bo-Peep without considering the narrative; without the text nearby, this image does not instantly bring any specific verse to mind. Looking at Richardson's other illustrations in this volume, one knows immediately which nursery rhymes they accompany. After further study, Little Bo-Peep's long strides, frantic look of desolation, and shepherd's crook give away her identity. Ultimately, the artist did stay within the framework of the storyline while heeding his urge to create a more lavish fantasy. And, like the other artists working during the apogee of the Golden Age, Richardson did much to fuse the narrative with the decorative in his work.

SING A SONG OF SIXPENCE
BEYOND THE GREAT DEPRESSION

During the years following the first world war, the Golden Age of children's books waned, finally fizzling to an end around 1920. After the onset of the Great Depression, modifications were inevitable for every business and every individual. This bleak episode in our history had lasting repercussions of monumental proportions, altering every aspect of life in America. In the publishing world, the Depression affected the actual production and content of children's books. The romantic and sentimental idealism that abounded into the 1920s came crashing to a halt when the social environment was dramatically recast. Amidst great cultural, economic, and political turmoil, the authors and artists reflected their time.

More often than not, authors wove stories that were realistic in attitude and explored family life and relationships within an immediate community while recreating the events and emotions of childhood. These stories observed life from a child's viewpoint, particularly focusing on love, security, and human nature. From these stories sprung hope, patience, and a strong belief in civility. Many illustrators amplified these books in an innately American way, reverting to simpler forms as well as less extravagant modes of production while following the narrative tradition of both the Ash Can School and the Social Realist movement. Although some children's books produced in the 1930s were sentimental in nature, many revealed the somber times. There were some discrepancies: usually these voices came from abroad.

During this time, the United States saw a steady influx of European artists who emigrated to escape the escalating oppressive political situation. Lured by the new glamor of Hollywood and New York, many of these artists found jobs as animators at the Disney Studio or as set or costume designers on Broadway. Those Europeans who strayed into the field of children's book illustrations left a significant mark. One of these was the Swiss-French artist, Roger Duvoisin, mentioned earlier, who came to America from Paris in 1925. Although he had hopes of designing scenery in Hollywood,[31] he was employed as a textile designer for a New York silk manufacturer until the company went bankrupt in the Great Depression.

Unemployed, Duvoisin began writing and illustrating children's books, first inspired by a story that his young son Roger, then age four, was trying to illustrate. By 1932, the elder Duvoisin's first book, *a little boy was drawing,* was published. It was the beginning of a wonderfully magical and prolific career. His cheerful characters—the lovable Petunia and the Happy Lion, for instance—as well as a brilliant palette, inventive use of space, and upright cursive that scrawls around the page work together to make Duvoisin's illustrations particularly inviting and childlike. In 1936, his *Mother Goose: A Comprehensive Collection of the Rhymes* (edited by William Rose Benét) was published, causing an uproar because of its riotous activity and vibrant colors. Critics worried: Might not these unruly scenes incite havoc rather than inspire proper behavior? But this engaging book proved to be quite popular, selling beyond expectations in a troubled time in America.[32] Each of the four hundred rhymes is accompanied with an illustration (forty in color, the others in black and white). In some cases there are two rhymes on a page, making it somewhat crowded and perhaps confusing for smaller children. And yet, looking at a page depicting two nursery rhymes, "Dickery, dickery, dare" and "The Jolly Miller" [cat. no. 42] it is difficult not to share the excitement and joy articulated by Duvoisin. In "Dickery, dickery, dare," a man has just grabbed onto the hind legs of a pink pig that is catapulting into space. Falling in midair, legs and arms horizontally parallel, he is about to land kerplunk! on his bottom.

Seemingly unaware of the riveting storyline above him, the Jolly Miller strides confidently along, with red striped hat, muttonchops, and rosy cheeks, toting a yellow sack on his shoulders. Poised in mid-stride, he has an insouciant air, singing, as the rhyme says, "I care for nobody, no! not I, If nobody cares for me." In this amusing image, Duvoisin has captured the essence of the poem; indeed, the Jolly Miller looks as if he had not a care in the world. Given the time in which this book was produced, "The Jolly Miller" and the other nursery rhymes helped to dispel the pervasive gloom of the '30s.

42. Roger Duvoisin (1904-1980). Born in Geneva, Switzerland; Came to the U.S. in 1927 "Dickery dickery Dare" and "The Jolly Miller," from *Mother Goose: A Comprehensive Collection of the Rhymes.* Edited by William Rose Benét [New York: The Heritage Press, 1936]. Jane Voorhees Zimmerli Art Museum, Rutgers, The State University of New Jersey, New Brunswick, New Jersey, Gift of Louise Fatio Duvoisin. Photo by: Jack Abraham

43a. (above) Antonio Frasconi (Born 1919). Born in Uruguay; Came to the U.S. in 1945. "This is the cow with the crumpled horn . . . ," from *The House that Jack Built* [New York: Harcourt, Brace & World, 1958]. Collection of Antonio Frasconi

43b. (below) Antonio Frasconi (Born 1919). Born in Uruguay; Came to the U.S. in 1945. Title Page from *The House that Jack Built* [New York: Harcourt, Brace & World, 1958]. © Antonio Frasconi, 1958. Collection of Antonio Frasconi

This is the Cow with the crumpled horn,
That tossed the Dog,
That worried the Cat,
That killed the Rat,
That ate the Malt,
That lay in the House that Jack built.

Voici la Vache avec la corne tordue,
Qui a lancé en l'air le Chien,
Qui a tourmenté le Chat,
Qui a tué le Rat,
Qui a mangé le Malt,
Qui se trouvait dans la Maison que Jacques a bâtie.

This is the House that Jack built.

Voici la Maison que Jacques a bâtie.

Since the publication of Duvoisin's cheery volume up to the present, numerous books of nursery rhymes have been published. There are many that emit that radiant spark first ignited by the artists working during the Golden Age and the decades that followed. One book in particular that transmits this special exuberance is "The House That Jack Built." In 1958, Antonio Frasconi's version of this tongue-tripping chant appeared and once again, the artist was able to demonstrate his patience and expertise in the tradition of woodcuts

51-53. Edward R. Emberley (born 1931). American. "The Drummer," "The Cannon," and "The General" from *Drummer Hoff* [New York: Simon & Schuster Books for Young Readers, 1967]. © Ed Emberley, 1967; Reprinted with the permission of Simon & Schuster Books for Young Readers, an imprint of Simon & Schuster Children's Publishing Division. Collection of Ed Emberley

[cat. nos. 43a and 43b]. With his vivid palette and use of folk imagery, Frasconi brings to life the long poem, while teaching children words through repetitive, rhythmic prose.

Drummer Hoff (1967) [cat. no. 51], adapted by Barbara Emberley and illustrated by Ed Emberley, is another tautologic tale augmented with brightly colored woodcuts. Similar in concept to "The House That Jack Built," *Drummer Hoff* documents the building of a cannon. Six soldiers take part in the fabrication of the weapon, "But Drummer Hoff fired it off." Illustrating each stage of the cannon's construction, Emberley produces a vivid chronicle of the event while echoing the amusing story with his distinctive forthright style. The bold colors and flat outlined forms are both reminiscent of folk paintings, stained-glass windows, and chapbooks. The figures are expressive and their facial features invite children's laughter. Like Frasconi, Emberley successfully puts simple words together with simple pictures in a mesmerizing way.

Another more recent volume of nursery rhymes is *Mother Goose* by Alice and Martin Provensen of 1976. In "Sing a Song of Sixpence" [cat. no. 46], twenty-three blackbirds roost in numbered boxes lining concentric octagons. In the center of the composition, a table serves as a clever device to indicate two separate chambers. On the left side, the king sits in "his counting house, counting out his money," while on the right, his queen is "in the parlor, eating her bread and honey." Through the window above the royal couple, the maid can be seen hanging clothes in the garden. Suddenly the twenty-fourth bird swoops down and snips her nose. This image is charming, albeit somewhat stiff and naive in its rendering. While the checkered tiles of the floor, the clothes, and the open window loosely parallel seventeenth-century Dutch genre paintings, the overall sense is that the Provensens were influenced not only by the traditional folk paintings of the Pennsylvania Dutch, but by creations from animated cartoons on which both artists had once worked.

Even today the memorable imagery of Crane, Caldecott, and their following enchants other artists illustrating nursery rhymes. One need only look quickly at "Mary, Mary, Quite Contrary" [cat. no. 48], depicted here by Arnold Lobel in his *Random House*

46. (left) Alice (born 1918) and Martin Provensen (1916-1987). American. "Sing a Song of Sixpence," from *Mother Goose* [New York: Random House, 1976]. © Alice Provensen, 1976; Reprinted with the permission of Random House, Inc. The Kerlan Collection, University of Minnesota
48. (above) Arnold Lobel (1933-1987). American. "Mary, Mary, Quite Contrary," from *The Random House Book of Mother Goose* [New York: Random House, 1986]. © Arnold Lobel, 1986; Reprinted with the permission of Random House, Inc. The Estate of Arnold Lobel

Mother Goose of 1986, to see the sense of whimsy that has been passed on to our times. A rather disheveled Mary surveys her garden in disbelief—rightly so, as it is in a state of boisterous upheaval. Above her head an overgrown vine of silver bells and cockleshells tinkles and twists down to its roots. Mary's flowers are truly wild: lifesize, each blossom boasts a merry face and fanciful bonnet. Intertwined in the stalks are tendrils of bells and shells. It is interesting to note that in his illustration for "My Lady's Garden" in *The Baby's Opera*, Crane depicts flowers that also sport faces, but they are constrained when compared to Lobel's. Even Pablo Picasso utilized this flower-face device in his portrait of his mistress, Françoise Gilot, entitled *La Femme-Fleur*, of 1946.[33] Truly, Lobel's riotous garden is not simply a tempting feast for bees, but a tribute to the great luminaries of the Golden Age.

"IT IS FUN TO HAVE FUN BUT YOU HAVE TO KNOW HOW."
EXTENDING TRADITIONS

Not only are the rhymes of Mother Goose a foundation for artists illustrating children's books, but these verses have spawned many other amusing rhymes that trigger a child's interest in reading. Many books use simple rhymes and uncomplicated illustrations to capture the attention of a young listener while teaching words, letters, numbers, or other essential information.

One such book, written by Bill Martin Jr, and illustrated with the lively collages of Eric Carle, introduces a vibrant menagerie that helps a child learn colors [cat. nos. 50a and 50b]. The chanting, repetitive nature of the text and the boldly rendered animals are particularly appealing to toddlers. Again, Carle is able to engross the small child in a merry game of listening, looking, and learning.

50a. Eric Carle (born 1929). American. Cover from *Brown Bear, Brown Bear, What Do You See?* written by Bill Martin Jr [New York: Henry Holt and Company, 1992]. © Eric Carle, 1992; Published with the permission of Eric Carle. Collection of the Artist; Loan arranged by R. Michelson Galleries, Northampton, Mass.

47. Hilary Knight (born 1926). American. "Owl and Pussycat out to Sea," from *The Owl and the Pussycat* [New York: Macmillan Publishing Company, 1983]. © Hilary Knight, 1983; Reprinted with the permission of Simon & Schuster Books for Young Readers, an imprint of Simon & Schuster Children's Publishing Division. Collection of Mr. Hilary Knight

Going backwards in time to the outlandish—and more sophisticated—verses and illustrations of the British author, Edward Lear (1812–1888), one sees a fresh and absurd approach to the world of nonsense. Extremely well-traveled, Lear also had a great interest in painting. Known more for his outrageously clever verses and droll cast of characters, this artist's natural skill as a painter of landscapes, animals, and portraits is often downplayed. Ultimately, it is the nonsense verses for which he is most remembered, and deservedly so. The combination of Lear's rhymes or limericks with simple pen-and-ink drawings simultaneously conveys both the ingenuous and satirical while engaging the attention of all audiences.

One of Lear's most beloved works is the story of *The Owl and the Pussy-Cat* (1867), which has been illustrated many times through the years by artists in both England and the United States. Hilary Knight illustrated his version of the poem with vibrant watercolors that are loosely and expressively rendered. One scene [cat. no. 47] shows the Owl and the Pussy-Cat in their pea-green boat. With spyglass tucked under his wing, the Owl strums his guitar with his feet while he reads a navigation chart. Perched in the bow, the Pussy-Cat writes down her proposal:

> Pussy said to the Owl, "You elegant fowl,
> How charmingly sweet you sing!
> Oh! let us be married! too long we have tarried:
> But what shall we do for a ring?"

Knight's enchanting illustrations truly delight the reader and convey the essence of Lear's musical poetry in a blithe and spirited manner.

45. Nancy Ekholm Burkert (born 1933). American. "Chippetty Tip, Chippetty Tip, Its Only Name is the Scroobius Pip," from *Scroobius Pip* [New York: Harper & Row, 1968]. © Nancy Ekholm Burkert, 1968. Lent by the Artist

A lesser known poem by Lear is *The Scroobious Pip*. Lear began working on it while on the island of Corsica in 1868. He died, however, without completing the tale, and it was unpublished until many years after his death. In 1953, the unfinished text appeared in a collection of Lear's work entitled *Teapots and Quails*. Subsequently the poet Ogden Nash added a line or two and Nancy Ekholm Burkert provided illustrations. In 1968, *The Scroobious Pip* was finally published in its present form. The Scroobious Pip is a mythical creature who is part beast, bird, fish, and insect. On the magical shores of the Jellybolee, the mysterious Pip sits, while all of the beasts in the world gather together. With his prodigious gift for lyrical cadences, Lear celebrates his love for nature in this story and Burkert, in her final image, pays homage to this passion [cat. no. 45]. The animals all wonder who and what the Scroobious Pip really is. In answer, the enigmatic character will only provide his cryptic answer with such phrases as: "Chippetty flip! Flippetty chip! My only name is the Scroobious Pip!"

Burkert's beasts romp, fly, and dance together merrily as they sing the last chorus:

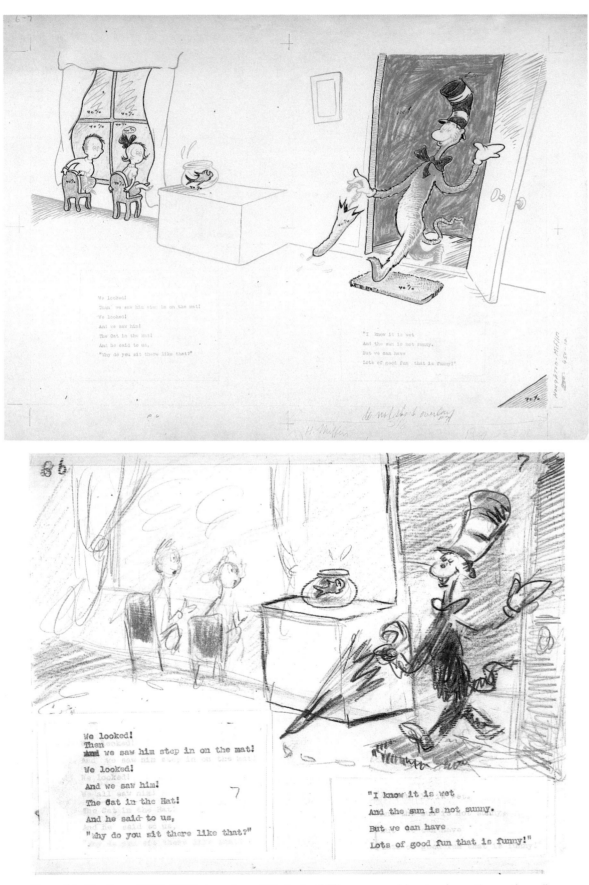

44a. and b. Dr. Seuss (1904-1991). American. "We looked! Then we saw him step in on the mat! . . . ,"
from *The Cat in the Hat* [New York: Random House, 1957]. Dr. Seuss Collection, Mandeville Special
Collections Library, University of California, San Diego. © TM 1957 Dr. Seuss Enterprises, L.P., ren.
1985

> "Chippetty tip! Chippetty tip!
> Its only name is the Scroobious Pip!"

Burkert is well-known for her facility in uniting her fluidly rhythmic imagery to a text, with the result that her illustrations are as significant as the storyline. In this image from *The Scroobious Pip*, her ability is clearly evident. With its delicate colors, meticulous attention to details, and teeming activity, this raucous scene captures the energy and exhilaration of Lear's poetry and demonstrates Burkert's own delight in presenting her chimerical vision.

It goes without saying that one of the most memorable and adored children's book authors is none other than Theodor Seuss Geisel, otherwise known as Dr. Seuss. Like Lear, his hilarious stories have captured the hearts of children of all ages around the world while encouraging literacy. Probably the best known of his books is the 1957 classic, *The Cat in the Hat.* In this harmlessly wicked caper, the Cat in the Hat strolls in to visit Sally and her brother who are at home alone with their goldfish on a rainy day [cat. nos. 44a and 44b]. The children and fish are quite startled by this uninvited intruder. The Cat simply says:

> "I know it is wet
> And the sun is not sunny.
> But we can have
> Lots of good fun that is funny!"

With his conspiring colleagues, Thing One and Thing Two, the Cat defiantly proceeds to wreak havoc, all the time trying to console the children (and fish) with the words:

> "Now! Now! Have no fear.
> Have no fear!" said the cat.
> "My tricks are not bad,"
> Said the Cat in the Hat.

The Cat has an amusing and busy day: his every activity launches the fish into a frantic state of apoplexy. The two children are caught between horror and intrigue; they are frightened but enthralled by their guest and his brazen partners-in-crime. And indeed, it is hard not to be mesmerized by this devilishly hyperactive Cat. All ends well, but not without some spills and tumbles. The mother returns to find a clean house and two children who seem to have had an uneventful day. Meanwhile, both reader and listener have been on the edge of their seats anticipating the worst. As with all of Dr. Seuss books, there is much to watch and absorb.

Dr. Seuss' genius prevails with an amazingly economical style. With his spontaneously rendered drawings in black, red, and blue, and just 222 words used in numerous permutations, the artist manages to capture expressions of fear, fascination, and frustration. Like the other books discussed, *The Cat in the Hat* offers a wealth of rich imagery in a very simple manner. But even more importantly, with this book Dr. Seuss released the young reader from the uninspired world of the *Dick and Jane* grammar school primers used in the 1950s to the exciting and limitless realm of make-believe.

Ultimately, an infant or toddler is exposed to many books such as those discussed above. Since the subject is infinite, this essay could only glance at some of the many tantalizing alphabet and nursery rhyme books that have been published through the years. After looking at those books which most successfully unify the text with the art, it becomes obvious that the illustrations are of utmost significance to the book as a complete unit and that the artist and author together provide equally meaningful components. Of tantamount importance is the fact that the alphabet and nursery rhymes play key roles in the learning process of a child, as evidenced by the quality, quantity, and variety of the material that has been produced. Finally, through these early books a young child is given a wealth of visual imagery *and* an invitation to dream. Under their spell, a child is granted spiritual and intellectual freedom while establishing the foundations for his or her future. In today's society, these roots extend around the world. Although the fast-paced technological community in which we live is providing tough competition for literature of all kinds, without early exposure to books, young people will lack the fundamentals necessary to take part in cybernetic advances.

This overview of picture books has laid the groundwork for a more exhaustive study of the art found in literature intended for older children. As the reader continues on to "Here and Now," one should remember the perceptive words of Dr. Seuss' famous feline:

> And look! With my tail
> I can hold a red fan!
> I can fan with the fan
> As I hop on the ball!
> But that is not all.
> Oh, no.
> That is not all . . . .'

III

H. Nichols B. Clark

Here And Now Then And There: Stories for Young Readers

69a. Esphyr Slobodkina (born 1908). Born in Siberia; Came to the U.S. in 1928. "Man Under Tree with Caps," 1940-47, from *Caps for Sale* [New York: William R. Scott, Inc., 1940]. ©Esphyr Slobodkina, 1947; The Kerlan Collection, University of Minnesota

Since the middle of the seventeenth century, individuals interested in the education of children have suggested that "pictures are the most intelligible books that children can look upon."[1] Picture books, in which image and text form an interactive whole, serve a particularly crucial function. Besides providing a basis for linguistic and literary competence through recitation of the alphabet and nursery rhymes, these volumes have a further purpose: either to introduce children to a wide range of factual experience or to foster their imaginations through fantasy. These antithetical approaches to children's books have fueled a debate over the bias against fairy tales which has raged for centuries and even persists today (see below, p. 159). This conflict between empiricism and fantasy has also extended in the twentieth century to the role of literature in education and child development.

Building on the ideas of such influential thinkers as William James and John Dewey, Lucy Sprague Mitchell, herself a pioneering force in the realm of progressive education early in this century, believed that children's literature should reflect the child's immediate world. She contended that freedom of expression, centered on empiricism rather than the remote world of fairy tales, was preferable in developing a child's imagination and, to this end, initiated her *Here and Now* books in 1921. Certain opposing views, influenced by Freudian thought and recently articulated by Bruno Bettelheim, took a more psychoanalytical bent and argued that a fanciful picture book offered an alternative to objective reality, which a young child was incapable of fully comprehending.[2] Moreover, Bettelheim theorized that picture books enabled the child to develop a rich and varied fantasy in images, a necessary precursor to a rich fantasy in words.

The third quarter of the nineteenth century experienced a proliferation of picture books made possible by the perfection of an economically viable color printing process developed by Edmund Evans. Under Evans' auspices, talents such as Walter Crane, Kate Greenaway, and Randolph Caldecott [cat. nos. 54a and 54b; see pp. 12-13] quickly dominated the field. Their efforts represented the first successful attempt to provide artistically superior and well crafted books at affordable prices, and these editions found immediate markets on both sides of the Atlantic.

FACT VS. FANTASY

At about the same time, America began to pay increased attention to literature for children, and the inauguration of *St. Nicholas* in 1873 heralded this commitment. Geared to a readership ranging in age from six to sixteen, the magazine, under the guidance of Mary Mapes Dodge, announced as the third point in a nine-point credo its desire to "inspire [readers] with an appreciation of fine pictorial art."[3] Dodge also aspired to "cultivate the imagination" and "prepare boys and girls for life as it is," with the intention of establishing a balance between fantasy and fact. Significantly, the editor asserted that illustration should possess a high degree of execution and be convincing. This emphasis on quality and objectivity was consistent with the prevailing criteria of

American artistic and literary attitudes and lent itself to the subsequent objectives of Lucy Sprague Mitchell.

Mitchell, considered by many to be extremely progressive, recognized that by the early 1920s America had become a predominantly industrialized and urban society and that the picture book should address this new reality; there was, however, a lingering taste for the pastoral convention epitomized in the goodness and optimism of Greenaway's overtly sentimental work. Although her illustrations for Browning's *Pied Piper of Hamelin* constitute a departure from her simple draftsmanship and pastel palette, they sustain the wistfulness for a "golden age" [cat. no. 55a].

SIMPLER TIMES

Even by 1910 the American farm was becoming something of a curiosity, and Elmer Boyd Smith set out to capture it for posterity in *The Farm Book* (1910) as well as *The Country Book* (1924). The image of the children dressed in their city clothes feeding a sow and her piglets nicely articulates the growing exoticism of farm life [cat. no. 56]. Undoubtedly influenced by Louis-Maurice Boutet de Monvel's *Jeanne d'Arc* (1896) with its draftsmanship and subtle coloration inspired by Art Nouveau precepts [cat. no. 57a;

55a. Kate Greenaway (1846-1901). British. "Where the waters rushed and fruit trees grew," Frontispiece for *The Pied Piper of Hamelin* [London: George Routledge and Sons, 1888]. ©The Pierpont Morgan Library, 1995. The Pierpont Morgan Library, Gift of Mrs. George Nichols, 1957.14

56. Elmer Boyd Smith (1860-1943). American. "The Pig Family," from *The Country Book* [Boston: Houghton Mifflin Company, 1924]. Kendra Krienke and Allan Daniel, New York City

MYTH, MAGIC, AND MYSTERY

58. Esphyr Slobodkina (born 1908). Born in Siberia; Came to the U.S. in 1928. "Nanny Goat and Horse," 1938 from *The Wonderful Feast* [New York: Lothrop, Lee & Shepard Company, 1955]. © Esphyr Slobodkina, 1955; Reprinted with the permission of Lothrop, Lee & Shepard Company, an imprint of William Morrow Northeast Children's Literature Collections, Archives and Special Collections Department, Senator Thomas J. Dodd Research Collection, University Library, University of Connecticut, Storrs

see p. 14], Smith created quintessentially American books with his own accomplished ingredients of exemplary draftsmanship, sensitive coloring, and informative detail.

This dedication to animal husbandry persisted well into the century and was even embraced by artists who had aligned themselves with some of the major contemporary movements. Esphyr Slobodkina, who had emigrated from Russia in 1928, espoused the modernist tenets of Surrealism and Constructivism and in the mid-1930s became a member of the American Abstract Artist group.[4] She brought her avant-garde commitment to geometric abstraction and subjective color to illustrating books. In 1938 Slobodkina collaborated with Margaret Wise Brown on *The Little Fireman*, whose content adhered to the empirical theories of Brown's mentor, Lucy Sprague Mitchell. Subsequently, Slobodkina embarked on an independent project, *The Wonderful Feast*, which she devised in 1938 but did not publish until 1955 [cat. no. 58]. In this idyll of barnyard life, the artist utilized the collage technique to create emphatic two-dimensional shapes reinforced by vibrant colors. Thus, bold invention infused fresh life into a seemingly retardataire subject.

Nostalgia for earlier, simpler times has never left us: this feeling is epitomized in the eloquent work of Barbara Cooney. Two examples, "Loading the Cart" from *The Oxcart Man* (1979) [cat. no. 59] and "Miss Rumphius Watching Children Gather Lupines" from *Miss Rumphius* (1982) [cat. no. 60], resound with the artist's deep and abiding love of familiar worlds—New Hampshire and Maine. In addition, these charming paintings reveal, through her emulation of the American folk art tradition, a sensitivity to ways of life and values that have all but disappeared. The artist reinforces her commitment to a more innocent worldview by working in a lucidly uncomplicated and direct style.

59. (below) Barbara Cooney (born 1917). American. "He packed the candles the family made," from *The Oxcart Man* [New York: The Viking Press, 1979]. ©Barbara Cooney Porter, 1979; Published by arrangement with Viking Penguin, Ltd. de Grummond Children's Literature Collection, University of Southern Mississippi
60. (above) Barbara Cooney (born 1917). American. "Miss Rumphius Watching Children Gather Lupine," from *Miss Rumphius* [New York: Viking Penguin, 1982]. ©Barbara Cooney Porter, 1982; Published by arrangement with Viking Penguin, Ltd. Lent by the artist; courtesy of the Bowdoin College Museum of Art, Brunswick, Maine

CITY LIFE

The pastoral tradition was challenged on many fronts in the twentieth century. The Ash Can School, under the leadership of Robert Henri, espoused an art that was immediate and direct and that chronicled life that revolved around the city. The industrialization of America inspired the American Precisionists, among whom numbered Charles Demuth and Charles Sheeler, to canonize the machine. Given impetus by the ideas of Lucy Sprague Mitchell, such attitudes also informed children's literature. Certain characters were inanimate objects that possessed human traits. *Little Toot*, by Hardie Gramatky, started plying the waters of New York harbor in 1939 [cat. no. 61]. A frivolous little tug, Toot gets his comeuppance from an older, wiser tug but shows his true mettle when he rescues an ocean liner in a storm. Gramatky successfully transferred his experience as an animator for the Disney studios to his children's books, and Toot was able to travel extensively in several subsequent volumes.

61. Hardie Gramatky (1907-1979). American. "Little Toot sees his reflection," from *Little Toot* [New York: G.P. Putnam's, 1939]. © Hardie Gramatky, 1939. Reprinted with the permission of G.P. Putnam's, an imprint of the Putnam & Grosset Group Spencer Collection; The New York Public Library; Astor, Lenox and Tilden Foundations

Works by a single artist, Virginia Lee Burton, sum up some of the issues at play. "No Steamshovels Wanted," from *Mike Mulligan and his Steam Shovel* (1939) [cat. no. 62], addresses the question of technological obsolescence, as the steamshovel is replaced by a more efficient diesel-powered model. It is not without consequence that Mike and his steamshovel, Mary Anne, are displaced from excavating foundations for skyscrapers in the city to finding a happy existence digging the cellar and providing the boiler system for a rural town hall. Burton pursues this confrontation of city and country in her award-winning *The Little House* (1942), which delineates the progression of a house's uncrowded pastoral location to encroachment and engulfment by development and its final salvation by relocation to pristine countryside [cat. no. 63; see p. 33]. In these stories, Burton anthropomorphizes the steamshovel and the house, thus nurturing a child's imaginative faculties, but she works in a clear, linear style and uses a convincing color scheme to reinforce the factual basis of the stories.

62. Virginia Lee Burton (1909-1968). American. "No Steam Shovels Wanted," from *Mike Mulligan and his Steam Shovel* [Boston: Houghton Mifflin Company, 1939] ©Virginia Lee Burton, 1939; Reprinted with the permission of Houghton Mifflin Company. Department of Special Collections, University of Oregon Library

64. Ezra Jack Keats (1916-1983). American. "Crunch, crunch, crunch, his feet sank into the snow," from *The Snowy Day* [New York: The Viking Press, 1962]. © Ezra Jack Keats, 1962; de Grummond Children's Literature Collection, University of Southern Mississippi

As America became increasingly urbanized, picture books dealt with this transformation until certain narratives assumed an exclusively metropolitan context. Among the earliest proponents of this genre was Ezra Jack Keats, who grew up in Brooklyn and cast a wide net around the city for his subject matter, firmly believing that all people (and children) wanted was "the opportunity to be people."[5] His first attempt to chronicle adventures in the city was *My Dog is Lost* (1960), which told of a young boy's search for his dog. Juanito looked all over Manhattan, as he ranged from Chinatown and Little Italy up Park Avenue to Harlem. Thus, new frontiers were being explored by a new cast of characters.

The book that really launched Keats' career and stands as one of the pivotal works in the realm of American children's literature is *The Snowy Day* (1962) which he wrote and illustrated. Inspired by the magical effect snow has on a city, Keats created his enduring character, Peter, a young African American, who reacts with universally wondrous delight at the snowfall which blankets and momentarily beautifies the city. Equally pivotal was the artist's use of collage, which became a liberating force for him in terms of extending his imagination and use of color. "Crunch, crunch, crunch, his feet sank into the snow" [cat. no. 64] captures the joy of making tracks in the snow and identifies the happy synergy of collage and paint, which produces an image that is vibrant yet reassuringly tranquil.

In 1966, Keats departed from his urban themes to create *Jennie's Hat* which further motivated him to explore the extensive possibilities of collage. Grounded in the important activity of daydreaming, the story centers around a young girl's desire to have her plain hat beautifully embellished. This is achieved through the kindness of birds, and the final result is a veritable cornucopia of materials [cat. no. 65]. This lyrical story provides an enchanting interlude to Keats' ongoing concern for recounting life in the city.

65. Ezra Jack Keats (1916-1983). American. "Jennie's Hat Being Decorated by Birds," from *Jennie's Hat* [New York: Harper & Row Publishers, 1966]. © Ezra Jack Keats, 1966; de Grummond Children's Literature Collection, University of Southern Mississippi

66. Ezra Jack Keats (1916-1983). American. "Peter chasing Letter," from *A Letter to Amy* [New York: Harper & Row Publishers, 1968]. © Ezra Jack Keats, 1968; de Grummond Children's Literature Collection, University of Southern Mississippi

In the fourth installment of Peter's adventures, *A Letter to Amy* (1968), Keats becomes more expressive with his use of acrylic paint and cut paper. "Peter chased the letter" [cat. no. 66] is considerably more atmospheric than the picture from *The Snowy Day*. The walls with their scumbled surfaces and graffiti, ranging from the authoritarian "Post No Bills" to the quasi-subversive line score for a stickball or stoopball game, resonate with the vital grittiness of urban experience. Keats conflates Peter's frantic pursuit of

67. John Steptoe (1950-1989). American. "Naw, my momma said he can't go in the park cause the last time . . . ," from *Stevie* [New York: Harper & Row Publishers, 1969]. Copyright © 1969, John Steptoe; Reprinted with the approval of the Estate of John Steptoe. The John Steptoe Collection

the letter so that his sequential movement reinforces the visual vibrancy of the technical process.

Despite Keats' commitment to chronicle the Black urban experience with sensitivity and compassion, he was unfairly castigated for representing stereotyped details and for not speaking with a Black voice.[6] While hindsight has defused these accusations, made during the emotionally charged years of the mid to late 1960s, an important voice

MYTH, MAGIC, AND MYSTERY

emerged from within the African-American community at this time. John Steptoe, also born in Brooklyn, was only nineteen when he published *Stevie*. Set in his neighborhood of Bedford-Stuyvesant, the story was of major consequence because it used the African-American dialect. Significantly, Steptoe admired and respected Keats for his pioneering efforts, although he lamented the reality that it required a white man to break the barrier in providing a dignified portrayal of African-American life in children's books.[7]

The drawings from Stevie, such as "Naw, my Momma said he can't go in the park . . . ," possess the unbridled energy of an adolescent youth who made them [cat. no. 67]. The use of heavy outlines elicited comparison with the work of the great French master Georges Rouault whom Steptoe had never heard of. While the dense composition and compressed, almost claustrophobic spatial structure share a certain affinity with this profoundly spiritual French artist, the art of comic books, whether in their newsstand form or in the monumental canvases of Roy Lichtenstein, offered the young artist a more immediate and accessible avenue of inspiration. Steptoe gives us the essence of the urban existence as he knew it first–hand; by means of poignant imagery and authentic dialogue, he provided the African-American child with a book they had never seen before—a story that was told about their turf in their terms. Consequently, John Steptoe and the African-American writers and artists who followed his lead opened up a whole new vista for their immediate audience and for the young audience at large.

ANIMALS AND PEOPLE

When dealing with the relationship of people and animals, the realm of the "here and now" must by necessity become elastic. There exists a litany of inventive stories firmly grounded in reality which often generate improbable situations. James Daugherty's *Andy and the Lion* (1938) blends fact and fantasy in the entertaining narrative of a young boy who takes a book out of the library and is transported into a retelling of *Androcles and the Lion*. Andy assumes the role of hero in taming his friend, who has escaped from the circus. The artist works in a vigorous style that chronicles rural America in a manner consistent with such regionalist artists as Thomas Hart Benton and John Steuart Curry. The depiction of Andy pulling the thorn transmits a feeling of Baroque energy with its interlocking diagonals and delineation of raw power [cat. no. 68] . Yet the pliers in Andy's back pocket signal preparedness, an American trait.

Equally liberal in its fusion of fact and fantasy is Esphyr Slobodkina's now legendary *Caps for Sale*, initially published in 1940 and reissued in 1947 with a broader range of color. In retelling this folktale for her nephew, the narrative considers the theme of the itinerant peddler, which has a rich history in American art. The idea of financial success through diligent entrepreneurship has long been cherished by Americans seeking to improve their lot; yet Slobodkina does not shy from depicting moments of discouragement or those of implausible levity, as the peddler, unable to sell any of his wares, takes a nap under a tree infested with cap-snatching monkeys [cat. nos. 69a and 69b]. The artist eschewed the more abstract geometry of her earlier books for a simpler style

68. James Daugherty (1889-1974). American. "Andy Pulling the thorn from the Lion's Paw," from *Andy and the Lion* [New York: The Viking Press, 1938]. © James Daugherty, 1938; Spencer Collection; The New York Public Library Astor, Lenox and Tilden Foundations

69b. Esphyr Slobodkina (born 1908). Born in Siberia; Came to the U.S. in 1928. "Monkeys in Tree with Caps," 1940-47, from *Caps for Sale* [New York: William R. Scott, Inc., 1940]. ©Esphyr Slobodkina, 1947; The Kerlan Collection, University of Minnesota

evocative of the great French naive master, Henri Rousseau, whose unrefined yet direct style had such an influence for the avant-garde.[8]

From this benign confrontation of man and monkeys, we turn again to instances of cooperation. Robert McCloskey based *Make Way for Ducklings* (1941) on a family of mallards he encountered in the Boston Public Garden and the traffic problems they created [cat. no. 70; see p. 34]. In pursuit of accuracy, McCloskey housed several mallards in his apartment so he could make detailed studies from life. His sketchbooks in the Boston Public Library bear this out and also reveal his attention to such locales as Louisburg Square [cat. no. 71]. Because the advent of World War II enforced economies which limited the use of color, McCloskey had to rely on his abilities as a draftsman to bring the fullest measure of expression to his work. The continued popularity of the book after fifty years speaks most tellingly of his success.

McCloskey imaginitively addressed an unfolding compatibility between man and animal in *Burt Dow, Deepwater Man* (1963). Chronicling the oft-times exasperating dealings of a Yankee sea salt with his dilapidated double-ender, Burt's story takes on a Jonah-like adventure into the belly of a whale. He escapes by drip painting à la Jackson Pollock, which causes the whale to burp him up [cat. no. 72]. McCloskey's choice of Abstract Expressionism to render the requisite reaction undoubtedly revealed his artistic bias, which was grounded in the humorous objectivity of his illustrations.

MAN AND NATURE

While *Burt Dow, Deepwater Man* considers the potential harmony between man and nature, children's literature also introduced young readers to man's helplessness in the

MYTH, MAGIC, AND MYSTERY

71. (left) Robert McCloskey (born 1914). American. Sketch for aerial view of Louisburg Square, ca. 1941. Courtesy of The Boston Public Library Print Department

72. (above) Robert McCloskey (born 1914). American. "Out of Whale's Mouth," from *Burt Dow, Deepwater Man* [New York: The Viking Press, 1963]. ©Robert McCloskey, 1963; May Massee Collection, William Allen White Library, Emporia State University

73. Charles Mikolaycak (1937-1993). American. "Jim waked. He clutched the bedclothes up to his chin . . . ," from *Shipwreck* [Chicago: Follett Publishing Co., 1974]. Copyright © Carole Kismaric Mikolaycak, 1995. The Kerlan Collection, University of Minnesota

Jim waked. He clutched the bedclothes up to his chin and lay listening. His bed trembled as the gale battered the house. But that had not waked him, nor was it the noise of the storm or the distant roar of the waves pounding the shore. It came again, the sound that had waked him, deep and insistent, the boom of the lifeboat gun, calling the lifeboat crew to its work.

face of nature's savage power. Charles Mikolaycak's illustrations for *Shipwreck* (1974) continue the tradition of this universal theme, which found its most notable expression in America through the work of Winslow Homer. While the story is set in author Vera Cumberlege's native England, the episode could take place in any fishing community. Mikolaycak handles the image of young Jim awakened by the boom of the lifeboat gun with an effective mixture of firm draftsmanship and delicate monochromatic wash [cat. no. 73]. His technical virtuosity recalls the woodcut illustrations of such nineteenth-century periodicals as *Harper's Weekly* to which Homer contributed.

TRAVEL

Since the late eighteenth century, travel accounts of such foreigners as the Marquis de Chastellux and Alexis de Tocqueville have offered informative windows into American life and customs. This literary genre occasionally can be found in children's books, most conspicuously in *Babar Comes to America* (1965), which recounted the visit of that lovable elephant of French origin by Laurent de Brunhoff who continued his father's initial efforts. Based in fact on the trip de Brunhoff made with his wife, the ensuing narrative focused on the vicissitudes of travel. Thus, we witness Babar employing a wide variety of conveyances ranging from a trolley car to a helicopter. Perhaps the most romantic vignette involves Babar traversing the Rockies by train [cat. no. 74]. The streamlined train, hurtling through a valley nestled between hills and larger peaks, represents the romance of the exploration and conquest of the American wilderness in ear-

74. Laurent de Brunhoff (born 1925). Born in Paris, France; Came to the U.S. in 1985. "Babar Crosses the Rockies," from *Babar Comes to America* [New York: Random House, Inc., 1965]. Courtesy of Norfolk Southern Corporation

lier times. This notion has provided an enduring theme for landscape painting since the second quarter of the nineteenth century, and de Brunhoff brings to his scene the same awe of nature and admiration for man's architectural achievements that Jasper F. Cropsey depicted in *Starrucca Viaduct* (The Toledo Museum of Art) exactly one hundred years earlier.

Even in this age of space exploration, the railroad continues to captivate our imaginations, and Donald Crews pays particular homage to the transportation of goods in *Freight Train* (1978). This drawing is a later variant on the original image, "Moving;" instead of a nondescript background, it suggests a pine forest in rugged terrain [cat. no. 75]. The blurred movement of the train conveys its brute force and recalls the eliding dynamism of the Italian Futurists, especially Giacomo Balla and Umberto Boccioni, who believed that "motion and light destroy the materiality of bodies."

The railroad station still imparts a feeling of excitement whether at the beginning or end of a trip. Tomi Ungerer portrays the bustle of a busy metropolitan depot in the moment of *The Beast of Monsieur Racine* (1971) when the creature and its captor disembark in Paris [cat. no. 76a]. The pomp and circumstance of the celebrated pair's arrival is nearly overwhelmed by the anonymous frenzy of the widely divergent throng of passengers crowding the platform—some of whom seem as exotic as the beast. Ungerer works with an economical yet energetic line, giving his characters unsettling physiognomies and scattering equally disturbing yet humorous episodes throughout the illustration. The bald man with three eyes in the lower right corner and the trunk carried by the porter at the left that is marked with a skull and crossbones and has blood seeping out of it are cases in point; these bizarre details confirm Ungerer's love of practical

75. (above) Donald Crews (born 1938). American. "Moving Freight Train," ca. 1986, variant of a drawing from *Freight Train* [New York: Greenwillow, 1978]. Mazza Collection Galleria, The University of Findlay

76a. (below) Tomi Ungerer (born 1931). Born in Strasbourg, France; Came to the U.S. in 1957 "Their arrival in Paris was a triumph," from *The Beast of Monsieur Racine* [New York: Farrar, Straus & Giroux, 1971]. © Tomi Ungerer, 1971; Donation Tomi Ungerer, Musées de la Ville de Strasbourg [Illust.]

77. Vladimir Radunsky (born 1954). Born in Russia; Came to the U.S. in 1982. "A lady came to the station with a pan, a divan . . . ," from *The Pup Grew Up!* [New York: Henry, Holt & Co., 1989]. © Vladimir Radunsky, 1989; Collection of Brenda Bowen

jokes (macabre as some of them are). The artist also pays tribute to his friend Maurice Sendak, whose arrival in Paris is heralded in a bold headline of the newspaper which the man at the far left is reading. In this story of a delightful practical joke, Ungerer employs a trenchant, satirical wit that bursts with raucous sensibilities.

From the bustle of this Parisian train station, we move to a quiet, almost eerie terminal where we learn that travel by rail also brings encounters with the unusual. In Vladimir Radunsky's illustrations for Samuel Marshak's *The Pup Grew Up!* (1989), the long-haired terrier, shown with its owner waiting for a porter at the railroad station [cat. no. 77], mysteriously changes into a Great Dane in the course of the journey. The artist's highly finished and coolly detached imagery recalls aspects of Surrealism, and the narrative irrationality would be consistent with the unusual turn of events in the story.

SANTA OR SAINT NICK AT NIGHT

The railroad can also transport readers into exotic realms, and there is a very special train that takes children to the North Pole on Christmas eve. Chris Van Allsburg's *The Polar Express* (1985) tells of this magical journey, and we are privy to the moment when the magnificent steam engine enters the highly industrialized North Pole [cat. no. 78]. By depicting a night scene with the architecture atwinkle with lights, Van Allsburg imbues the image with an appropriate sense of magic and poetry.

The personage of Santa Claus has enjoyed a rich literary and visual history in America, receiving its major impetus from the publication in 1823 of Clement Moore's poem "A Visit from St. Nicholas," which catapulted the jolly arbiter of children's for-

78. Chris Van Allsburg (born 1949). American. "The Polar Express Entering the North Pole," from *The Polar Express* [Boston: Houghton Mifflin Company, 1985]. © Chris Van Allsburg, 1985; Reprinted with the permission of Houghton Mifflin Company. Justin G. Schiller (Personal Collection)

tunes into the limelight. Artists such as Robert Weir initiated the visual response, and the political caricaturist, Thomas Nast, created one of the most enduring images in the second half of the nineteenth century. In our own time, Dr. Seuss invented one of the most poignant antitheses to Santa in *How The Grinch Stole Christmas* (1957) [cat. no. 79]. Dr. Seuss uses the despicable Grinch as a latter-day Scrooge to belittle the modern materialism of Christmas and to emphasize the genuine spirit of a celebration.

One of the most recent treatments of the doings and undoings of Santa Claus is William Joyce's *Santa Calls* (1993), which relates Santa's summons of a boy, his sister, and best friend for an Oz-like adventure in Toyland that carries a lesson of brotherly love. In the scene of the trio's first audience with Santa Claus [cat. no. 80], we encounter a visual extravaganza worthy of a Busby Berkeley film of the 1930s, as a chorus line of snowmen stand ready to break into a spectacular dance number. The handling of the figures as well as the costumes and imaginative details communicate Joyce's admiration for the work of Winsor McCay—in this instance the comic strip, *Little Nemo in Slumberland*. Santa, with his monocle and watch fob, assumes an unusually patrician demeanor, which is effectively dispelled by the huge chocolate-chip

Then he slid down the chimney. A rather tight pinch.
But, if Santa could do it, then so could the Grinch.
He got stuck only once, for a moment or two.
Then he stuck his head out of the fireplace flue
Where the little Who stockings all hung in a row.
"These stockings," he grinned, " are the first things to go!"

79. Dr. Seuss (1904-1991). American. "The grinch comes down the chimney to steal everything while the WHOS sleep," from *How The Grinch Stole Christmas* [New York: Random House, 1957]. © 1957 TM Dr. Seuss Enterprises, L.P., ren. 1985. Dr. Seuss Collection, Mandeville Special Collections Library, University of California, San Diego

80. William Joyce (born 1957). American. "Mrs. Claus Led Them into an Enormous Room," from *Santa Calls* [New York: HarperCollins Publishers, 1993]. © William Joyce, 1993. Collection of William Joyce

cookie that he holds in his right hand. This central image is emblematic of the zest, humor, and originality of the entire book. Joyce's treatment of Santa's kindness and wisdom results in honoring a major character and icon who bridges the worlds of the "here and now" and the "then and there."

ANIMALS WITH HUMAN CHARACTERISTICS

The distinction in a child's mind between fact and fantasy is undoubtedly tenuous, and picture books, for the most part, make little attempt to clarify these boundaries. Nevertheless, countless books engage the reader in a wonderful world of imagination that carries beyond the "here and now." Animals who assume human characteristics have fascinated audiences since Aesop first created his fables in ancient Greece (see below, p. 201). In England at the turn of the century, Beatrix Potter helped revolutionize this model, and her success was due in great measure to a profound knowledge of animals and a commitment to convey her stories, such as *The Tailor of Gloucester*, in a direct and forthright manner [cat. no. 81a; see p. 22]. Significantly, Potter was deeply impressed by *Uncle Remus: His Songs and His Sayings*, which appeared in England by 1881, and she even fashioned some of her own designs for these stories.[9] Her original tales of rabbits and mice, however, secured her reputation both in England and abroad.

Other works such as Kenneth Grahame's *The Wind in the Willows* (1908) and A.A. Milne's books of the 1920s about Christopher Robin and his beloved bear, Pooh, also told enchanting stories with animals. Ernest H. Shepard immortalized both Grahame's and Milne's endearing characters, with those of Milne assuming universal appeal. The reader is as captivated by the illustrations as by the text; "Pooh Marooned with Ten Pots of Honey" [cat. no. 82a] depicts the hapless bear on a tree limb with his precious ambrosia. Although Shepard renders the scene from behind, the viewer fully realizes Pooh's intense concentration on his life-sustaining supply. All comes right, of course, and after one or two more adventures reiterating Pooh's inherent guilelessness and

82a. Ernest H. Shepard (1879-1976). British. "Winnie Pooh Marooned with Ten Pots of Honey," from *Winnie the Pooh* [New York: E. P. Dutton, 1926]. The Pierpont Morgan Library, Gift of Mr. and Mrs. Malcolm P. Aldrich, 1960.18

goodness, Christopher Robin throws him a wonderful party with all of his friends in attendance [cat. no. 83]. The drawings are as spare and succinct as the author's text, but they are equally convincing in their ability to bridge the real and imaginary worlds.

Numerous American artists embraced this artistic outlet, and one of the most popular was Harrison Cady. The son of a naturalist, Cady spent much of his boyhood studying animal and insect life. Among his best-known works are the illustrations for Thornton W. Burgess' collection of bedtime stories which include such characters as "Peter Rabbit with Uncle Billy Possum" (1914) [cat. no. 84; see p. 25]. Cady becomes more fanciful in his renderings of these animals than were Potter or A.B. Frost (see below, p. 186), and consequently his appealing creatures assume more comic personalities. He also developed a satiric style for his depictions of insects, exemplified in "Woodland Serenade" [cat. no. 85]—done for *St. Nicholas* in 1907—in which he also transformed human types into animals, creating an equally vivid array of personalities, which echo Palmer Cox's *Brownies* (see below, p. 117).

Not all portrayals of animals intended for children possessed Cady's degree of levity. Artists such as Charles Livingston Bull and Paul Bransom carried the legacy of Sir Edwin Landseer's ennobled animal kingdom into the realm of children's literature, and others, including Boris Artzybasheff, conceived an imagery influenced by avant-garde ideas. His collaboration with author and poet Padraic Colum on a book entitled *Creatures* (1927) offered a variety of animals described in verse and captured in strikingly beautiful drawings, and "The Jack Daw" is characteristic [cat. no. 86]. The bold interplay between blacks and whites and the sharp angular forms reflect the influence of avante-garde Russian art as well as the cool stylization of the unfolding Art Deco aesthetic.

The plausible action of a bird perched in a tree is turned into the totally improbable behavior of an elephant in Dr. Seuss' *Horton Hatches the Egg* (1940) [cat. no. 87]. Horton performs this function as a kindness to an irresponsible bird, and Dr. Seuss enhances the remarkable plot with a cast of animals that defy zoological classification.

85. (right) Harrison Cady (1877-1970). American. "Woodland Serenade," 1907, for *St. Nicholas*. Prints and Photographs Division, The Library of Congress
86. (above) Boris Artzybasheff (1899-1965). Born in Kharkov, Ukraine; Came to the U.S. in 1919. "The Jack Daw," from *Creatures* [New York: The Macmillan Company, 1927]. Reprinted with the permission of Simon & Schuster Books for Young Readers, an imprint of Simon & Schuster Children's Publishing Division. Courtesy of The Boston Public Library Print Department, John D. Merriam Collection

It is this wonderful combination of whimsical rhyme and image that has generated so many ardent fans of Dr. Seuss, and his message about responsibility is easily acceptable since it is couched in such entertaining terms.

If Dr. Seuss' imagery benefited from his experience of creating cartoons, then some of Gustaf Tenggren's later work was influenced by his years with the Disney studios in the late thirties. His work for Golden Books, beginning in 1942, particularly underscored the Disney legacy. His first and most successful effort, *The Poky Little Puppy* [cat. no. 88; see p. 37] embodies this impact with plump stuffed-animal figures delineated

All alone Horton sat
And he guarded and tended
The egg. But his troubles
Were far, far from ended.
While he sat there so gently,
So faithful, so kind,...
Three hunters were sneaking
Up softly behind.

with crisp outlines and set against flat fields of color. The exploits of the adventurous little spaniel still hold enormous appeal for many young readers.

By way of contrast, Clement Hurd, like Artzybasheff, adapted modernist ideas to animal imagery. Study in Paris during the early 1930s brought him in contact with Ferdinand Léger and an inventive approach to formal design and bold use of color. Hurd's subsequent encounters with avant-garde figures in New York included Margaret Wise Brown, whose star was rapidly rising as an established author of children's books. After several successful joint efforts, including *The Runaway Bunny* (1942), they collaborated on *Goodnight Moon* in 1947 [cat. nos. 89a and 89b]. This latter book about the ritual of going to sleep combines a crispness of language enhanced by a clear, reductive geometry of forms and bright, joyous colors.[10] Hurd also recognized the specific needs of children and gave them ample opportunity for visual exploration and comparison as he chronicled how the room changed with time. Dismissed as overly sentimental by that influential institutional arbiter of taste, the New York Public Library (who did not order a copy of the book until 1973), *Goodnight Moon* withstood this potentially mortal slight and became such a classic in the field that it has earned the ultimate accolade of being parodied in Sean Kelly's *Boom, Baby Moon* (1993), illustrated by Ron Hauge.

87. Dr. Seuss (1904-1991). American. "They laughed and they laughed," from *Horton Hatches the Egg* [New York: Random House, Inc., 1940]. © TM 1940 Dr. Seuss Enterprises, L.P., ren. 1968 Dr. Seuss Collection, Mandeville Special Collections Library, University of California, San Diego

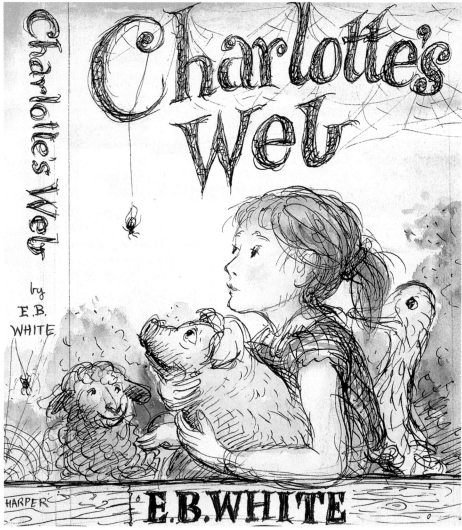

89b. (above) Clement Hurd (1908-1988). American.
"Bedtime," from *Goodnight Moon* [New York:
Harper & Row Publishers, 1947]. The Kerlan
Collection, University of Minnesota
90. Garth Williams (born 1912). American.
Alternate cover for Charlotte's Web, ca. 1952. By
E. B. White [New York: Harper & Row Publishers,
1952]. Estate of Ursula Nordstrom

The indifference of Anne Carroll Moore, (retired children's librarian at the New York Public Library and principal reviewer for *The Horn Book*) to *Goodnight Moon* was tame, however, compared to her attempt in 1945 to suppress E. B. White's first children's book *Stuart Little*, with illustrations by sculptor turned caricaturist, Garth Williams. Moore could not abide the idea of a human family giving birth to a mouse. Once again her judgment was fallible, and the book's success eventually gave rise to an equally beloved story, *Charlotte's Web* (1952). An exquisitely finished alternate to the final cover design introduces us to the central cast of characters as Fern and Wilbur look apprehensively at Charlotte as she descends from the "C" in her name [cat. no. 90]. Williams' draftsmanship is sure, and he captures the salient elements of each character with an economy of means.

Close in artistic spirit and execution to Williams' illustrations were Lillian Hoban's drawings of Frances, the endearing badger who first appeared in 1960 with drawings by Williams. "It was breakfast time, and everyone was at the table" from *Bread and Jam for Frances* (1964) opens the narrative, which deals with breaking Frances of a monolithic diet [cat. no. 91]. The picture is a paean to domestic harmony, in which the morning meal is depicted as the epitome of a leisurely repast. The velvety pencil strokes have a soft lithographic quality which literally and figuratively reinforces the warm and fuzzy tenor of the story.

Equally sympathetic is Tasha Tudor's *Corgiville Fair* (1970), which chronicles the festivities of this annual event in a small town inhabited by corgis, cats, rabbits, and goblins known as boggarts. The panoramic illustration of the fair [cat. no. 92] contains myriad details in carefully delineated watercolors that convey the spirit of celebration as well as the artist's trademark aura of well-being.

The adventures of animals is so pervasive that we can even find stories set within museums. In *Norman the Doorman* (1959) Don Freeman gives us the endearing char-

91. Lillian Hoban. American. "Family Eating Bread and Jam," from *Bread and Jam for Frances* [New York: Harper & Row Publishers, 1964]. © Lillian Hoban, 1964; Northeast Children's Literature Collections, Archives and Special Collections Department, Senator Thomas J. Dodd Research Collection, University Library, University of Connecticut, Storrs
92. Tasha Tudor (born 1915). American. "There was the Big Tent . . . ," from *Corgiville Fair* [New York: Thomas Y. Crowell Company, 1971]. © Tasha Tudor, 1971; Collection of Col. Thomas Tudor

There is the Main Tent where Vegetables, Fruit, Preserves, Flowers and Fancywork are shown. The Poultry Shed, the Goat and Guinea Pig Barns. The Ginger Beer Stand, the PeepShow and the Merry-go-Round, with a Calliope and dashing wooden Goats with flowing beards. There are runaway pigs and lost Puppies and TabbyCats selling Cotton Candy, and Boggarts with Patent Medicine Remedies, and old Corgis with Trained Fleas. It is WONDERFUL!

93. (below) Don Freeman (1908-1978). American. Preliminary idea for "Norman Lecturing to Guests at the Majestic Museum," ca. 1959, preliminary idea for *Norman the Doorman* [New York: The Viking Press, 1959]. May Massee Collection, William Allen White Library, Emporia State University

94. (right) Petra Mathers (born 1945). Born in Germany; Came to the U.S. in 1968. "'Yes,' she said and flung the covers back. Victor's heart jumped and his knees gave way," from *Victor and Christabel* [New York: Alfred A. Knopf, Inc., 1993]. © Petra Mathers, 1993; Reprinted with the permission of Alfred A. Knopf, Inc., an imprint of Random House, Inc. Collection of Petra Mathers

96. (bottom) William Steig (born 1907). American. "Zeke leaving the family living room having put them to sleep with his harmonica playing," from *Zeke Pippin* [New York: HarperCollins Publishers, 1994]. Collection of Holly M. McGhee

acter of Norman, a mouse, who guides friends and family, such as his cousins the Petrinis, through the museum's storage. This preliminary idea [cat. no. 93] reveals how Freeman reversed the composition to accommodate its placement on a different page and how he changed the subject of the painting from a lion to a sad clown. The setting of the book permitted the artist to interject a wide range of art-historical references in an often humorous vein.

Equally implausible but no less enchanting is Petra Mathers' story of *Victor and Christabel* (1993) which tells of a shy crocodile, working as a museum guard, who falls in love with a young, female crocodile in a painting. The canvas that appears mysteriously on the museum's doorstep and subsequently under Victor's domain is based on Vittore Carpaccio's *Saint Ursula's Dream* (ca. 1495) which hangs in the Galleria Dell'Accadèmia in Venice. In this variation on the Pygmalion story, which Mathers combined with the fairy tale story of an enchanted princess, Victor, through his unwavering devotion, breaks the spell and wins the heart of Christabel [cat. no. 94]. Early in the book, Mathers pays homage to Kurt Schwitters and the Orphism of Robert and Sonia Delaunay by including examples of their work in the galleries. In the climactic scene of Christabel's release from the canvas, the pure forms of objects magically suspended in air and the even applications of color provide a composition that brings Wassily Kandinsky's Bauhaus abstractions to mind. While these art–historical references are appropriate to the story's museum context, they ultimately serve to capture the narrative's magic.

William Steig has entertained readers of *The New Yorker* for over six decades with his delightful cartoons, and he has also enthralled children of all ages for three decades with his wonderful tales filled with humorous fantasy.[11] *Sylvester and the Magic Pebble* (1969) secured his reputation, and books such as *The Amazing Bone* (1976) and *Dr. De Soto* (1982) affirm Steig's exalted position as well as demonstrate his commitment to the underdog. In "Dr. De Soto fastened his extractor to the bad tooth," we witness the huge disparity in size between the fox and the two mice [cat. no. 95; see p. 39]. Nevertheless, guile neutralizes this imbalance, and the mice devise a way to perform their good services without risk of injury. The economical composition and efficient line conspire with a vivid text to give the narrative a visual amplitude that recalls the pioneering efforts of Randolph Caldecott.

With an illustrious career well established, Steig has lost none of his luster. In a recent work, *Zeke Pippin* (1994), the artist-author gives us a splendid yarn of a pig playing a magic harmonica that puts its audience to sleep. When Zeke first performs for his family, he storms out of the room, incensed at their soporific reaction [cat. no. 96]. Here again, Steig's signature tremulous draftsmanship brings energy and zest to his renditions. He, too, is not immune to art-historical reference, as he satirizes Antonio Canova's *Three Graces* (1810–1815) with a porcine variation. Readers of all ages gravitate unwaveringly to Steig's stories for their witty implausibility and delectable artistry.

WHIMSICAL STYLE, IMPROBABLE ADVENTURES

Equally preposterous narratives involved humans, and one of the earliest masters in this genre was Peter Newell. In addition to refreshing new interpretations of Lewis Carroll and Mother Goose (see above, p. 58), Newell attempted producing books with different properties such as odd shapes, and even holes. *The Hole Book* (1908) possesses a proto-Surreal quality as a bullet—fired by a disobedient child—passes through a variety of locales, including a pet shop, where the transaction for a parrot is interrupted by a group of mice escaping through the bullet hole [cat. no. 97a]. In the original art work, Newell glued a small disk of shiny black enamel paint on the drawing to mark the bullet's path.

Contemporary artists admire Newell's whimsical style, and Richard Egielski reinterprets *The Little Father* (1985)—by Gelett Burgess, one of Newell's contemporaries best known for his "Goops" (see below, p. 118)—in a style reminiscent of the earlier artist. The story tells of the magical shrinking properties of india ink when drunk, and Egielski captures the theatrical expression and bold outline consistent with cartoon imagery that informed Newell's style [cat. no. 98]. In original works such as *Louis the Fish* (1980), written by Arthur Yorinks, the admiration for Newell is also apparent. In this delightfully bizarre story of a butcher who turns into a fish, the moment "Louis dreams he is attacked by various meats" [cat. no. 99] conveys a marvelously Surreal sense of Louis struggling with his grip on reality as he is surrounded by an array of angry chops, steaks, and salamis. The artist cleverly offsets the brouhaha on the street by the placid pisciform clouds that gently float by in the night sky. Through his own wit and skillful draftsmanship, Egielski brings fresh expression to Newell's legacy.

97a. (top) Peter Newell (1862-1924). American. "Pet Shop with Mice Escaping," from *The Hole Book* [New York: Harper Brothers, 1908]. Philip Hofer Bequest, Department of Printing and Graphic Arts, Houghton Library, Harvard University
98. (middle) Richard Egielski (born 1952). American. "I fancy that he shrank/Because of all the India ink that Mr. Master drank," from *The Little Father* [New York: Farrar, Straus, and Giroux, 1985]. © Richard Egielski, 1985; Collection of Richard Egielski
99. (right) Richard Egielski (born 1952). American. "Louis attacked by hamburgers, salamis, roast beefs, etc.," from *Louis the Fish* [New York: Farrar, Straus, and Giroux, 1980]. © Richard Egielski, 1980; Collection of Richard Egielski

And so he went back over the sunny hills and down through the cool valleys, to show all his pretty kittens to the very old woman.

It was very funny to see those hundreds and thousands and millions and billions and trillions of cats following him.

One of the seminal books dealing with improbability and animals was Wanda Gág's first children's book, *Millions of Cats*, which appeared in 1928. Gág employed a simple yet imaginative stylization in her imagery to create intelligible and humorous vignettes that were enhanced by the sophisticated fusion of picture and text [cat. no. 100]. The artist believed that her illustrations for children's books should be held to the same high standards as other work she produced. This criteria reflected a desire to endure, and *Millions of Cats* continues to give enormous pleasure today.

From millions of cats we turn to hats and *The 500 Hats of Bartholomew Cubbins* (1938), by Dr. Seuss. Again, magic is in the air as the deferential Bartholomew cannot show his respect to the king because of a hat that keeps replacing itself [cat. no. 101]. Here, too, the outrageous storyline is perfectly complemented by zany drawings which contribute to creating a superb sense of fantasy.

Escape from reality into worlds of enchantment anchors much of the best in children's literature, and another book that has made a lasting impression is Crockett Johnson's *Harold and the Purple Crayon* (1955). Harold's adventures with his magic crayon take the reader far and wide: on picnics, over mountains, and even into the city [cat. no. 102]. Johnson's approach is a true stroke of genius, since he creates pictures as a child would create them; consequently, they can see the story in their own visual language. In a sense, this was the modernist aesthetic coming back on itself, since so many twentieth-century artists believed that the most original art was possible only by creating it as a child would.

In 1963 there emerged from the reassuring never-neverland surveyed thus far a purposefully unsettling and even terrifying book by Maurice Sendak, *Where the Wild Things Are*. Sendak has emerged as one of the major creative forces in children's book illustration, and *Where the Wild Things Are* was pivotal to establishing this reputation.[12] Like Ezra Jack Keats, Sendak grew up in Brooklyn, and the urban experience provided an

100. Wanda Gág (1893-1946). American. "Old Man Confronted by Cats in a Landscape," from *Millions of Cats* [New York: Coward, McCann & Geohegan, 1928]. Reprinted with the permission of Coward-McCann, an imprint of the Putnam & Grosset Group. The Kerlan Collection, University of Minnesota

101. Dr. Seuss (1904-1991).
American. "Bartholomew Arrives at
Top of the Tower," from *The 500
Hats of Bartholomew Cubbins* [New
York: Vanguard Press, 1938]. © TM
1938 Dr. Seuss Enterprises, L.P., ren.
1965. Dr. Seuss Collection,
Mandeville Special Collections
Library, University of California, San
Diego

important foundation to his artistic vision. By his own admission, Sendak's aesthetic was based in great part on the movies he saw in the late thirties and early forties: *King Kong*, the musicals of Busby Berkeley, the comedies of Laurel and Hardy, and the animated films of Walt Disney.

Where the Wild Things Are deals with parent-child conflict, anger, fantasy, escape, and, ultimately, reconciliation. The book was controversial, considered by some adults to be too scary and threatening; but the Caldecott committee's voice prevailed, and the book enjoys unprecedented success in many languages. In addition to a strong dose of

MYTH, MAGIC, AND MYSTERY

102. Crockett Johnson (1906-1975). American. "He made lots of buildings full of windows," from *Harold and the Purple Crayon* [New York: Harper & Row Publishers, 1955]. Northeast Children's Literature Collections, Archives and Special Collections Department, Senator Thomas J. Dodd Research Collection, University Library, University of Connecticut, Storrs

He made lots of buildings full of windows.   He made a whole city full of windows.

imagery taken subliminally from *King Kong,* Sendak works in pen and ink, employing ample cross-hatching that pays tribute to the early nineteenth-century graphic tradition in Europe. One of the artist's attention-getting devices was a series of double-page spreads without text at the center of the book which is preceded by the crowning of Max and his declaration to "let the wild rumpus start" [cat. no. 103]. Possibly signifying Max's fury, which renders him unable to speak, these "rumpus" images vibrantly convey a child's quest for empowerment far more forcefully than words.

If *King Kong* insinuated itself into *Where the Wild Things Are,* then Busby Berkeley, Laurel and Hardy, Mickey Mouse, and a healthy dollop of Winsor McCay's comic strip *Little Nemo in Slumberland* provided the visual ingredients for *In the Night Kitchen* (1970). *Little Nemo* was a revelation to Sendak, who first saw McCay's work in an exhibition at The Metropolitan Museum of Art in 1965; it sent him back to study the popular art of his childhood. The use of frames—derived from these researches—implies a sense of

103. Maurice Sendak (born 1928). American. "Make him King of all the Wild Things/Let the Rumpus Start," from *Where the Wild Things Are* [New York: Harper & Row Publishers, 1963]. © Maurice Sendak, 1963. Courtesy, Maurice Sendak and The Rosenbach Museum & Library

104. (above) Maurice Sendak (born 1928). American. "And they put that batter up to Bake a Delicious Mickey-cake," from *In the Night Kitchen* [New York: Harper & Row Publishers, 1970]. © Maurice Sendak, 1970. Courtesy, Maurice Sendak and The Rosenbach Museum & Library
105. (below) Chris Van Allsburg (born 1949). American. "Monkeys Steal food, Miss one turn," from *Jumanji* [Boston: Houghton Mifflin Company, 1981]. © Chris Van Allsburg, 1981; Reprinted with the permission of Houghton Mifflin Company. Collection of Chris and Lisa Van Allsburg

animation or comic books exemplified in a close-up double spread of the Mickey-cake being put in the oven by the trio of Hardyesque bakers [cat. no. 104]. The ambiguity of kitchen as cityscape enhances the dream imagery, and Sendak's fanciful highrise architecture embellished with kitchen utensils anticipates postmodern architecture of the late seventies and eighties. This book, too, was controversial as adults objected to Mickey's precise nudity and the book's implicit sexuality. Sendak refused to capitulate to this criticism and favored *In the Night Kitchen* over *Where the Wild Things Are*, considering it more profound.

Chris Van Allsburg's highly imaginative work also proves that children enjoy material that may prove unsettling to adults. *Jumanji* (1981) tells the story of a brother and sister who play a jungle adventure board game that lurches them in and out of reality. The move "Monkeys steal food, miss one turn" leads the players to the kitchen where monkeys are pillaging the room [cat. no. 105]; these are not the lovable characters typified by Curious George (see below). Van Allsburg combines the hermetic stillness of Caspar David Friedrich with Max Klinger's penchant for the bizarre into what the artist himself terms a "gentle surrealism." The extraordinary draftsmanship and expressive use of shadows provide a convincing hyperreality, while the suspended animation reinforces the scene's metaphysical quality.

Less disturbing because of his use of comic relief is the work of David Wiesner. The artist often takes his reader to the far side of reality with weird storylines containing mutated flora and fauna. In *Tuesday* (1991), squadrons of frogs on magic-carpet lilypads pass through Somewhere, U.S.A., leaving puzzlement and paranoia in their wake [cat. no. 106]. The pictures are rendered in a cool palette with a precise clarity that renders the image even more compelling and eerie.

Similar principles hold true for *June 29, 1999* (1992), in which giant vegetables begin to fall to earth, possibly as the result of a high school student's experiment with growing seedlings in the ionosphere. In "At last, the blue ribbon at the state fair is mine!", the cabbage in Tony Kramer's field is worthy of the photorealist still lifes of Ben Schonzeit, and its enormity gains added dimension by the spectator's worm's-eye view [cat. no. 107]. Here again, the light-hearted narrative defuses any potentially sinister element one can encounter in science fiction; even the extraterrestrials are disarmingly benign.

Another contemporary of Van Allsburg and Wiesner who delights in the outrageously improbable is William Joyce. His work is distinguished from the other two by a greater emphasis on humor at the expense of the bizarre. *Dinosaur Bob and his Adventures with the Family Lazardo*, first published in 1988 and expanded in 1995, offers a delightful peek into the imaginative world of a lovable and talented apatosaurus. Discovered in Egypt by the Lazardo family, Bob is adopted by them and brought back to southwestern Virginia. Evocative of Winsor McCay's *Gertie the Dinosaur*, an animated film which appeared in 1914, *Dinosaur Bob* is a period piece set in 1929, and Joyce captures the spirit of the age with great gusto and wit. "'Hooray!' yelled the Lazardos, and they

106. (above) David Wiesner (born 1956). American. "Frogs Flying on Lilypads," from *Tuesday* [New York: Clarion Books, 1991]. ©David Wiesner, 1991; Reprinted with the permission of Clarion Books, an imprint of Houghton Mifflin Company. Collection of David Wiesner

107. (below) David Wiesner (born 1956). American. "At last, the blue ribbon at the state fair is mine!," from *June 29, 1999* [New York: Clarion Books, 1992]. © David Wiesner, 1992; Reprinted with the permission of Clarion Books, an imprint of Houghton Mifflin Company. Collection of David Wiesner

launched into the Hokey Pokey" blends the properties of animation and the comic strip with the tight regionalist style of Grant Wood to create a composition that is cinemagraphic as well as suggestive of an era [cat. no. 108].

In addition to their gigantic size, dinosaurs command the attention of children because they lived so long ago, thus leaving a lot to the imagination. Otherworldly animals have always held fascination for young and old as well, and dragons occupy a place of honor in this category (see below, p. 145). A recent anthology of poems by Jack Prelutsky with pictures by Peter Sís entitled *The Dragons Are Singing Tonight* (1993) attempts to blur the lines of disbelief regarding these creatures. "I Made A Mechanical Dragon" [cat. no. 109] offers the artist's tongue-in-cheek assessment of American technology in the guise of a mechanical construction according to the do-it-yourself tradi-

MYTH, MAGIC, AND MYSTERY

108. (above) William Joyce (born 1957). American. "'Horray!' Yelled the Lazardos and they launched into the Hokey Pokey," from *Dinosaur Bob*, rev. ed. [New York: HarperCollins Publishers, 1995]. © William Joyce, 1995. Collection of William Joyce

109. (below) Peter Sís (born 1949). Born in Brünn, Czechoslovakia; Came to the U.S. in 1982. "I Made a Mechanical Dragon," from *The Dragons Are Singing Tonight* [New York: Greenwillow Books, 1993]. © Peter Sís, 1993; Reprinted with the permission of Greenwillow Books, an imprint of William Morrow. Collection of Peter Sís

tion of Rube Goldberg. The visual humor is infectious and recalls the superb quasi-surreal animation of *Monty Python and His Flying Circus.*

Sís also uses animals and magic in a story to educate his daughter about her Czech heritage. Inspired by Czechoslovakia's liberation from Communist rule, *The Three Golden Keys* (1994) weaves adventure with legend, and a black cat with magic eyes plays a major role. In "I follow the determined cat back across the ancient bridge" [cat. no. 110; see p. 41], the viewer looks at the scene through a convex lens with the spectral framework of the hot-air balloon as a filter. The pale blue tonality and prevalent mist contribute a fugitive and mysterious atmosphere to the setting. The hovering apparition of a fish with trumpet snout being rowed by oarsmen with feathers underscores the surreal, dreamlike state of the narrative and recalls the icthyoid fantasies of Hieronymus Bosch and David Teniers the Younger (see below, p. 175). Sís was directly inspired by a print he saw in a book; etched by an 18th-century Frenchman named Bresse, it depicts a balloon in the form of a fish making a flight between two Spanish cities in 1784.[13]

Animals unquestionably have a magical effect on people, and house pets such as dogs and cats are no exception. In Carol Purdy's *Mrs. Merriwether's Musical Cat* (1994) with illustrations by Petra Mathers, a stray cat exerts a remarkable influence on a group of piano students devoid of talent. "Suddenly a stray cat leaped onto the piano . . ." depicts the moment of transformation when the cat jumps from the window onto Mrs. Merriwether's piano [cat. no. 111]. Mathers works in her familiar style, creating simplified forms that comprise flat shapes. She assembles a carefully articulated formal

111. Petra Mathers (born 1945). Born in Germany; Came to the U.S. in 1968. "Suddenly a stray cat leaped onto the piano," from *Mrs. Merriwether's Musical Cat* [New York: G. P. Putnam's Sons, 1994]. © Petra Mathers, 1994; Reprinted with the permission of G. P. Putnam's Sons, an imprint of the Putnam & Grosset Group. Private Collection

MYTH, MAGIC, AND MYSTERY

arrangement whose visual dynamics are as integral to the production as the pictorial narrative.

The same formal aesthetic, predicated upon shape and color that Mathers created with her brush, Vladimir Radunsky achieved with hand-colored cut paper for the re-issue of Bill Martin Jr's *The Maestro Plays* (1994) [cat. no. 112]. The bold areas of color and disparities of scale create a visually arresting picture filled with whimsy. The pictorial effect of this collage motif possesses a modernist quality that recalls the early illustrations of fellow Russian Esphyr Slobodkina done in much the same manner.

Emily Arnold McCully also used magic in conjunction with piano lessons in *The Amazing Felix* (1994). Felix neglects his practice in favor of learning magic tricks; he carries the day and earns the admiration of his father through his prestidigitation. The story commences with an ocean voyage, and the title page shows Felix with his mother and sister about to board a large ocean liner [cat. no. 113]. Set in the twenties, the picture captures the flavor of the period, and the setting, awash with cars, tugboats, ships, and factories, is a virtual hymn to the industrial age championed by such American Precisionists as Charles Sheeler and Charles Demuth as well as French posters.

McCully created a less improbable storyline in her earlier award-winning *Mirette on the High Wire* (1992), blending fact with fiction as she remembered her childhood. She transformed her initial idea for a biography of the daredevil Blondin to accommodate her own treacherous tree-climbing youth. The story tells of a young girl who persists in learning to walk the tightrope from a guest in her mother's boarding house. The beautifully rendered watercolors are redolent of late nineteenth-century Paris, and "Mirette raced into Bellini's room" [cat. no. 114], with its deep perspective and shad-

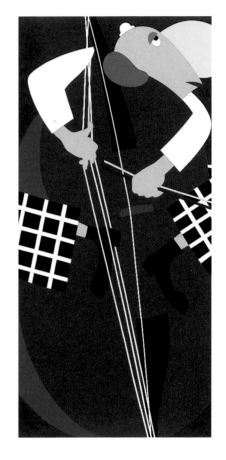

112. (above) Vladimir Radunsky (born 1954). Born in Russia; Came to the U.S. in 1982. "But suddenly, he's playing wildly . . . he slaps the strings," from *The Maestero Plays* [New York: Henry, Holt & Co., 1994]. © Vladimir Radunsky, 1994. Collection of Vladimir Radunsky
113. (left) Emily Arnold McCully (born 1939). American. "The Family Arrives at the Ship," from *The Amazing Felix* [New York: G. P. Putnam's Sons, 1993]. © Emily Arnold McCully, 1993; Reprinted with the permission of G. P. Putnam's Sons, an imprint of the Putnam & Grosset Group. Collection of Emily Arnold McCully

114. Emily Arnold McCully (born 1939). American. "Mirette Raced into Bellini's Room," from *Mirette on the High Wire* [New York: G. P. Putnam's Sons, 1992]. © Emily Arnold McCully, 1992; Reprinted with the permission of G. P. Putnam's Sons, an imprint of the Putnam & Grosset Group. Collection of Emily Arnold McCully

The Banquet

115. Will H. Bradley (1868-1962). American. "Peter Poodle," Frontispiece for *Peter Poodle, Toy Maker to the King* [New York: Dodd, Mead & Company, 1906]. Lent by The Metropolitan Museum of Art, Gift of Fern Bradley Dufner, 1952 © Metropolitan Museum of Art, 1995

owy ambience, recalls on a benign level *Le Viol* (c. 1868–1869), by Edgar Degas (Philadelphia Museum of Art).[14] Mirette's breathless intensity as she rushes through the door is entirely consistent with her impetuous nature.

FOLKTALES AND TRADITIONS

Certain books grew out of the folk and fairy tale tradition and could find a place in either camp. From his youth, Will H. Bradley developed an abiding interest in printing and design. Deeply influenced by Aubrey Beardsley, the English Arts and Crafts movement, and French Art Nouveau, Bradley was among the first artists to produce posters in this country, and he brought his myriad talents to writing, illustrating, and designing for children's books. The frontispiece for *Peter Poodle, Toy Maker to the King* [cat. no. 115] reflects his consummate sense of design in which the highly stylized forms produce a complex pattern that strikes a balance between the intricacy of mediæval manuscript illumination and the reductive geometry of a modernist aesthetic.

Folk art also played an important role in children's book illustration, and artists who immigrated to America used it as a way to maintain ties to the country and culture they left behind. One of the earliest attempts to portray Eastern European folk motifs were the illustrations the husband and wife team of Maud and Miska Petersham created for Margery Clark's *The Poppy Seed Cakes* published in 1924 [cat. no. 116]. Miska's Hungarian background inspired these productions, which abound in colorful peasant designs as well as a well-scrubbed veneer and cheerful good humor of the characters themselves. To be sure, reality was a far cry from these wishful remembrances. The Petershams brought a bold sense of two-dimensional pattern and bright palette to their task and quickly became an important force in American illustration.

From Eastern Europe we move to Scandinavia and Ingri and Edgar Parin d'Aulaire's *Ola*, which first appeared in 1932. The cover captures the Nordic folk tradition, evidenced in Ola's colorful costume, complete with ski cap and brightly

116. Maud Petersham (1890-1971) and Miska Petersham (1888-1960) Born in Hungary; Came to the U.S. in 1912). "The Goat Was Not Easy to Catch," from *The Poppy Seed Cakes* [Garden City, L.I.: Doubleday, Doran and Company, 1924]. Mazza Collection Galleria, The University of Findlay

117. Ingri Parin d'Aulaire (1904-1980) Born in Konigsberg, Norway; Came to the U.S. in 1929 and Edgar Parin d'Aulaire (1898-1986) Born in Munich, Germany; Came to the U.S. in 1929. "Cover," for *Ola* [Garden City, L.I.: Doubleday, Doran and Company, 1939]. Courtesy of The Boston Public Library Print Department

trimmed overalls [cat. no. 117]. They were extremely catholic in their choice of subject matter, which ranged from Greek and Norse myths to American history (see below, p. 151), and their art possessed a clarity and richness of detail that appealed to the inquisitive reader.

Artists have also paid considerable attention to traditions springing from folk and pagan rituals. Halloween is one of the most beloved of holidays and generates great artistic appeal because of its potential for scary imagery. While Tasha Tudor includes ghosts, witches, and goblins in the Halloween drawing for her charming book of holidays, *A Time to Keep* (1977), she tempers the potential for fright in order to reassure her younger readers [cat. no. 118]. Nevertheless, children come away with a vivid sense of the occasion that triggers the imagination.

CAST OF CHARACTERS

In children's literature there are certain figures who will endure on the basis of their endearing personalities and memorable behavior. In the early 1880s Canadian–born Palmer Cox created his band of "Brownies," odd little creatures with skinny legs and bulbous heads and bodies [cat. no. 119a; see p. 17]. They wore distinctive costumes which covered a wide range of ethnographic stereotypes that also symbolized America as a melt-

118. Tasha Tudor (born 1915). American. "October," from *A Time to Keep* [New York: Rand McNally & Company, 1977]. © Tasha Tudor, 1977; Reprinted with the permission of Checkerboard Press. Collection of Col. Thomas Tudor

ing pot fueled by democratic ideals (with the exception of the black color barrier).[15] Brownies pervaded American popular culture and even spawned a camera.

Another set of characters who also came on the scene at the end of the century were Gelett Burgess' "Goops" [cat. no. 120a; see p. 18]. Characterized by cookie-cutter shapes and balloon heads that parodied the Art Nouveau aesthetic, Goops achieved widespread exposure through their appearance in *The Lark* and *St. Nicholas* and graduated to books on juvenile manners soon thereafter. Burgess accompanied his whimsical drawings with lively doggerel that gently carried a firm message concerning acceptable behavior.

In 1918, Johnny Gruelle created Raggedy Ann as a memorial to his recently deceased daughter Marcella. Two years later Ann's brother Raggedy Andy appeared, and over the next twenty years they embarked on numerous adventures including a trip to Cookie Land [cat. no. 121]. These lovable rag dolls with button eyes and irresistible personalities continue to enchant children today.

AMIABLE ANIMALS

In addition to elfin-like creatures and dolls, certain animals have captured the hearts of children. In 1936 a dog and a bull entered the lives of young children. Otto [cat. no. 122], created by William Pène du Bois, was an enormous dog who used his size and strength to perform good deeds. *The Story of Ferdinand*, written by Munro Leaf

121. Johnny Gruelle (1880-1938). American. Cover, for *Raggedy Ann in Cookie Land* [Chicago: P. F. Volland & Co., 1931]. Kendra Krienke and Allan Daniel, New York City

122. William Pène du Bois (1916-1993). American. Cover, for *Giant Otto* [New York: The Viking Press, 1936]. Private Collection, Courtesy of Illustration House

124. Palmer Cox (1840-1924). Born in Granby, Quebec, Canada; Came to the U.S. in 1863. "The Bull Broke Through the Gate," from *The Brownies Around the World* [New York: Century Co., 1894]. Prints and Photographs Division, The Library of Congress

and illustrated by Robert Lawson, tells the splendid story of a bull who would rather sit and smell flowers than perform futile heroics in the ring [cat. no. 123a; see p. 34]. Incidentally, Palmer Cox, in 1894, had alerted children to the destructive power of this animal in "The Bull Broke through the Gate," from *The Brownies Around the World* [cat. no. 124]. Moreover, Ferdinand's pacifist position would have had a special impact for many who shuddered at the folly of the Spanish Civil War.

From the bullrings of Spain, we move to the jungles of Africa where the man in the yellow hat found *Curious George* in 1940 [cat. no. 125]. Hans Augusto Rey and his wife Margret concocted no end of unauthorized adventures for this mischievous monkey; among the first was an accidental flight with balloons [cat. no. 126].

A turtle named Yertle has entertained many young readers, and once again Dr. Seuss is responsible for this imaginative invention. Motivated by ambition and greed, Yertle orders a tower of turtles to be built under him in order to expand the horizons of his kingdom [cat. no. 127]. While this carapaced creature and his subjects defy orthodox zoology, they are pure Seuss in their expressive personalities.

Balloons have proven a favored form of transportation (see below, p. 150), and even larger specimens of the animal kingdom availed themselves of this unpredictable

125. (left) Hans Augusto Rey (1898-1977). Born in Hamburg, Germany; Came to the U.S. in 1940. "George Sees Yellow Hat," from *Curious George* [Boston: Houghton Mifflin Company, 1940]. © Margret E. Rey, 1940; Reprinted with the permission of Houghton Mifflin Company. de Grummond Children's Literature Collection, University of Southern Mississippi

126. (right) Hans Augusto Rey (1898-1977). Born in Hamburg, Germany; Came to the U.S. in 1940. "George Floating Over City with Balloons," from *Curious George* [Boston: Houghton Mifflin Company, 1940]. © Margret E. Rey, 1940; Reprinted with the permission of Houghton Mifflin Company. Department of Special Collections, University of Oregon Library

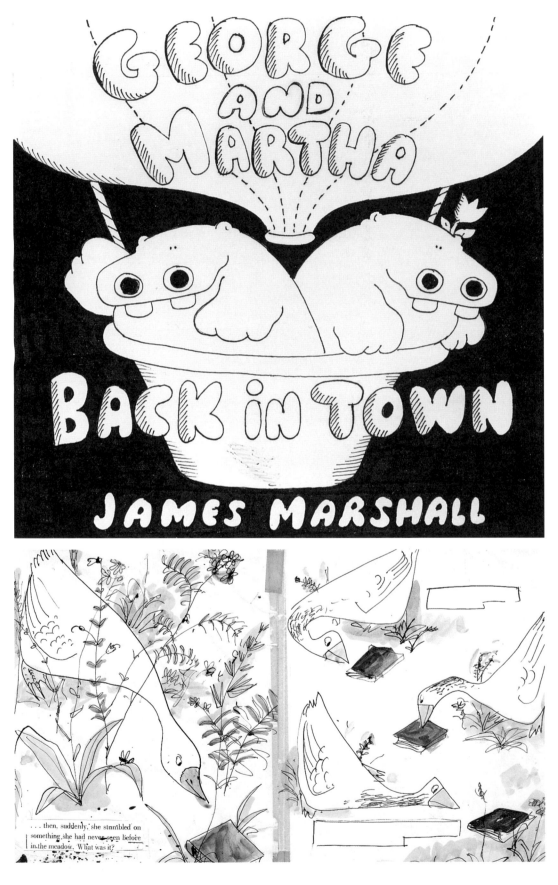

127. (above) Dr. Seuss (1904-1991). American. "Then Yertle the Turtle was perched up so high," from *Yertle the Turtle and Other Stories* [New York: Random House, 1950]. © TM 1950 Dr. Seuss Enterprises, L.P., ren. 1977 Dr. Seuss Collection, Mandeville Special Collections Library, University of California, San Diego

128. (upper right) James Marshall (1942-1992). American. Cover, for *George and Martha Back in Town* [Boston: Houghton Mifflin Company, 1972]. © James Marshall, 1972; Reprinted with the permission of Houghton Mifflin Company. Northeast Children's Literature Collections, Archives and Special Collections Department, Senator Thomas J. Dodd Research Collection, University Library, University of Connecticut, Storrs

129. (lower right) Roger Duvoisin (1904-1980). Born in Geneva, Switzerland; Came to the U.S. in 1925. "Then suddenly she stumbled on something she had never seen before," from *Petunia* [New York: Alfred A. Knopf, Inc., 1950]. Jane Vorhees Zimmerli Art Museum, Rutgers, The State University of New Jersey, Gift of Louise Fatio Duvoisin. Photo by: Jack Abraham

130. Ludwig Bemelmans (1898-1962). Born in Meran, Tyrol, Austria, Came to the U.S. in 1914. "They left at half past nine in two straight lines," from *Madeline* [New York: The Viking Press, 1939]. Collection of Mr. and Mrs. Benjamin Eisenstat

132. Hilary Knight (born 1926). American. Alternate Cover, for *Eloise in Paris* [New York: Simon and Schuster, 1957]. © Hilary Knight, 1996. Collection of Mr. Hilary Knight

method of flight. In *George and Martha Back in Town* (1972), James Marshall's popular pair of hippopotamuses, who are his answer to the odd couple, descend into their second book via balloon [cat. no. 128].

How often does a child get called "a silly goose" by a teasing parent? And who inevitably comes to mind but Roger Duvoisin's flibberty-gibbet *Petunia* (1950) [cat. no. 129]. She assumes an air of self-importance when she discovers a book, but her conceited ignorance brings nothing but trouble. Happily, Petunia's brush with arrogance broadcasts a meaningful message about the importance of learning to read.

DIFFERENT KINDS OF FAMILIES

Finally, there are some memorable human characters. Ludwig Bemelmans emigrated from the Austrian Tyrol via Paris to New York at the outbreak of World War I in 1914 and achieved enduring fame with *Madeline*, who made her debut in 1939. The words

131. Hilary Knight (born 1926). American. "Eloise with Skibberdee," 1954, unpublished drawing for *Eloise* [New York: Simon and Schuster, 1955]. © Hilary Knight, 1996. Collection of Mr. Hilary Knight

and pictures effectively reinforce each other to give us a succinct view of a little girl growing up in a Paris boarding school [cat. no. 130]. Such was her appeal, that Madeline enjoyed numerous interesting exploits told in additional stories.

Another little girl, capable of all sorts of trouble, is *Eloise*, who descended on the Plaza Hotel in New York in 1955. Written by Kay Thompson and illustrated with clever pen and ink drawings by Hilary Knight, Eloise terrorizes the staff of the hotel and keeps her nanny constantly on guard [cat. no. 131]. Eloise is also well-traveled and makes journeys—first class, no doubt—to Paris and Moscow [cat. no. 132]. In this series written for "precocious grown-ups," an unusual theme for children's books emerges: a rich kid who is seemingly abandoned by her parents. To her credit, Eloise is undaunted by this unhappy state of affairs, but it proves a sad commentary on child-rearing practices within a certain social strata.

SILLY FAMILIES

Young readers also delight in characters possessed of total silliness, and James Marshall's Stupid family rises to the top of this category. In a relentless visual barrage of ridiculous juxtapositions, this earnest but absurd family bubbles happily through life. No activity they organize is safe from some ludicrous concatenation of lunacy [cat. no. 133; see p. 44], and the artist is careful to ensure that what we witness is a silly rather than malicious stupidity. Marshall recognized a child's love of the outlandish juxtaposition and provided his audience with a rich smorgasbord of inanity.

In this chapter, we have looked at a wide-ranging selection of stories that are tethered to the past, present, and future. Many stories were conceived to engage a response founded on empirical principles, while many demanded the full release of the reader's imagination. In all the outstanding examples surveyed, text and picture were carefully calibrated to create a harmonious aural and visual experience. Author and artist have taken their craft very seriously, and many artists have mined rich veins of art history to assist in equipping the young child with a solid foundation of visual literacy. In an age where increasing emphasis is being placed on imagery, nurturing these fundamental tools takes on added significance, and children's books will continue to play a critical role in education.

IV

H . Nichols B . Clark

HIGH ADVENTURE AND FANTASY: ART FOR ALL AGES

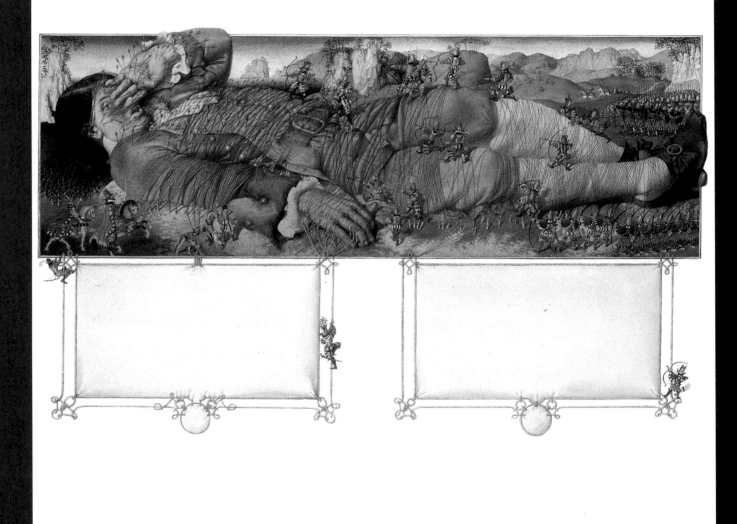

134. Gennady Spirin (born 1948). Born in Russia; Came to the U.S. in 1991. "I must have slept a long time," from *Gulliver's Adventures in Lilliput* [New York: Philomel Books, 1993]. © Gennady Spirin, 1993; Reprinted with the permission of Philomel Books, an imprint of the Putnam & Grosset Group. Collection of Sara Jane Kasperzak

CLASSICS

There is a body of "classic" literature that appeals to children and adults alike, albeit on different levels. *The Pilgrim's Progress*, published between 1678 and 1684 by the English author and preacher John Bunyan, was a forceful allegory of good and evil. By the nineteenth century, it was the best-selling book in America after the Bible, and the young republic's citizenry saw parallels between the tortuous journey of the Christian soul on earth and those travails encountered by the pioneers in the American wilderness.[1] Other older works that held great sway were Daniel Defoe's *Robinson Crusoe* (1719), which inspired another favorite among children, Johann Wyss' *Swiss Family Robinson* (1812, translated 1814). Both these novels, with their delineation of ingenious and self-reliant survival, held particular cachet for a youthful nation facing similar challenges. Jonathan Swift's *Gulliver's Travels* (1726) also enjoyed a dual response. It has intrigued adults with its satire and captivated children with its fantasy and recently was published in a form adapted for children with superb illustrations by Gennady Spirin. The magical watercolor paintings, such as that of Gulliver lashed down and pierced by hundreds of Lilliputian arrows [cat. no. 134], recall Northern Renaissance manuscript illuminations with their exquisite sense of detail and atmospheric landscape. They embody the recurring infatuation with fantasy that even a classic piece of literature over 250 years old can convey.

The early nineteenth century witnessed a wave of emotionally-charged creative outpouring called Romanticism, which swept Europe and America. In literature, for example, the historical novels of Sir Walter Scott held great appeal for older children, and the plays of William Shakespeare enjoyed revived interest through the publication in 1807 of Charles and Mary Lamb's *Tales from Shakespeare*. These works provided fertile ground for artistic interpretation, and many painters, both European and American, based their subjects on episodes from these and other narratives. Indeed, artists continued to subscribe to the ranking of painting categories codified by the French Academy in the seventeenth century where types of subject matter which used the imagination—allegory, history, religion, and literature—were deemed superior to work which simply recorded the external world—portraiture, landscape, and still life.

ILLUSTRATING LITERATURE

From the outset, painting in Colonial America centered around the pragmatism of portraiture, which could be justified as recording a likeness, whether for personal posterity or for relatives back in England. After the Revolution, as the young republic struggled to develop, the arts were still regarded as a luxury. By the second quarter of the nineteenth century, however, Americans began to seek an identity and recognized that literature and art could assist them in advancing this goal through the description of local customs and topography. Perhaps enlightened Americans also understood that artistic maturity signaled ascendance into the fraternity of civilized states.[2]

Literature occupied higher status than the visual arts in early nineteenth-century

America; thus, writers supplied subject matter to artists who could fashion an interpretation that already benefited from widespread exposure to thousands of readers. Washington Irving and James Fenimore Cooper provided many of the most notable points of departure.[3] Works such as Irving's *A History of New York from the Beginning of the World to the End of the Dutch Dynasty*, or "Rip Van Winkle," as well as any of Cooper's *Leatherstocking Tales* were commercial successes that articulated the American spirit and described its physical realms. Most renderings, such as Asher B. Durand's *Dance on the Battery in the Presence of Peter Stuyvesant* (1838) [Museum of the City of New York], John Quidor's *Ichabod Crane Flying from the Headless Horseman* (ca. 1828) [Yale University Art Gallery], Charles Bird King's *Rip Van Winkle Returning from a Morning Lounge* (ca. 1825) [Museum of Fine Arts, Boston], or Thomas Cole's *Scene from "Last of the Mohicans"* (1827) [New York State Historical Association, Cooperstown, New York], existed independently of their sources and would have been known only through the limited venue of exhibition—usually in one of the major metropolises such as New York, Philadelphia, or Boston—before entering a private collection or returning to the artist's studio.

This isolated and limited approach began to shift as a market for illustrated books developed in the early decades of the nineteenth century. As noted, Washington Irving provided fertile territory, and even Washington Allston departed from his more elevated and ethereal compositions to create two comic pieces in 1817 for his good friend's *A History of New York* in which he emphasized the differences in characters by expressive physiognomic contrast.[4] In spite of his allegiance, Allston's approach, as well as that of Durand, has been considered too refined, whereas the energetic, flamboyant style of Quidor most successfully captures the literary zest of Irving's pen.[5]

Written under the pseudonym of Diedrich Knickerbocker, *A History of New York*, despite its satire, voiced Irving's affection for the cultural heritage embodied in Dutch New York. This work, published in 1809, was overshadowed at the end of the next decade by two stories from *The Sketch Book of Geoffrey Crayon, Gent.* which appeared in 1820. "The Legend of Sleepy Hollow," pitting the Yankee Ichabod Crane against the Backwoodsman Brom Bones, contributed a mythology and folklore of the Hudson Valley to the literary canon, while "Rip Van Winkle" borrowed from a German folk tale to create one of the most enduring characters in American literature.[6] Thus, Irving echoed the unfolding interest in traditional folk tales in Europe, disseminated in great part through the German Romantics. The American author's immediate success, in the words of Joshua Taylor, "attests to the eagerness of the [American] public at this moment to find an imaginative inheritance to complement the now legendary military and political past."[7]

The artist who brought book illustration to a significant level of achievement in America during this period was Felix Octavius Carr Darley. His illustrations of Irving's writings in the late 1840s were instrumental in establishing his reputation.[8] In 1848 the managers of the American Art-Union, a short-lived organization founded to promote American art, commissioned Darley to create illustrations for *Rip Van Winkle* and *The*

135. Felix O.C. Darley (1822-1888). American. "Rip Amusing Children," from *Rip Van Winkle, designed and etched [on stone] by Felix O. C. Darley for the Members of the American Art-Union* [New York: n.p., 1848]. Munson-Williams-Proctor Institute, Utica, New York

Legend of Sleepy Hollow.[9] Published as pamphlets with text and six plates of outline renderings designed and etched on lithographic stone, these publications were distributed as premiums for the art lotteries of 1848 and 1849.

RIP VAN WINKLE

"Rip Amusing Children" [cat. no. 135] depicts and reveals the delightful chaos of irresponsibility that he symbolizes. Children surround him like the Pied Piper and share his enjoyment in floating a small homemade boat in a washtub. The porch on which they congregate is a jumble of ladders and rakes leaning askew against walls with harnesses and yokes on pegs gathering dust, while foliage crawls higgledy-piggledy up the side of the house. This disheveled scene underscores the neglect that Rip accords to his daily responsibilities. The costumes and architectural details, such as the leaded casement window and impressive strap hinges of the shutter, are convincingly accurate. Darley's hand is sure, and he demonstrates an innate ability to blend the requisite ingredients of illustration, narration, and imitation, so that his interpretation both reinforces and enhances the text. Darley is not without his own humor, as the mother hen with chicks scratching for food on the porch may allude to Rip's ongoing description as "hen-pecked." In sum, Rip Van Winkle embodies that element of American character which desires to escape from work and responsibility, and his appealing personality has endured with a power to move and entertain us still.[10]

136. N. C. Wyeth (1882-1945). American. "It was with some difficulty that he found his way to his own house," from *Rip Van Winkle* [New York: David McKay, 1921]. Millport Conservancy

Both "Rip Van Winkle" and "The Legend of Sleepy Hollow" generated significant sales within both the United States and England; they attracted sustained interest in visual interpretation as well.[11] Moreover, these stories were not immune from artistic versions abroad. The Englishman Arthur Rackham illustrated an edition of *Rip Van Winkle* in 1905 and brought to his rendering the delightful caricature and anthropomorphic nature that defines his work. Without question, the narrative of the lovable sloth received one its most important treatments at the hands of N. C. Wyeth.

Having studied with Howard Pyle (see below), Wyeth established his reputation with illustrations for Robert Louis Stevenson's *Treasure Island* (1911), *Kidnapped* (1913), and *The Black Arrow* (1916), as well as for other books in the series of Scribner Classics. Subsequently, Wyeth was pursued by other publishers, and in 1921 he illustrated *Rip Van Winkle* for David McKay. Among his most powerful images must rank the illustration to the text "It was with some difficulty that he found the way to his own house . . . ," [cat. no. 136] where Rip, after his twenty-year nap in the Catskills, returns to a post-Revolutionary America and finds his house in an advanced state of disrepair. Wyeth, conscious of the need for a bold sense of pattern for reproductive purposes, set Rip in the doorway and created a strong sense of light and shadow. The serpentine branches of the sycamore tree silhouetted against the mottled blue sky in the background underscore this schematic quality. Rip's long hair and beard as well as tattered clothes and puzzled expression poignantly capture his predicament. Curiously, he no longer carries the replacement firelock, and instead supports himself with a walking staff. No reason for this artistic liberty has come to light, and Wyeth's departure from the traditional iconography begs further investigation, especially since he liked to collect curios in the interest of accuracy.

The story has attracted myriad artists interested in bringing their own viewpoint to the text, and the shelves of most libraries offer a host of options. These range from Gustaf Tenggren in 1944 and Maud and Miska Petersham in 1951 [cat. no. 137] to the caricaturist David Levine in 1963 and Leonard Everett Fisher in 1966—to name but a few. The work by the Petershams also depicts Rip's finding his house gone to decay; it is executed in pen and ink and reflects a facile draftsmanship. The summary treatment of the setting and even the figures themselves confirm the Petershams' concern for the total design of a book. Through the use of outline, there is a flattening of form which provides greater sympathy to the typography of the text. Although a bit freer in handling, the execution harkens back to some of their earliest work, notably for Carl Sandburg's *Rootabaga Stories* (1922) (see below, p. 191), which codified their dedication to tenets of simplicity, economy, and clarity of expression in the illustrative process.

In recent years, Rip Van Winkle has continued to garner attention, and Thomas Locker adapted the story in 1988 [cat. no. 138]. Locker's approach places greater emphasis on the visual experience, and the artwork virtually takes precedence over the pared down text. Artistically, he reveals a strong debt to seventeenth-century Dutch landscape and genre painting, which parenthetically had significant impact on American

137. Maud Petersham (1890-1971) and Miska Petersham (1888-1960). Born in Hungary; Came to the U.S. in 1912. "He Found His House Gone to Decay," from *Rip Van Winkle* [New York: MacMillan, 1951]. Reprinted with the permission of Simon & Schuster Books for Young Readers, an imprint of Simon & Schuster Children's Publishing Division. Department of Special Collections, University of Oregon Library

138. Thomas Locker (born 1937). American. "Rip Returns home," from *Rip van Winkle* [New York: Dial Books, 1988]. © Thomas Locker, 1988. Collection of Thomas Locker

artists in the nineteenth century. Locker's tight, meticulous style, with its emphasis on rendering the material world, offers an intriguing comparison with an artist whom he holds in high esteem, N.C. Wyeth.[12]

In his admiration of Wyeth, Locker also works on a large scale; his canvases measure 32 x 40 compared to Wyeth's 40 x 30 inch dimension. Presumably, each artist anticipated a life for their paintings beyond the reproductive process, in which they were reduced by a factor of more than four, and gave them a physical presence worthy of easel painting. The reductive process is deceiving, especially since Locker's work reads like a Dutch cabinet picture—intimate in both size and scale. Its stagelike setting, with complex system of horizontals and verticals leading to the mountainous countryside beyond, echoes the simpler yet bolder compositional format of Wyeth. Locker's attention to detail, achieved through a precise handling of the paint and reflecting his desire to convey such textures as the pine flooring or Rip's ragged clothes, is made feasible by the advances of reproductive technology. Wyeth, by contrast, was constricted and had to content himself with a bolder massing of form. Each has their merits, and both aspire to transcend mere illustration.

MYTH, MAGIC, AND MYSTERY

As criteria emerged in the second quarter of the nineteenth century for that which was typically "American," central ingredients consisted of elements of the colloquial and the self-made.[13] One of the great proponents of these tenets was Mark Twain, and another character of American literature who has entered the pantheon of legendary figures is Huckleberry Finn. Twain recognized that his novel would be controversial, but he also firmly believed that it would become a classic. The literature on this story is enormous and defies the scope of this essay.

Adventures of Huckleberry Finn (1884) tells the tale of an uncivilized boy who eschews respectability while discovering a moral fineness through his friendship with a runaway slave, Jim, who shows him love, acceptance, and respectability. Through a mischievous boy who embodies a carefree spirit and self-reliance, the book articulates some distinctly American traits. Just as Rip Van Winkle shunned responsibility, Huck disdained an accepted code of behavior and rejected conformity through his adventures with Jim. The outcome is all the more understandable since the so-called respectable society of the Mississippi Valley ranked Huck just above Jim on the social scale.

Twain personally selected Edward W. Kemble, a young illustrator who was just beginning to gain a reputation with his drawings for *Life* magazine, to illustrate *Adventures of Huckleberry Finn*. Despite Twain's criticisms, the original drawings remained virtually unaltered, and the frontispiece [cat. no. 139] stands as the image most associated with Huck.[14] The "hero" dominates the composition as he holds a rabbit that he has just shot and looks out at the viewer with a mixture of good-natured pride and defiance. This pen and ink drawing succinctly captures his roguish character, which is visually reinforced by the tattered straw hat and shabby clothes. Despite Twain's initial misgivings, Kemble's drawings contributed meaningfully to the text.

Like "Rip Van Winkle," *Adventures of Huckleberry Finn* has attracted the attention of numerous illustrators, regardless of its controversial nature. From little-known Worth Brehm, who provided very fine illustrations for a 1923 edition, to extremely popular artists, such as Norman Rockwell and Thomas Hart Benton, many have gravitated to the opportunity. In his introductory note to the deluxe Limited Edition Club offering published in 1942, Benton hailed Kemble's illustrations as the definitive interpretation—with some reservations about aspects of his draftsmanship.[16] He also praised Kemble for understanding his function of providing visual stimulants rather than literal depictions and for measuring the appropriate balance between text and image.

Thus, it may have been fitting to approach a draftsman to illustrate the hundredth anniversary edition, and Barry Moser was a logical choice. Moser selected the medium of wood engraving to create his illustrations. The work conveys his facile ability to evoke his subject and manifests the suggestive element that Benton admired in Kemble. "Never Saying a Word" [cat. no. 140] depicts Huck and Jim standing waist

139. (left) E. W. Kemble (1861-1933).
American. Frontispiece, for
Adventures of Huckleberry Finn [New
York: Charles L. Webster & Co.,
1884]. The Mark Twain House,
Hartford, Ct.

140. (right) Barry Moser (born 1940).
American. "Never Saying a Word,"
from *Adventures of Huckleberry Finn*
[West Hatfield, Mass.: Pennyroyal
Press, 1985]. © Barry Moser, 1984;
Published with the permission of
Barry Moser. Courtesy of R.
Michelson Galleries, Northampton,
Mass.

deep in the water with their raft, looking off in different directions. And yet, through the compositional overlapping of their figures, they are inextricably connected, physically and psychologically. Significantly Moser has imbued Jim with a dignity and monumentality that departs from so many earlier stereotypical characterizations.

BAD BOYS AND GOOD GIRLS

The perceptive characterization exemplified in Kemble's frontispiece for *Adventures of Huckleberry Finn* coincided with the unfolding development of a literature looking at the world through the eyes of children. While Huck's behavior may have pushed the definition of mischief to its limits, he did, nevertheless, form part of the litany of lovable miscreants who graced the pages of books and stories in the late nineteenth and early twentieth centuries. Thomas B. Aldrich's *The Story of a Bad Boy* first appeared in 1869 with illustrations by the virtually forgotten Sol Eytinge, Jr. The book chronicles the semi-autobiographical adventures and tribulations of a wholesome, albeit mischievous boy, who suffers through adolescence in a New England town by the sea just prior to the Civil War. The reader shares his rites of passage, and these daily exploits entertain and enlighten. The book was reissued in 1894 with illustrations by Arthur Burdett Frost, who had studied with Thomas Eakins and William Merritt Chase. At this juncture, Frost was on the threshold of garnering universal acclaim with his renderings for

Uncle Remus (see below, p. 186). The full-page plates for *The Story of a Bad Boy* were executed in watercolor and gouache and exhibit a loose painterly technique. "The Initiation" [cat. no. 141] depicts a moment of high drama for the chapter "I Become an R.M.C." (Rivermouth Centipede), which tells of the hero's initiation into a schoolboy's secret society. The image shows young Bailey just before he is unceremoniously dumped into the hogshead (which seemed like a fall of two miles), enduring the incantations of the twelve fantastically dressed initiates. Frost cleverly captures the moment of high suspense, reinforced by the grotesque masks reminiscent of the Belgian Symbolist painter, James Ensor. This ceremony anticipates the escapades of the equally lovable and misguided Penrod, whom Booth Tarkington introduced to the world in 1914.

This theme of the tribulations of male adolescence continues into our own time and received one of its most insightful and entertaining readings in the early 1940s at the hand of Robert McCloskey, who had recently scored a triumph with his *Make Way for Ducklings* (1941) (see above, p. 90). *Homer Price* (1943), which he also wrote and illustrated, consisted of a series of vignettes recounting modern tall tales in the mythical town of Centerburg (situated somewhere in the heartland of the Middle West). James Daugherty identifed Homer as a member of that formidable gang of boys in American fiction and recognized McCloskey's place in the artistic tradition of E. W. Kemble, A. B. Frost and Peter Newell.[16]

Written soon after America had gone to war, the book heralds the foibles, resourcefulness, and ingenuity of American youth. Like the genre painters of the nineteenth century, those chroniclers of everyday life, McCloskey provides us with a window to the America of the period. The depiction of Homer building a radio in his room [cat. no. 142] not only informs us about the state of technology—notice the vacuum tubes—but also treats us to a thoroughly detailed inventory of a young boy's room. Although technology and fashion have changed the appearance of certain objects considerably, the central ingredients to be honored remain essentially the same: sports heroes, modes of transportation, and school allegiances. To McCloskey's great credit, there is as much humor and warmth in the finely crafted drawings as there is in the vivid text, and he, too, provides us with an engaging and enduring chronicle of boyhood.

GENTILITY

As Huck, Tom, Bailey, Penrod, Homer, and so many others signified youth's relentless struggle with issues of decorum, Penrod's creator, Booth Tarkington, also provided a contrasting counterpart, the angelic Georgie Bassett. His type, too, had already entered the literature, most notably via *Little Lord Fauntleroy* by Frances Hodgson Burnett in 1886. This character, immortalized by Reginald Birch, became the paradigm of the Victorian child—to the distress of many a young boy. "Mr. Mordaunt Held the Small Hand as He Looked Down at the Child's Face" [cat. no. 143], constitutes an amplification of the original pen and ink drawings of the 1886 edition with lush watercolors for

141. Arthur Burdett Frost (1851-1928). American. "The Initiation," from *The Story of a Bad Boy* [Boston: Houghton Mifflin Company, 1894]. Courtesy of The Boston Public Library Print Department, John D. Merriam Collection

142. Robert McCloskey (born 1914). American. "Homer Building a Radio," from *Homer Price* [New York: The Viking Press, 1943]. © Robert McCloskey, 1943; May Massee Collection, William Allen White Library, Emporia State University

143. Reginald Bathurst Birch (1856-1943). Born in England; Came to the U.S. in 1880. "Mr. Mordaunt Held the Small Hand as he Looked Down at the Child's Face" from *Little Lord Fauntleroy* [New York: Charles Scribner's Sons, 1916]. Reprinted with the permission of Atheneum Books for Young Readers, an imprint of Simon & Schuster Children's Publishing Division. Betsy B. Shirley Collection of American Children's Literature, The Beinecke Library of Yale University

the 1916 reissue. The opulent interior, replete with Grand Manner portrait in the style of Anthony van Dyck, echoed the splendor of the aristocratic English country house. The sympathetic gaze between Mr. Mordaunt and Fauntleroy, a vision of sartorial stylishness in velvet and lace, captured the saccharine sentimentality of this literary genre.

144. Reginald Bathurst Birch (1856-1943). Born in England; Came to the U.S. in 1880. "Gaily the troubador touched the guitar," from *Little Men* [Boston: Little Brown & Co., 1901]. Courtesy of The Boston Public Library Print Department

145. Jessie Willcox Smith (1863-1935). American. "The Girls Reading," from *Boys and Girls of Bookland* [New York: Cosmopolitan Book Corporation, 1923]. Collection of the Brandywine River Museum, Gift of the Women's Club of Ardmore, Haverford, Pennsylvania

English by birth, Birch immigrated to America in 1880 and illustrated many of the best selling books of the period that originated on either side of the Atlantic. He gravitated to literature espousing gentility, and another example of his facile style is an illustration for Louisa May Alcott's *Little Men* (1871) entitled "Gaily the troubador touched the guitar" [cat. no. 144], which Birch created for the 1901 edition. Alcott, in this sequel to *Little Women* (1868), also based the narrative on family experience and depicted the character and ways of her nephews living in Concord, Massachusetts. Alcott explores the idea that boys are free to explore, expound, and evade the responsibilities of daily life, while "little women" are conditioned for subservience and self-sacrifice. In this record of "Daisy's Ball," a tea dance, it is not insignificant that Birch dominated the

146. Barbara Cooney (born 1917). American. "The Nightly Sing at the Piano," from *Little Women* [New York: Crowell, 1955]. © Barbara Cooney, 1955. Courtesy of The Boston Public Library Print Department

foreground with the youngest girl offering refreshment to her guest, who, in turn, seems to expect such treatment. This polarity was part of the social matrix, and the avoidance of responsibility by young boys emerges as a central theme, whether the child is respectable or not.

Little Women established Alcott's reputation and provided her financial security. It also attracted widespread artistic interest, ranging from Birch and Jessie Willcox Smith to Barbara Cooney. Smith, who began her career as a kindergarten teacher, went on to study with Thomas Eakins and Thomas Anschutz at the Pennsylvania Academy of the Fine Arts. Subsequently she was one of Howard Pyle's first students at the Drexel Institute, and he had a profound influence on her.[17] Smith's depictions for the 1915 edition of *Little Women* were signature works. She created "The Girls Reading" [cat. no. 145] for Nora Archibald Smith's *Boys and Girls of Bookland* in 1923.[18] While changing the designs of the dresses from the original illustrations and making the scene a bit more generic, Smith still manages to capture the aura of well-being, even in the family's reduced circumstances, and evokes a sense of the expected role for young women that contradicted Alcott's true headstrong and assertive personality. Smith, with her commitment to evoking the innocence of youth, was especially sensitive to this subject matter.

Barbara Cooney created scratchboard illustrations for a 1955 edition, and her depiction of the girls holding their nightly sing by the piano reaffirms the sense of values and code of behavior with which these young women were instilled [cat. no. 146]. The delicate use of line, which sympathetically articulates form, also captures the spirit of the text. *Little Women*, with its multiple levels of meaning, continues to enchant both in print and, more recently, in film, and artists such as Smith and Cooney have contributed to the rich visual legacy.[19]

HIGH ADVENTURE

While the material surveyed in this chapter has dealt almost exclusively with themes taken from American settings, there evolved considerable demand for adventure stories which cut across geographical and temporal boundaries. Essential in expanding these horizons is Howard Pyle, who fathered America's "golden age of illustration," which extended from 1875–1925. Born of a Quaker family in Wilmington, Delaware, the young Pyle convinced his parents to allow him to pursue an artistic career, a vocation frowned upon by the Quaker religion. Although his artistic education was far from memorable, Pyle recalled his fascination with pictures in books as a child.[20] He initially produced drawings for magazines and came into contact with such kindred spirits as Edwin Austin Abbey and Arthur Burdett Frost.

At the outset, Pyle occasionally gravitated to American themes such as *Yankee Doodle* (1881) [cat. nos. 147a and 147b; see p. 18]. Inspired by a variant text, which did not even include the verse most people know today, Pyle created a publication in a format and style reminiscent of the illustrated poems and stories of Walter Crane, Randolph

This is the way that one in Cap and Motley stops for awhile along the stony Path of Life to make you laugh.

148. Howard Pyle (1853-1911). American. "This is the way that one in Cap and Motley stops for awhile along the stony Path of Life to Make you Laugh," ca. 1883, from *Pepper and Salt* [New York: Harper & Brothers, 1886]. Collection of the Brandywine River Museum, Museum Volunteers' Purchase Fund, 1985

Caldecott, and Kate Greenaway. His original watercolors possess a spare yet animated outline that convey the requisite blend of mirth and graphic lucidity.

By the early 1880s, Pyle was also writing and illustrating his own books. Among the works that garnered the most positive reaction were *The Merry Adventures of Robin Hood* (1883), *Pepper & Salt, or Seasoning for Young Folk* (1886), *The Wonder Clock* (1888), *Otto of the Silver Hand* (1888) and the King Arthur books; they were all lauded for their vivid narrative and synthesis of text, illustration, and book design. *Pepper and Salt* embodies Pyle's desire to recraft European legends, and the frontispiece, "This is the way that one in Cap and Motley stops for awhile along the stony Path of Life to make you laugh," [cat. no. 148], epitomizes the theme of this exhibition and book: that children love to be entertained whether by music or by story (signified by the book which lies open at the jester's feet).

One of Pyle's most enduring efforts—it is still in print today—is *The Merry Adventures of Robin Hood*, which first appeared in 1883. These lively tales, set in mediæval

150. (above) Walter Crane (1845-1915). British. "The Golden Bird," from *Household Stories from the Collection of the Bros. Grimm* [London: Macmillan & Co., 1882]. Mazza Collection Galleria, The University of Findlay

149. (right) Howard Pyle (1853-1911). American. "Robin Shooteth His Last Shaft," from *The Merry Adventures of Robin Hood* [New York: Charles Scribner's Sons, 1883]. Reprinted with the permission of Scribner, an imprint of Simon & Schuster. From the Collection of the Central Children's Room, Donnell Library Center, The New York Public Library

152. (opposite) N. C. Wyeth (1882-1945). American. "The Passing of Robin Hood," from *Robin Hood* [New York: Charles Scribner's Sons, 1917]. Reprinted with the permission of Atheneum Books for Young Readers, an imprint of Simon & Schuster Children's Publishing Division. From the collection of the Central Children's Room, Donnell Library Center, The New York Public Library

England, gave full throttle to the reader's imagination. The illustrations emulated the print tradition of the Northern Renaissance, as well as Walter Crane's black and white illustration. The final image, "Robin Shooteth His Last Shaft" [cat. no. 149], with its accomplished draftsmanship and sensitivity to typography, echoes Crane's formative influence, exemplified in "The Golden Bird," [cat. no. 150], which appeared in *Household Stories from the Collection of the Bros. Grimm* (1882) [cat. no. 151; see p. 11]. Crane was associated with the Pre-Raphaelite Brotherhood, who inspired a revived interest in mediævalism and craftsmanship. Eschewing the mechanical conveniences of the Industrial Revolution, these artists concentrated on achieving the highest degree of artistic and aesthetic results. These lofty tenets were instrumental in galvanizing Pyle's creative attitudes.

In the climactic image, Robin rests against his dear companion Little John and prepares to determine his grave site by letting loose a final arrow. The details suggest authenticity, while the meaningful iconography, especially the hourglass and crucifix on the mantel, implies Robin's mortality and salvation. With the inclusion of what appear to be cranes flying by the window to the left, Pyle may have paid his own per-

153. (above left) N. C. Wyeth (1882-1945). American. "One more step, Mr. Hands," said I, "and I'll blow your brains out!," from *Treasure Island* [New York: Charles Scribner's Sons, 1911]. Reprinted with the permission of Atheneum Books for Young Readers, an imprint of Simon & Schuster Children's Publishing Division. Lent by the New Britain Museum of American Art, Harriet Russell Stanley Fund

154. (above right) John R. Neill (1877-1943). American. Unpublished illustration for *Treasure Island*, 1914. Collection of Natalie Neill Mather

155. (right) Frank Schoonover (1877-1972). American. "Siege of the Round-House," from *Kidnapped* [New York: Harper & Brothers, Publishers, 1921]. Collection of General Edward R. Burka

sonal homage to the English master, since Crane often incorporated the bird into his signature.

Howard Pyle's illustrations for *Robin Hood* also permit us to consider the transfer of leadership of what has become known as the Brandywine School, since his disciple, N.C. Wyeth, elected to create a set of illustrations in 1917. "The Passing of Robin Hood" [cat. no. 152] depicts the same episode in a far simpler though equally evocative setting. Wyeth, using brush rather than pen, employs a bold massing of forms and interplay of light and shadow to enhance the moment, but it has been rightly argued that Pyle's romantic vision and dramatic composition were instrumental in the formation of Wyeth's artistic approach.[21]

Dictated, in part, by Pyle's premature death in 1911 at the age of fifty-eight, Wyeth's ascension may have been secured anyway by the appearance that year of his illustrations for Robert Louis Stevenson's *Treasure Island.* These compelling works established his national reputation. " 'One more step, Mr. Hands,' " said I, " 'and I'll blow your brains out!' " [cat. no. 153] epitomizes Wyeth's illustrative approach with his dramatic extrapolation from the text. In this action-packed chapter near the end of the novel, Wyeth selects the moment of crucial confrontation between Jim and the nefarious Israel Hands. The worm's–eye view and steeply pitched angle of vision, as well as the powerful interplay of diagonals, visually reiterate the literary tension of the episode. Consistent with Wyeth's working method, the painting is large, measuring 47 x 38 inches and consequently undergoes substantial reduction for reproduction in the book.

Not all interpretations of *Treasure Island* were keyed to the published text, and some found their way into the mainstream by way of illustrated magazines. One such example is John R. Neill's evocative variant of the rendering which appeared in the *Pictorial Review* in 1914 [cat. no. 154]. Neill, in this painterly watercolor recalling Reginald Birch's flowing style, alludes to the vivid images that well up in the reader's mind. The picture, then, is more an insight into the effects of literature on the imagination and how this stirring genre of romance and drama could enthrall the youth of the day.

Among Howard Pyle's students who had a measurable impact of his own was Frank Schoonover. Schoonover opted for art school rather than the ministry and, through his attendance at the Drexel Institute, earned one of the coveted scholarships at Pyle's summer school in Chadds Ford, Pennsylvania. From the outset of his career, Schoonover manifested a love of the outdoors and traveled extensively in northern Canada to better understand the frontier. He also traveled to Europe to enhance his artistic education and responded enthusiastically to Italian art and architecture. In addition to magazine illustration, Schoonover wrote articles and stories as well as illustrating over 200 classics and children's books. This prodigious output covered a broad range of subject matter which tended toward outdoors adventures.

Schoonover could not escape the allure of Robert Louis Stevenson, and in 1921 he created for the cover and frontispiece of *Kidnapped* his visualization of "The Siege of the Round-House," in which David Balfour and Alan Stewart fend off the insurrec-

156. (right) Frank Schoonover (1877-1972). American. "Fritz Striding with flamingo," from *Swiss Family Robinson* [New York: Harper & Brothers, Publishers, 1921]. Collection of General Edward R. Burka

157. (below) Trina Schart Hyman (born 1939). American. "Then they heard a hideous roaring that filled the air with terror," from *Saint George and the Dragon* [Boston: Little, Brown and Company, 1984]. © Trina Schart Hyman, 1984. Collection of Trina Schart Hyman

tionists aboard their ship. Subscribing to Pyle's dictum to "capture the moment just before the ultimate drama and you have captured the essence," Schoonover selects the instant when David is about to fire a pistol for the first time. The artist successfully captures the youth's tentativeness which is tempered with a resolute determination [cat. no. 155]. Curiously, Schoonover's treatment considers the anticipation and consequently is more psychological than either his mentor's, which graphically depicts Alan running his sword through Mr. Schuan's body (Delaware Art Museum), or Wyeth's, which depicts the same furious engagement (Brandywine River Museum). Stylistically, the debt to Pyle and Wyeth is clear, as the simple, well-defined forms create a compelling mood. Schoonover has, however, employed a fuller and richer palette that is more colorful than the earlier and earthier tones of his Canadian and Western subjects.

Schoonover's love of adventure is also engagingly articulated in his cover and frontispiece for the 1921 edition of *Swiss Family Robinson* which portrays Fritz, the eldest boy, striding through the woods in the company of the tamed flamingo [cat. no. 156]. Bird and youth walk in step, and this sense of harmony suggests the enlightened approach that the family has taken in regards to their habitat. Furthermore, Fritz is armed with bow and arrow, having quickly realized that the supply of shot and powder was finite and that he may need a different weapon over the long run. Thus, Wyss was thinking in Darwinian terms well before 1859, when the Englishman's controversial theory of evolution first came to light. Stylistically, the painting is consistent with the scene from *Kidnapped*, with its equally rich palette and energetic brushwork. A prolific artist, Schoonover in 1921 alone produced work for over ten books. His contribution to the genre of illustration was not limited to his making art but also revolved around his teaching. He founded an art school in Wilmington in 1942 and taught there until 1968, when he was ninety-one. Thus, he continued the tradition of his mentor well into our own time.

Significantly, Howard Pyle's formative legacy endures today, both in terms of content and style. Many artists profess this heritage, and among the most accomplished and acclaimed is Trina Schart Hyman whose art for Margaret Hodges' adaptation of the legend of *Saint George and the Dragon* epitomizes this tradition as well as evokes the influence of Arthur Rackham [cat. no. 157]. The illustration shows the hero in the literal heat of battle with the flame-throwing dragon while everyone around him flees. The quality of Hyman's line, though somewhat bolder because of the added use of watercolor, resonates with the inspiration of Pyle's masterful technique. The mullion-pane structure provides a literal and figurative window into the romantically charged story of knights of old, which holds its own in the face of competition of such intergalactic heraldry as *Star Wars*.

IN THE REALM OF THE FAIRIES

If the visionary world of science fiction dominates "fantastic" literature today, magical otherworldly realms have long captivated readers. In the last century, Victorian

England, with its rapidly growing urban and industrialized society, was especially susceptible to a world of chimerical dreams and fantasies.[22] Anchored in the creations of William Blake, this synergistic literary and visual genre attained enormous popularity in the second half of the nineteenth century and early decades of the twentieth.

Lewis Carroll's *Alice's Adventures in Wonderland*, published in 1865, was written for children but appealed as potently to adults on a different level. The book offered a virtual warp of time and space in the guise of a dream and probed the potentially darker sides of the unconscious well before Freud. Of the more than 100 artists who have attempted to illustrate Carroll's classic, the original artist, Sir John Tenniel, and subsequently Arthur Rackham emerge as the most admired. Tenniel's work, such as " 'The Hatter' " and ' "A Mad Tea-Party' " [cat. no. 158a; see p. 9], survives in exquisitely finished graphite drawings and reflects the artist's influence on the American Henry Louis Stephens (see above, p. 15). The reader easily identifies with Alice's puzzlement and discomfiture.

Carroll's *Alice's Adventures in Wonderland* was inspired by a story that did not sustain similar allure. Charles Kingsley, the British cleric, novelist, and social reformer, published *The Water Babies* in 1853, and the book is considered to mark the beginning of the English literary fairy-tale tradition. Written for his youngest child, the work stands as a children's classic, despite its overladen symbolism and dated quality. Perhaps stimulated by Baron de la Motte-Fouqué's *Undine* or Hans Christian Andersen's "Little Mermaid," earlier in the century, the hero's drowning and subsequent adventures beneath the waters of the Thames convey the narrative into a mystical world of aqueous imagery.

The story received possibly its most memorable visual interpretation in 1916 with the edition illustrated by Jessie Willcox Smith. The artist considered these illustrations to be her best work and donated them to the Library of Congress.[23] The paintings reflect some of the decorative quality of her early work, which was informed by Japanese prints, posters, and possibly the color prints of Mary Cassatt.[24] To achieve the requisite ethereal effects, she utilized a complex technique of oil over varnished watercolor. Emotionally, "Mrs. Bedonebyasyoudid" provides a mixture of humor and anxious repulsion [cat. no. 159]. One cannot help but smile at her spiky seaweed coiffure and green-lensed spectacles, while the vignette of Tom's being fed a pebble because of his own malicious actions underscores the book's moralizing themes.

The liberated innocence of childhood plays an important role in fantasy literature. The successful stage production of *Peter Pan* was first performed in London in 1904. It evolved from an episode in J. M. Barrie's *The Little White Bird* (1902), as did the author's prose offering, *Peter Pan in Kensington Gardens*. Published in 1906, this story benefited enormously from the superb illustrations by Arthur Rackham. Peter's adventures range from the airborne excitement of trying to reach Kensington Gardens by means of a kite propelled by birds [cat. no. 160; see p. 22] to the earthbound "Butter is got from the roots of old trees" [cat. no. 161]. These exquisite drawings

embody Rackham's consummate ability to mingle the refined and delicate with the grotesque and foreboding.

Peter Pan, like so many other children's favorites, entered the realm of popular culture by means of movies and especially the animated films of Walt Disney. Happily, the illustrated book was not buried by these passive forms of entertainment, and *Peter Pan* has enjoyed artistic interpretation in recent years. Perhaps the most notable illustrations have been created by Trina Schart Hyman. "Up and down they went, and round and round" [cat. no. 162] is a delightfully dizzying insight into the Darling children's first experience of flight. Hyman has carefully constructed the composition so that the centrifugal feeling is reinforced by the judicious positioning of children, folds in sheets and quilts, and other seemingly mundane objects in the room. The vertiginous arrangement echoes the Baroque tradition of bursting the boundaries of the frame, while the compressed space and cropped forms reflect the compositional impact of photography. Thus, the artist has captured through formal means the wonder of this "fantastic" experience of flight which captivates all children.

At the same time that Barrie was enchanting British audiences with his sprite who defied adulthood, L. Frank Baum was entrancing the American public with a tale of fairy lore considered a worthy successor to Carroll's *Alice* books, namely—*The Wonderful Wizard of Oz* (1900).[25] This hallucinatory invention fabricated of commonplace American

159. Jessie Willcox Smith (1863-1935). American. "Mrs. Bedonebyasyoudid," from *The Water Babies* [New York: Dodd, Mead & Company, 1916]. Prints and Photographs Division, The Library of Congress

161. Arthur Rackham (1867-1939). British. "Butter is got from the roots of old trees," 1905, from *Peter Pan in Kensington Gardens* [London: Hodder & Stoughton, 1906]. Beinecke Rare Book Library, Yale University

162. Trina Schart Hyman (born 1939). American. "Up and down they went, and round and round," from *Peter Pan* [New York: Charles Scribner's Sons, 1980]. © Trina Schart Human, 1980; Reprinted with the permission of Atheneum Books for Young Readers, an imprint of Simon & Schuster Children's Publishing Division. Collection of Trina Schart Hyman

materials has endured despite repeated efforts at suppression. In fact, the more rigorous the repression, the more intense became the appeal of Oz, and the 1939 film with Judy Garland and company all but assured it cult status. The illustrations for the original edition published in 1900 were created by William Wallace Denslow. Denslow's career, like his personal life, was a bit of a roller coaster ride, but at the turn of the century, when he was collaborating with L. Frank Baum, he ranked as one of the most important illustrators working in the Midwest. His style was formed as much by an interest in Japanese prints as it was by the British models of Walter Crane, Kate Greenaway, and Randolph Caldecott. "The Soldier with the Green Whiskers Led them Through the Streets" (into The Emerald City) [cat. no. 163], with its bold sense of outline that effectively flattens the forms, demonstrates the importance two-dimensional design held for Denslow, who was among the first to combine this element with color. The artist also captures the outlandish whimsy of the tale as he humorously interprets the green spectacles that the entire party—even Toto—wear to protect their vision in The Emerald City. Other details such as flowers growing out of the soldier's rifle and the bow on his beard underscore the illogicality of the proceedings.

The Wonderful Wizard of Oz has had no shortage of reissues; legions of artists have illustrated it. Among the most successful attempts must rank Charles Santore's luxurious watercolors for an edition published in 1991. His depiction of the intrepid travelers' passage through The Emerald City [cat. no. 164] reveals an imposing bastion cast in an emerald-green hue; this architectural extravaganza recalls the Art Nouveau curvilinearity and fantasy of the Catalan architect Antonio Gaudí. This penchant for sublime theatricality augmented Santore's homage to the exuberantly imaginative sets of the 1939 movie. In making reference to Gaudí, Santore indicated that he was trying to imagine what architecture L. Frank Baum might have envisioned for his Utopian city, and to Santore, Gaudí was the most avant-garde and visionary architect working at the turn of the century.[26] The intense light reinforces the figures' sense of wonderment, and there is a hyperreality that imbues Santore's drawing with a decidedly metaphysical and surreal feeling that successfully captures the dreamlike quality of the narrative.

To his chagrin, Baum found that the public could not get enough of Oz, and its appeal put him in a literary straitjacket. Among the many sequels was *The Road to Oz*, published in 1909, which contained illustrations by the highly talented John R. Neill. In one of the culminating episodes, the reader witnesses "Drinking the Health of Princess Ozma of Oz" [cat. no. 165] in which a festive banquet is about to commence. Santa Claus toasts the princess' health before the feast begins, and we behold a sumptuously laid table at which many familiar characters are seated: the Tin Woodman in the right foreground, the Scarecrow at left center with Jack Pumpkinhead opposite, and Dorothy adjacent to the standing Princess. Neill, with his deft draftsmanship, creates a visual cornucopia which sparkles with crystal stemware and jewel-like architectural details. He truly transports us to a wonderland.

163. (below left) W. W. Denslow (1865-1915). American. "The soldier with the green whiskers led them through the streets," from *The Wonderful Wizard of Oz* [Chicago: George M. Hill Company, 1900]. Print Collection, Miriam and Ira D. Wallach Division of Art, Prints and Photographs; The New York Public Library Astor, Lenox and Tilden Foundations

164. (above) Charles Santore (born 1935). American. "The soldier with the green whiskers led them through the streets," from *The Wizard of Oz* [New York: JellyBean Press, 1991]. © Charles Santore, 1991; Published with the permission of Charles Santore. Collection of Olenka and Charles Santore

165. (below, right) John R. Neill (1877-1943). American. "Drinking the Health of Princess Ozma of Oz," from *The Road to Oz* [Chicago: Reilly & Britton Company, 1909]. Private Collection

166. William Pène du Bois (1916-1993). American. "Jettisoning Ballast from 'The Globe'," from *The Twenty-one Balloons* [New York: The Viking Press, 1947]. Mazza Collection Galleria, The University of Findlay

167. Nancy Ekholm Burkert (born 1933). American. "Everyone can have some!," from *James and the Giant Peach* [New York: Alfred A. Knopf, Inc., 1961]. © Nancy Ekholm Burkert, 1961; Reprinted with the permission of Alfred A. Knopf, Inc., and imprint of Random House, Inc. Lent by the Artist

Fantasy has and will always captivate readers young and old, and there are certain vehicles that seem especially suited for such flights of fancy. Jules Verne's *Around the World in Eighty Days* (1873) may have set the standard in the late nineteenth century. Not surprisingly, the balloon emerges as the conveyance of choice in numerous stories under discussion. Just as the Wizard sought to effect his escape from Oz in a balloon, it was the intention of Professor William Waterman Sherman to fly across the Pacific Ocean by this method of transport in William Pène du Bois' *The Twenty-One Balloons*, published in 1947. The book, a delightful blend of scientific truth and nonsense, profited enormously from the author's polished pen and ink drawings. "Jettisoning Ballast from 'The Globe'" [cat. no. 166] displays a precision of detail that anchors the work in the real world, while the objects suspended in midair defy gravity and belief. Just before publication, Pène du Bois was astounded to learn of the similarity between *The Twenty-one Balloons* and F. Scott Fitzgerald's "The Diamond as Big as the Ritz," which appeared in 1922. While he could offer no explanation, save secrecy in the pursuit of diamonds, the legacy of the two narratives is an instance of richly parallel imaginations.

Roald Dahl, known to adults for his marvelously malicious short stories, is the author of some of the most widely read children's books today, including *Charlie and the Chocolate Factory* (1964) and *James and the Giant Peach*, first published in 1961. This mercurial tale of James Henry Trotter and a mutant peach who embark on a series of adventures includes an airborne trip across the Atlantic Ocean in which the peach resembles an inverted balloon. The fable culminates in a ticker tape parade up Fifth Avenue in New York City, and Nancy Ekholm Burkert's "'Everyone can have some!'" captures the triumphant James and his insect companions in tandem with the enormous fruit [cat. no. 167]. The insects are worthy of the great French caricaturist J.–J. Grandville and his admirers, Henry Louis Stephens and John Tenniel, for their unsettling anthropomorphic quality. The peach, riding on a flatbed truck, reminds one of the giant inflated balloons of the Thanksgiving Day parade, and the artist has incisively suggested the feeding frenzy that is about to unfold. The regimen of Burkert's training is rooted in an exquisite detail, precision, and delicacy which harkens back to the craftsmanship of the Northern Renaissance.[27]

HISTORY

As well as exploring far-off realms of fantasy, children's books often provide the young with their first exposure to history. One of the most interesting examples is *Daniel Boone: Historic Adventure of an American Hunter Among the Indians* (1931), produced by Esther Averill and Lila Stanley, Americans living in Paris. Feodor Rojankovsky, a Russian who had never been west of Paris, created the illustrations. The artist brought a typically European romantic notion of American Indians and wilderness, fueled by the writings of James Fenimore Cooper, to the task. The scene, "By the campfire at night [Boone] talked with a trader named Finley . . ." [cat. no. 168], depicts Daniel

Boone (1734–1820) seated on a stump at the lower left and Finley leaning against a tree with a British military camp shown in the background. Rojankovsky used colored pencils and achieved a clarity which is augmented by the angularity of his modernist tendencies.

Abraham Lincoln (1809–1865) became a popular subject in the late thirties and early forties, and perhaps he was lionized to overshadow the tyranny of Hitler's oppressive policies. Ingri and Edgar Parin d'Aulaire published their award-winning picture-book in 1939, and "Abe Reading by the Fire" [cat. no. 169] is as romantic in interpretation as Rojankovsky's in capturing the well-documented motivation and aspirations of the young Lincoln. The apparition of the soldier on horseback along with a statue of a Greek or Roman orator in classical toga in the smoke of the fire allude to Lincoln's bravery and prowess as a public speaker. Such details as these repeatedly enhance the narrative.

James Daugherty illustrated Carl Sandburg's *Abe Lincoln Grows Up* in 1928 and subsequently worked on several other projects dealing with American history. His illustrated biography of Lincoln appeared in 1943 and earned him the coveted Newbery

168. (left) Feodor Rojankovsky (1891-1970). Born in Mitava, Russia; Came to the U.S. in 1941. "By the campfire at night he talked with a trader named Finley . . . ," from *Daniel Boone: Historic Adventure of an American Hunter among the Indians* [Paris: Domino Press, 1931]. The Kerlan Collection, University of Minnesota
169. (right) Ingri Parin d'Aulaire (1904-1980). Born in Konigsberg, Norway; Came to the U.S. in 1929 and Edgar Parin d'Aulaire (1898-1986). Born in Munich, Germany; Came to the U.S. in 1929. "Abe Reading by the Fire," from *Abraham Lincoln* [Garden City, L.I.: Doubleday, Doran and Company, 1939]. The Kerlan Collection, University of Minnesota

170. James Daugherty (1889-1974). American. "Lincoln Leading the Parade in the Wake of Emancipation," from *Abraham Lincoln* [New York: The Viking Press, 1943]. © James Daugherty, 1943. May Masse Collection, William Allen White Library, Emporia State University

Medal. The text was intended for older readers, and the images formed commanding narratives in their own right. "Lincoln Leading the Parade in the Wake of Emancipation" [cat. no. 170] demonstrates Daugherty's powerful draftsmanship which reverberates with the muscular energy of such American regionalists as Benton and Curry and descends ultimately from the expressive power of Michelangelo. Although the depiction of the African Americans in the lower left corner and the young boy walking beside Lincoln is handled with a sensitivity tempered by an inevitable sense of stereotype, the artist's inclusion of empty liquor bottles, in hindsight, was most unfortunate. Daugherty, no doubt, meant to convey the spirit—or spirits—of celebration, but the formal juxtaposition with the figures at the left has resulted in an interpretation he surely did not intend. In the previous decade he had created illustrations for *John Brown's Body* by Steven Vincent Benét as well as artwork for a retelling of *John Henry*; his gravitation to these subjects suggest a decided sympathy for African Americans.

As noted previously, African-American children have enjoyed a rich proliferation of pertinent literature in recent years, and part of the market includes books about important figures. Among the outstanding current accomplishments in this genre is Andrea Davis Pinkney's *Dear Benjamin Banneker* (1994), illustrated by her husband, Brian. Benjamin Banneker (1731–1806) was the son of a freed slave in Maryland. He owned a tobacco farm and was a self-taught scientist. Banneker produced an almanac between 1792 and 1802 and served on George Washington's commission to plan and build the new capital on the Potomac river. The image of Benjamin riding along the shore of the Chesapeake Bay depicts one of his jaunts to gather information for the almanac, and Pinkney practically casts Banneker in the guise of an equestrian statue [cat. no. 171] .

171. Brian Pinkney (born 1961). American. "Benjamin Banneker riding along the shore of the Chesapeake," from *Dear Benjamin Banneker* [New York: Gulliver Books, 1994]. © Brian Pinkney, 1994; Reprinted with the permission of Gulliver Books, an imprint of Harcourt Brace & Company. Collection of Brian Pinkney

MYTH, MAGIC, AND MYSTERY

172a. Robert Lawson (1892-1957). American. "Ben flying Kite with Amos on Knee," from *Ben and Me* [New York: Dell Publishing Co., 1939]. © Robert Lawson, 1939, renewed 1967 by John W. Boyd. Reprinted with permission of Little, Brown and Company. Betsy B. Shirley Collection of American Children's Literature, The Beinecke Library of Yale University

Certainly, Banneker's accomplishments were worthy of such a monument. Interestingly, the artist employs the demanding scratchboard technique, because he felt it allowed him to sculpt as well as draw.

Intellectual curiosity and inventiveness made Banneker a product of his time. He corresponded with Thomas Jefferson, and his scientific bent also connects him with one of the great diplomats, philosophers, and inventors of the eighteenth century, Benjamin Franklin (1708–1790). Captured in a wonderfully mercurial book by Robert Lawson titled *Ben and Me* (1939), Franklin's sound judgment is revealed to be dependent on the wisdom of a mouse, Amos. Not all the adventures were happy ones for Amos, and "Ben Flying a Kite with Amos on His Knee" represents their friendship before a serious breach occurred over Franklin's use of Amos in experiments with kites, lightning, and electricity [cat. no. 172a]. This pen and ink drawing signals Lawson's hallmark style of precise attention to detail with a humorous anecdotal quality.

DRIVEN BY DREAMS

Pursuing the realm of technological innovation into the twentieth century, America won the race to master flight, but Louis Blériot (1872–1936) made a major contribution to the field on behalf of France. He was the first aviator to fly across the English channel. Alice and Martin Provensen recounted this adventure in *The Glorious Flight, Across the Channel with Louis Blériot, July 25, 1909* (1983). A double-page spread early on shows the trials and tribulations of *Blériot V* and *Blériot VI* [cat. no. 173], complete with crash landings. Appropriate to the period of the French aviator's achievement, the Provensens worked in a naive style reminiscent of the French customs official and "Sunday" painter, Henri Rousseau. The simple charm of their attempt to capture the untutored yet honest vision of Rousseau accords perfectly with the trial and error nature of Blériot's achievement.

173. Alice (born 1918) and Martin Provensen (1916-1987). American. "Bleriot V and VI," from *The Glorious Flight: Across the Channel with Louis Blériot July 25, 1909* [New York: The Viking Press, 1983]. © Alice Provensen, 1983. Mazza Collection Galleria, The University of Findlay

History is often driven by the pursuit of a dream. This was the case for Blériot as well as for a Chinese immigrant from Canton who grew up in the American Southwest. Bong Way "Billy" Wong (1933–1969) was instilled with the conviction he could be anything he wanted to be. Although Billy's aspiration to become a great basketball star was stymied by his size, a visit to Spain opened his eyes to the graceful yet dangerous and controversial sport of bullfighting. Ignoring the belief that only Spaniards could become true matadors, Billy persevered and became the first Chinese bullfighter.

Allen Say recounted this motivational story in *El Chino* (1990) with spare text and scintillating watercolors. The artist beautifully composed and richly colored Billy's initial encounter with a young bull [cat. no. 174]. The high horizon line and careful arrangement of forms reflect Say's devotion to Far Eastern principles of design, while the assured handling of paint contributes a profound stillness and earnest concentration which underscore the tension and impending drama.

Subsequently, Say indulged himself in some poignant family history. *Grandfather's Journey* (1993) delineates his grandfather's life in Japan and America and exposes the conflicts involved in bridging two cultures. One of the most evocative images depicts his grandfather as a young man, traveling across America and posing with a group of men of varying backgrounds who symbolize the country's function as a melting pot [cat. no. 175]. The slight tilt his of grandfather's head intimates a vulnerability reiterated in the almost comic bagginess of his suit—undoubtedly an equally new experience in haberdashery. Say's handling of the watercolor medium is again deft and sure, and he employs a limited palette that nevertheless produces a rich visual experience. In our selective review of people who have made history, we have seen how an individual's deeds assured them long-lived recognition.

In this consideration of High Adventure and Fantasy for older readers, we have explored themes that are distinctly American and some that are more universal. While the physical settings and ways of life may have evolved dramatically, these works are bound together by the single most compelling ingredient: the ability to trigger the imagination and let the mind roam free into seemingly unimaginable realms. In virtual lock-step with this literary practice, the art of illustration has provided a wide range of

MYTH, MAGIC, AND MYSTERY

interpretation in an equally wide array of stylistic and technical approaches. Consequently, the artists who work in this genre play a crucial role in introducing individuals, young and old, to a visual language that is predicated upon extraordinarily high standards. Just as the best stories endure, so will this art of high caliber assume its rightful place in the lexicon of eminent artistic achievement, and the disparate bodies of literature exemplified here are bound together by a connective tissue of artistic interpretation which heralds their ingredients of "myth, magic, and mystery."

174. Allen Say (born 1937). Born in Yokohama, Japan; Came to the U.S. ca. 1953. "Sure enough, the first rancher I saw gave me the nod," from *El Chino* [Boston: Houghton Mifflin Company, 1990]. © Allen Say, 1990; Reprinted with the permission of Houghton Mifflin Company. Collection of Allen Say

175. Allen Say (born 1937). Born in Yokohama, Japan; Came to the U.S. ca. 1953. "He met many people along the way," from *Grandfather's Journey* [Boston: Houghton Mifflin Company, 1993]. © Allen Say, 1993; Reprinted with the permission of Houghton Mifflin Company. Collection of Allen Say

V

H . Nichols B . Clark

HAPPILY EVER AFTER . . . :
FAIRY TALES, FABLES,
AND MYTHS

180. James Marshall (1942-1992). American. " 'My turn!,' cried the younger step-sister, thrusting her pudgy foot at the prince," from *Cinderella* [Boston: Little, Brown and Company, 1989]. © James Marshall, 1989, Reprinted with the permission of Little, Brown and Company. Northeast Children's Literature Collections, Archives and Special Collections Department, Senator Thomas J. Dodd Research Collection, University Library, University of Connecticut, Storrs

In 1974 Iona and Peter Opie, pioneering scholars of the world and words of childhood, suggested that the existing literature on fairy tales was so sizable that if piled on end it would rival the beanstalk that Jack climbed to reach the sky.[1] There has been little surcease in the intervening twenty years, and scholars have subjected these durable stories to a broad spectrum of interpretation ranging from psychoanalytic and psychosexual to structuralist and feminist.[2] While this essay will address some of these issues, textual readings have been minimized in favor of visual interpretation. Here, too, the Opies recognized that a tale's illustrations often reflect the era in which they were depicted, effecting the setting, appearance of characters, and even influencing a story's popularity.[3]

COLLECTIONS

Whether myth, legend, folk or fairy tale, these stories have existed for thousands of years as vehicles to explain the seemingly inexplicable.[4] Until relatively recently, the tales were handed down and disseminated through an oral tradition. These narratives offered solace, hope, and instruction, and they were often laced with an ingredient of magic. The earliest known collections of stories emanated from the East with the Hindu anthology known to Western audiences as *Fables of Bidpai*, dating from the third century A.D.[5] The earliest known European volume, a collection of tales and jests, was published in Venice in two parts from 1550 to 1553. It was, however, through the efforts of Charles Perrault and Mme. d'Aulnoy that the fairy tale entered the realm of literature. Perrault's eight stories, *Histoire ou Contes du temps passé. Avec des Moralitez*, in 1697, enjoyed a particular success that still endures today.

FAIRY TALES

The literary life of the fairy tale was not without problems. Many adults—and it was they who determined what was available to children—believed that narratives espousing magic and the supernatural were unhealthy and thought it was dangerous for children to have access to literature that permitted the imagination free play.[6] This attitude was especially prevalent in the second half of the eighteenth century which, under the soubriquet of the Age of Reason, attempted to codify and order the natural world. The Protestant and particularly Puritan strongly opposed the perceived frivolity and fantasy of such tales, and there were many especially vociferous opponents in America. Among the best known was "Peter Parley," the pseudonym for Samuel Goodrich, who, beginning in 1827, dedicated himself to attacking fairy tales and publishing books filled with facts, technical descriptions, and scientific observations. Parley's efforts inspired numerous imitators in England, and by the 1840s, there was a considerable body of literature deemed suitable for children, though perhaps not by the children themselves.

Despite these concerted efforts to suppress the fairy tale, the genre prospered. With the Romantic Age in the early nineteenth century emerged a fascination with the past, resulting in a flowering of revival styles. Consequently, folklore was accorded a vital role in defining the texture of a country's cultural heritage, and stories began to be recorded, collected, and published. The German brothers and philologists, Jacob and Wilhelm Grimm began publishing their *Kinder- und Haus-Märchen* in 1812, and their efforts inspired the serious collecting of folk and fairy tales throughout Europe and elsewhere.[7]

Just as well known and loved as the Grimms and their fairy tales was not a collector but a creator. Hans Christian Andersen came from a humble background for whom storytelling was a central form of entertainment. His modest career as an author transformed radically in 1835 with the publication of *Tales Told for Children*. Such stories as "The Princess on the Pea," "The Little Mermaid," and "The Ugly Duckling," continue to enthrall readers young and old.

THE ILLUSTRATED FAIRY TALE

176b. George Cruikshank (1792-1878). British. "Cinderella and the Glass Slipper," from *The Fairy Library* [London: David Bogue, 1854]. Rare Books and Special Collections, Princeton University Library

As fairy tales from the various sources of Perrault, Grimm, Andersen, and others gained popularity in the nineteenth century so did the demand for their illustration. One of the benchmark publications was Edgar Taylor's translation of *Grimm's Fairy Tales* in 1823 which included twenty-two etched illustrations by the highly regarded artist George Cruikshank. His success in this field induced him to reinterpret several stories in the 1850s to reflect his conversion to total abstinence from alcohol.[8] Although controversial, the images have endured, and the title page of *Cinderella and the Glass Slipper* (ca. 1854) [cat. nos. 176a and 176b; see p. 8], here reproduced in its published form as well as a finished drawing, reflect the artist's faithful attention to detail enlivened by a spirited sense of design. The coupling of Cinderella and her benevolent fairy godmother in the kitchen conveys a rustic yet mysteriously "gothic" sensibility which sets an appropriate tone for the story.

CINDERELLA

It is fitting to commence the artistic discussion of this section with "Cinderella," since it enjoys a place among the oldest stories on record and has entered the literature in over 700 variants.[9] Among the earliest known interpretations is a Chinese version which dates from around A.D. 850, and happily it has been recently retold and illustrated.[10] "Cinderella" was in America by the late eighteenth century in the form of a chapbook (a small portable pamphlet), and it was one of the earliest such stories to be illustrated by an American.

Felix Octavius Carr Darley brought illustration to a level of esteem in America.[11] In 1846 he began producing over 100 designs to be reproduced in Eleanor Fenn's series of *Grandfather Lovechild's Nursery Stories*. Two of the works interpreted "Cinderella" [cat. nos. 177a (see p. 14) and 177b] demonstrate his fondness for realism. While Darley has attempted to evoke a sense of fantasy through costume and action in a tight, linear style, there is something stilted in the image; he found his true *metier* in juvenile literature and the emerging American mythologies of Irving and Cooper (see above, pp. 123ff).

Given "Cinderella's" popularity, there is no shortage of artistic interpretation that could provide sufficient material for its own exhibition. In this current, highly selective survey, we have chosen to look at some very disparate stylistic renderings that speak to children in the eras in which they were created. Leonard Weisgard illustrated the story in 1938 and gives us a Cinderella who resonates with the Big Band Swing Era [cat. no. 178] and the accompanying quest for independence by young women. Indeed, this Cinderella, with her narrow-waisted dress offset by leg-of-mutton sleeves and daringly short, flaring striped skirt, thick high-heeled shoes (which contradict any properties of glass), and tightly-permed coiffure, could easily have shared a stage with those singing sensations, the Andrews Sisters. By contrast, the prince's emissary retains a greater fidelity to courtly appearance consistent with the story, although the decoration on his waistcoat suggests an admiration of American folk art. This is even more apparent in Cinderella's ball gown, with its birds and tulips, echoing the flat stylization of *fraktur* painting. This sensitivity to Americana was entirely consistent with the growing interest in such folk art, while the emphasis on flat, geometric forms also implies a desire to keep in step with the current Art Deco aesthetic.

177b. (left) Felix O.C. Darley (1822-1888). American. "Cinderella Trying on Slipper" from Lawrence Lovechild, *Grandfather Lovechild's Nursery Stories. Fred Fearnought* [Philadelphia: George B. Zieber, 1847]. Rare Books and Special Collections, Princeton University Library

178. (above) Leonard Weisgard (born 1916). American. "Cinderella Trying on Slipper," from *Cinderella* [Garden City, L.I.: Doubleday, 1938]. © Leonard Weisgard, 1938. Department of Special Collections, University of Oregon Library

179. Marcia Brown (born 1918). American. "Cinderella Going to Ball," from *Cinderella* [New York: Charles Scribner's Sons, 1954]. © Marcia Brown, 1954; Reprinted with the permission of Atheneum Books for Young Readers, an imprint of Simon & Schuster Children's Publishing Division. Mazza Collection Galleria, The University of Findlay

Marcia Brown, in her adaptation, from the mid-1950s [cat. no. 179], returns to an eighteenth-century milieu both in setting and costume. Her evocation of the French Rococo in emphasizing the aristocratic opulence of silks and satins is achieved through nervous line, delicate colors, and scintillating surface worthy of those French paradigms Jean-Antoine Watteau and Jean-Honoré Fragonard. In America the fifties were a decade of chiffons and satins, as the country settled into a peacetime prosperity (albeit tempered by the tension of the unfolding Cold War). Quite possibly, in the wake of World War II and the Korean conflict, the escapism of fairy tales took on an added measure of importance in soothing the American psyche.

The decade of the sixties brought about a social revolution which challenged the status quo embodied in the Eisenhower era, and a new radicalism entered the arts. This renegade element entered the stream of fairy tale interpretation in the delightfully outrageous work of James Marshall. His renderings for *Cinderella*, executed in 1989 [cat. no. 180], have an amusingly satirical quality worthy of the British tradition of Thomas Rowlandson and George Cruikshank. The spoiled step-sister, replete with rouge and beauty mark (wishful thinking), pouts while straining to get her over-sized foot into the delicate slipper and exudes an expressive brio that defines Marshall's work. This facet of humor as entropy challenges the status quo and, in making us laugh involuntarily, exhorts us not to take ourselves too seriously. Marshall, through his visual esprit, knocks literature and tradition off its pedestal, and it falls on our level. He does not disparage the stories in the process; he simply makes them more accessible by means of sidesplitting humor.

A variant of "Cinderella" comes to us by way of the Brothers Grimm: Charlotte Huck's *Princess Furball*, illustrated by Anita Lobel, which also appeared in 1989. Derived from the German tale, "Many Fur," it recounts the elevation of a young woman from menial labor to her proper station in life. Lobel, in the episode of the prince slipping the ring onto the princess' finger [cat. no. 181], works in a reductive style of bold, simple outlines and broad areas of local color which connect the work to the tradition of folk art. This conscious use of a naive yet direct and legible style visually reinforces the vividness of the ancient oral convention.

MYTH, MAGIC, AND MYSTERY

181. Anita Lobel (born 1934). Born in Cracow, Poland; Came to the U.S. in 1952. "While they were dancing, he slipped a tiny gold ring on her finger," from *Princess Furball* [New York: Greenwillow Books, 1989]. © Anita Lobel, 1989; Reprinted with the permission of Greenwillow Books, an imprint of William Morrow. On loan by the artist

"Cinderella" also enjoys African interpretations. John Steptoe gravitated to African folk tales that provided a vision of the land and people of his ancestors. *Mufaro's Beautiful Daughters* (1987) is dedicated to the children of South Africa and takes its inspiration from a folk tale collected and published in 1895 by G. M. Theal in his *Kaffir Folktales*. The story which has affinities with "Cinderella" pits pride against humility and selfishness against generosity in the guise of a father (Mufaro=happy man), who

182. John Steptoe (1950-1989).
American. "On the seat of the great
chief's stool lay the little garden
snake," from *Mufaro's Beautiful
Daughters* [New York: Lothrop, Lee
& Shepard Books, 1987]. Copyright
© 1987, John Steptoe; Reprinted
with the approval of the Estate of
John Steptoe. The John Steptoe
Collection

offers the king a choice of his daughters (Manyara=ashamed and Nyasha=mercy). The monarch is searching for a suitable bride for the prince (Nyoka=snake). All the names are taken from the Shona language, and details in the pictures were inspired by the ruins of an ancient city found in Zimbabwe as well as the flora and fauna of the region.[12] We clearly see Steptoe's stimulus in the picture of Nyasha encountering the snake (who is actually the prince Nyoka) on the great chief's throne [cat. no. 182]. There is a greater sense of naturalism than in his earlier work, and the viewer marvels at the rich detail, such as cracks and weathering in the stone, which speaks not only to fidelity but also to a spiritual atmosphere of place and ritual. Whether consciously or not, Steptoe captures that moment of peak drama—just before the snake transforms itself—an ingredient that was so important to Howard Pyle. The poignance in all the illustrations for this remarkable book confirms how special the material was for the artist.

PUSS IN BOOTS

If the events in "Cinderella" are controlled by magic, then those of another of Perrault's great tales, "Puss in Boots," are fueled by the use of one's wits. This tale of

　　　　　　　　　　　　　　　　　　　MYTH, MAGIC, AND MYSTERY

184. Marcia Brown (born 1918). American. "Puss Blowing Trumpet," Frontispiece for *Puss in Boots* [New York: Charles Scribner's Sons, 1952]. © Marcia Brown, 1952; Reprinted with the permission of Atheneum Books for Young Readers, an imprint of Simon & Schuster Children's Publishing Division. de Grummond Children's Literature Collection, University of Southern Mississippi

cunning was epitomized in Walter Crane's pioneering interpretation of 1873 [cat. no. 183; see p. 10] in which he surrounds the text with a series of visual episodes culminating in Puss' outwitting the ogre by changing him into a mouse. Crane's importance to the American tradition of illustration has been discussed elsewhere (see above, pp. 10ff), and his influence has effected a broad spectrum of American artists ranging from Howard Pyle to Marcia Brown.

Brown, who created her *Puss in Boots* in 1952, saw it in terms of an exuberant Baroque aesthetic consistent with the way in which Perrault initially recorded the story.

The frontispiece [cat. no. 184] shows the crafty cat in seventeenth-century costume worthy of the heroes of Alexandre Dumas' *The Three Musketeers*. Puss stands magisterially with his right paw on his hip while literally and figuratively blowing his horn with his left. The bold pattern of his hat is offset by the wispy plumes that sprout from it and the dentil-like quality of his ruff collar; the polygonal geometry of his red boots is balanced by the sweeping curves of his tail and sash. The composition is a masterful exercise in color, draftsmanship, and two-dimensional design, which pay tribute to Crane as well as Baroque conventions.

LITTLE RED RIDING HOOD

Certain stories blend magic and guile. The tale of "Little Red Riding Hood" has long enjoyed universal popularity with especial success in America since the late eighteenth century.[13] In the following century, the narrative often appeared as a conflation of the Perrault and Grimm versions. Not surprisingly, most tellings contained strong moral overtones which addressed Red Riding Hood's actions and their consequences.

In 1903, W. W. Denslow, riding on the success of his illustrations for L. Frank Baum's *The Wonderful Wizard of Oz* (1900) (see above, pp. 148ff), produced *Denslow's Little Red Riding Hood*. The artwork, such as "Little Red Riding Hood Meeting the Wolf in the Woods" [cat. no. 185], is vintage Denslow with its strong sense of design. The bold outline, creating broad unmodulated areas, flatten the composition and reflect his debt not only to such British sources as Randolph Caldecott and Walter Crane but also to Japanese prints. The attenuation of the wolf provides a nice foil to the squat, triangular presence of Red Riding Hood. As in Arthur Rackham, the trees in the background are anthropomorphized and look on with bemused expressions. This last element defines the fanciful element of Denslow's approach.

As the twentieth century progressed, the moral implications of the story were increasingly downplayed, although never completely subsumed.[14] In 1972 Beatrice Schenk de Regniers created a version in verse, "for boys and girls to read themselves."[15] Edward Gorey created the drawings and brought his clever draftsmanship to the project. The depiction of the wolf, who leans casually against the bedstead and polishes off the cake, having already ingested Red Riding Hood, is executed in a spare and controlled hand [cat. no. 186]. By means of strategic shading, such as the head of the wolf, Gorey insinuates the brutal terror of the episode into his interpretation.

Trina Schart Hyman acknowledged her source in the Grimm version for her own retelling and illustration in 1983. She infuses her pictures with wit and a sense of nineteenth-century Americana [cat. no. 187]. The ladder-back chair in the left foreground, patchwork quilt on the bed, exposed-beam ceiling, framed alphabet sampler, and woodstove in the room beyond all lend a quaintness to the scene. The framed sampler may also constitute a visual *double-entendre*, since it could be read as an eyechart for the imposter grandmother before closer scrutiny reveals its true identity. The curtain of the

185. W. W. Denslow (1856-1915). American. "Little Red Riding Hood meets Wolf," from *Denslow's Little Red Riding Hood* [New York: G. W. Dillingham, 1903]. de Grummond Children's Literature Collection, University of Southern Mississippi

MYTH, MAGIC, AND MYSTERY

186. Edward Gorey (born 1925). American. "And the wicked wolf, without more ado, ate Red Riding Hood and the little cake, too," from *Red Riding Hood* [New York: Atheneum, 1972]. © Edward Gorey, 1972; Reprinted with the permission of Atheneum Books for Young Readers, an imprint of Simon & Schuster Children's Publishing Division. Collection of Edward Gorey, Courtesy of Gotham Book Mart Gallery, New York City

canopy bed is tied back to permit us to enter the scene and recalls a device that was popular in seventeenth-century Netherlandish genre painting. In addition to a refined sense of composition, Hyman enhances the episode by capturing the tension of the moment with her lively draftsmanship and vibrant color. Thus, her lineage from the Pyle tradition is patently apparent in this illustration.

"Little Red Riding Hood," like "Cinderella," boasts universal sources. Ed Young created a distinguished version in 1989: *Lon Po Po: A Red Riding Hood Story from China*. Young grew up in China where he read a lot of folk tales and legends, also disseminated through Peking opera.[16] Young feels very strongly about his approach to bringing these Chinese tales into Western culture; they have to "feel like China" and contain a certain authenticity.

In the Chinese version, it is the mother who goes off to visit her mother while leaving her three daughters behind. The young girls are forced to contend with a wolf who

"Good morning, Grandmother," she called. But there was no answer. Then she went quietly into the bedroom and pulled the bed-curtains back. There lay her Grandmother. But she had drawn her shawl down over her face, and she looked very odd. Red Riding Hood couldn't help but stare.

"Grandmother! What big, hairy ears you have grown!" she said.

"The better to hear you with, my dear."

187. (below) Trina Schart Hyman (born 1939). American. "Little Red Riding Hood Approaching Wolf in Bed," from *Little Red Riding Hood* [New York: Holiday House, 1983]. © Trina Schart Hyman, 1983. Collection of Trina Schart Hyman

188. (above) Ed Young (born 1931). Born in Tianjin, China; Came to the U.S. in 1951. "Shang and Sisters in Tree Looking Down at Wolf," from *Lon Po Po, A Red-Riding Hood Story from China* [New York: Philomel Books, 1989]. © Ed Young, 1989; Reprinted with the permission of Philomel Books, an imprint of the Putnam & Grosset Group. Collection of Ed Young

has tricked his way into their house. The illustration depicts the moment when the three sisters have escaped to the safety of a gingko tree while the wolf looks plaintively and hungrily up at them [cat. no. 188]. Young brings to the picture a decidedly Asian aesthetic with the bold diagonal of the tree limb which bisects the sheet. The three children form a dense compositional element as they look down at the predator from their precarious perch. The wolf, by contrast, is the lone element in the lower two-thirds of the design, and his placement is critical to ensure a harmonious configuration. The loose, vaporous washes and chalky pastels further affirm the composition's spatial ambiguity, and the mysterious atmosphere evokes Chinese screen painting, further underscored by the illustration's organization into panels. Thus, Young provides a valuable contribution to the litany of "Little Red Riding Hood" by supplying us with an exquisite rendering.

SNOW WHITE

In turning to another of the stories chronicling a young girl who has to overcome adversity to assume her rightful place, we encounter an instance of adult/parent as adversary. "Snow White," as we know her today, originally appeared under the name "Snow Drop" in the Edgar Taylor translation of the Grimm's *German Popular Stories*.[17] The tale tells of a parent who is destroyed by jealousy of a child who surpasses her, and according to Bruno Bettelheim, the implications are patently Oedipal.[18]

An artist who concluded his career contributing to the Walt Disney Studio was the Danish-born Kay Nielsen, who went to Hollywood in 1936 and remained to work with Disney.[19] In 1925, while still living in Europe, Nielsen illustrated a group of the Grimm's tales, including "Snow Drop," and chose the moment when the dwarfs mourn her as she lies in state in her glass casket [cat. no. 189]. This painstakingly rendered watercolor recalls Northern Renaissance manuscript illumination—even to the use of gold paint—but the stylized nature and anatomy resonates with an Art Deco aesthetic. The dwarfs have a sculptural quality that reminds one of Romanesque architectural decoration. Snow Drop, too, is handled in a tight, linear fashion which reflects Nielsen's ongoing debt to the Art Nouveau manner of Aubrey Beardsley, and this elegant stylization became a central ingredient of Nielsen's art.

The Disney interpretation became so ingrained into the public awareness that serious artistic treatment lapsed for nearly thirty years.[20] One of the most ambitious and beautiful attempts in recent memory is Nancy Ekholm Burkert's illustrations to Randall Jarrell's translation, which appeared in 1972. The return of the dwarfs to their newly ordered household [cat. no. 190a] and the wicked stepmother in her laboratory concocting the poison for the apple [cat. no. 190b; see p. 40] epitomize Burkert's concern for recording the specifics of nature with clarity and precision, while at the same time articulating her attraction to a metaphysical presence in which the natural is at one with the supernatural.[21] Burkert's artistic sources range from manuscript illumination of the Middle Ages to the English fine art tradition of illustration embodied in artists extend-

ing from Walter Crane and Arthur Rackham. For *Snow White and the Seven Dwarfs*, she was especially captivated by the Flemish masters of the fifteenth and sixteenth centuries and by one of her favorite works, *The Portinari Altarpiece* by Hugo van der Goes. Certainly the physiognomies of the dwarfs echo those of the shepherds in the central panel of the Flemish master's work, and the Majolica vase of daylilies on the table reiterates the prominent placement of flowers in the altarpiece. They carry the same symbolic implication of purity, just as the basket of cherries Snow White holds refers to her sweetness of character.[22] In the laboratory scene, the artist's symbolic references are also accurate, and Burkert prominently displays a mandrake root lying on the table as well as reproduced in the illustrated herbal. The root's narcotic properties have been known since antiquity, as was the need for careful dosage to prevent a deep painless sleep from turning into an eternal one.[23]

Both paintings contain a wealth of pertinent detail that rewards the viewer who is willing to spend extended periods of time perusing the work. Even in the early 1970s, Burkert's approach was an anomaly in the face of a rapidly accelerating pace of life. In her highly sophisticated images, there is a cool, cerebral, and detached quality, and Burkert's interpretation assumes almost Apollonian proportions in Nietzschean terms.

If Burkert's representation of *Snow White and the Seven Dwarfs* is Apollonian, then Maurice Sendak's in *The Juniper Tree* (1972) is surely Dionysian. The single illustration for the story is visually potent, with a complexity bordering on the claustrophobic, and it pulsates with an almost bestial intensity.[24] The project, initiated in 1962, was eleven years in the process, but it stands as one of Sendak's most ambitious and satsfying undertakings. "Snow White" [cat. no. 191] occupied him for the better part of four months during which he came to realize that the more familiar the story, the greater the challenge in interpreting it.

Sendak's thorough preparation included acquiring the most meaningful editions of the stories, as well as choosing to visit the German regions from which the Brothers Grimm purportedly gathered their material. In discounting the French sources, this German expedition also brought him before the work of the Northern Renaissance masters, Albrecht Altdorfer, Albrecht Dürer and Matthias Grünewald, all of whom impressed him profoundly.

Sendak gradually distilled his artistic inspirations for the project. As well as George Cruikshank's illustrations for Grimm, Sendak was particularly moved by the powerful simplicity of Dürer's *Small Passion* (1509–1511), a series of thirty-six woodcuts and title page based on the life of Christ, and the engraved works of a third Grimm brother Ludwig Emil.[25] He emulated both German artists' innovative, dense cross-hatching, which made his own pen and ink drawings look like wood engravings, and he also imitated the formal convention of having the figures strain to burst their boundaries. What results is an intense visual experience with everything pushed right up to the front of the picture plane. The viewer, in fact, becomes the telltale mirror and is mesmerized by the haunting stare of the stepmother. Other details signal the narrative flow. The

Opposing page: **191.** (left) Maurice Sendak (born 1928). American. "Snow White and the Seven Dwarfs," from *The Juniper Tree and Other Tales from Grimm* [New York: Farrar, Straus and Giroux, 1973]. © Maurice Sendak, 1973. Courtesy, Maurice Sendak and The Rosenbach Museum & Library
189. (right) Kay Nielsen (1886-1957). Born in Copenhagen, Denmark; Came to America in 1936. "Snow Drop," from *Hansel and Gretel and Other Stories* [London: Hodder & Stoughton, 1925]. Courtesy of The Boston Public Library Print Department, John D. Merriam Collection
190a. (below) Nancy Ekholm Burkert (born 1933). American. "Snow White with basket of fruit, talking to Dwarfs," from *Snow White and the Seven Dwarfs: A Tale from the Brothers Grimm* [New York: Farrar, Straus and Giroux, 1972]. © Nancy Ekholm Burkert, 1972. Lent by the Artist

192. Gustaf Tenggren (1896-1970). Born in Magra, Sweden; Came to the U.S. in 1920. "Jack Stealing Gold," 1930, from an unpublished version of *Jack and the Beanstalk*. The Kerlan Collection, University of Minnesota

partially eaten apple sits in front of an anguishing dwarf while behind him, Snow White reclines and gazes out in a soporific trance. Dominating the back wall is an owl set within a rectangular frame. Is it a picture? Is it a window? Is it a mirror? The owl was a common symbol in seventeenth-century Netherlandish genre painting, especially the work of David Teniers the Younger. Significantly, the owl here does not represent wisdom but rather drunkeness, sleep and, by extension, death. It is no accident that the owl's gaze reiterates that of the stepmother. Thus, in a drawing of diminutive size but vast formal and emotional magnitude, Sendak gives us a compact, complex, and compelling record of this ageless tale.

MYTH, MAGIC, AND MYSTERY

193. Gustaf Tenggren (1896-1970). Born in Sweden; Came to America in 1920. "Rapunzel in the Tower," from "Rapunzel" in *The Tenggren Tell-It-Again Book* [Boston: Little, Brown and Company, 1942]. The Kerlan Collection, University of Minnesota

FOREIGN ARTISTS

The art of illustration in America has benefited greatly from foreign influences. Gustaf Tenggren was born in Sweden and came to America at the age of twenty-four. Although his formative influences were Scandinavian, he devoted much of his mature artistic energy to melding Swedish and American cultures and visual traditions.[26] From his initial vantage point in Cleveland, Ohio, Tenggren quickly realized that his predilection for trolls, steeped in fantasy as well as Arthur Rackham and various nineteenth-century Nordic artists—especially John Bauer, was not what the American public wanted. Thus, he rapidly assimilated an American imagery which included caricature. His "Jack and the Beanstalk" [cat. no. 192], painted in 1930, pushes a sense of terror almost to the limit. The massive giant slumbers in a chair crafted with animal skull armrests, and his clawlike left hand, pointed ears, jagged teeth, and ominous shadow cast against the wall suggest a raw, demonic power. All of this brute savagery is mitigated by the sausage-shaped nose which provides some much-needed comic relief. Jack is equally ludicrous with his diminutive size. But this disparate juxtaposition underscores the triumph of brains over brawn. Jack's pixielike rendering takes on the properties of a cartoon character, which reflects Tenggren's adaptability and anticipates his association with Walt Disney later in the decade.

Tenggren worked for the Walt Disney Studios between 1936 and 1939, overlapping briefly with Hardie Gramatky, Kay Nielsen, and Martin Provensen, and contributed to aspects of *Snow White and the Seven Dwarfs*, *Pinocchio*, *Bambi*, and *Fantasia*, among others. This experience solidified Tenggren's penchant for precise drawing, pastel colors, doll-like figures, and fantasy landscapes.[27] Much of this aesthetic appears in his books of the 1940s such as *The Tenggren Tell-It-Again Book*, which was published in 1942. One of the more striking images in this anthology is "Rapunzel" where the heroine looks despondently out from the window of her pencil-shaped tower [cat. no. 193]. Rapunzel's hair cascades down in wavy rivulets and curls up at the bottom in a manner that reiterates the branches of the highly stylized trees in the left foreground. The old witch comes directly from Tenggren's animation repertoire as well as Wanda Gág's *Tales from Grimm*, and he takes obvious delight in letting the old crone's nose repeat the elongated shape of her pointing right index finger. The reductive aspect of the landscape, which denies spatial recession, affirms Tenggren's admiration for the modern aesthetic embodied in such disparate sources as Georgia O'Keeffe's precisionist landscapes, crystalline forms of American Regionalists such as Grant Wood, and Paul Manship's elegantly stylized Art Deco sculpture.[28] At the same time, Tenggren never relinquished his Nordic roots, and it was this synthesis of the old and the new that infuses his work with such visual vibrancy.

NEW ENGLAND STOCK WITH OLD ENGLAND SOURCES

By contrast, Tasha Tudor has deep New England roots, and her preference for pen and ink and soft, ethereal watercolors retains an allegiance to the tradition of Randolph Caldecott, Walter Crane, Beatrix Potter, and Edmund Dulac. She elected to evoke the ideals, beauty, and sentiment of a bygone era, and this devotion is borne out in the type of book she has chosen to illustrate: Frances Hodgson Burnett's *The Secret Garden* (1962) and *The Little Princess* (1963); Robert Louis Stevenson's *A Child's Garden of Verses* (1947) and *Fairy Tales from Hans Christian Andersen* (1945), among others. From the last publication comes a tender realization of an episode in "The Real Princess," in which the flaxen-haired guest is about to ascend the enormous mound of colorful mattresses and feather beds that have been placed over a pea [cat. no. 194]. This ploy was intended to

test her royalty by assessing the sensitivity of her skin. Her finely chiseled features stand in telling contrast to the ample countenance of the housekeeper. This affable matron is accompanied by her young candle-bearing son, whose inclusion underscores the artist's sentimental advocacy of domestic harmony. Tudor is deeply interested in theater and costume, and she brings a fanciful sense of the stage set to her delicate execution.

SORCERY AND WITCHCRAFT

Sorcery and witchcraft have long provided compelling subject matter for children and adults alike. Wanda Gág's adaptation and translation of the Grimm's *The Sorcerer's Apprentice* was published posthumously in 1947 and reissued in 1979 with illustrations by Margot Tomes. While the image of the apprentice gathering ingredients is somewhat unsettling, the facing illustration where he enters the sorcerer's library [cat. no. 195] truly captures the look and ambience of such workshops in the numerous depictions of alchemists by David Teniers the Younger.[29] The creature suspended from the ceiling was a common image alluding to the false science of alchemy, while the glass vessels represent various working tools such as alembics (distillation flasks) and bell jars. The

194. (left) Tasha Tudor (born 1915). American. "The Real Princess," from *Fairy Tales from Hans Christian Andersen* [New York: Henry Z. Walck, Incorporated, 1945]. © Tasha Tudor, 1945. The Kerlan Collection, University of Minnesota
195. (right) Margot Tomes (1917-1991). American. "The boy was almost beside himself with curiosity," from *Wanda Gág's The Sorcerer's Apprentice* [New York: Coward, McCann & Geoghegan, Inc., 1979]. © Margot Tomes, 1979; Reprinted with the permission of Coward-McCann, an imprint of the Putnam & Grosset Group. The Kerlan Collection, University of Minnesota

196. (above) Leo (born 1933) and Diane Dillon (born 1933). American. Cover for *The Porcelain Cat* [Little, Brown and Company, 1987]. © Leo and Diane Dillon, 1987. Private Collection
197. (below) Margot Zemach (1931-1989). American. "Between times, she scratched a Tune on a fiddle," from *Duffy and the Devil* [New York: Farrar, Straus and Giroux, 1973]. © Margot Zemach, 1973. Collection of Kaephe Zemach-Bersin

bell jar in this depiction is especially disconcerting since it contains an homunculus and telegraphs the sorcerer's sinister intentions. The mortar and pestle and chart on the wall also amplify the eerie setting. Tomes uses a system of very fine parallel hatchings and cross-hatchings which, like Maurice Sendak's work earlier in the decade, simulates an engraving. Since Teniers' work was widely distributed through engravings, this was an appropriate reference.

Recently the distinguished artistic team of Leo and Diane Dillon illustrated an original story of sorcery, *The Porcelain Cat* (1987). The cover illustration [cat. no. 196] introduces the central characters and announces the artists' stylistic preference for this undertaking. The framing device and furniture design recall the organic curvilinearity of the Vienna Secession, which the artists had seen recently in an exhibition in New York, while the flat areas of color suggest an equivalent debt to poster design of this period. The sorcerer's workshop contains all the requisite paraphernalia, and many of the pictures are filled with hidden images that visually reinforce the wizardry of the narrative.

The sorcerer's association with the devil yields two more stories in which this malevolent figure is surprisingly outwitted. The first is a Cornish version of the "Rumpelstiltskin" story, which was retold and illustrated by Harve and Margot Zemach in 1973. *Duffy and the Devil* was based on a popular play performed in Cornwall, England, during

MYTH, MAGIC, AND MYSTERY

the Christmas season in the nineteenth century. The plot centers around an indolent lass named Duffy who captures the heart of the local squire by weaving exceptional clothes for him with the assistance of the devil. Duffy extricates herself from her bargain with the help of the housekeeper, Old Jone, who learns the devil's name by her own devious means. While Harve convincingly captured the dialects, Margot caught the Cornish character and details in a vibrant combination of line and color reminiscent of Thomas Rowlandson [cat. no. 197]. The image reverberates with the work of such American contemporaries as Maurice Sendak and William Steig, and Zemach's fluctuating line weight also recalls the energetic draftsmanship of Howard Pyle's *Yankee Doodle* drawings (see above, p. 18). In giving us a witches' cancan, the artist creates an image of irrepressible wit, and one readily understands the squire's desire to join the fun.

Zemach's boisterous rendering of the story constitutes a very different approach from Paul Zelinsky's interpretation of the Grimm's version of "Rumpelstiltskin." The artist, in retelling the tale, assiduously researched the various texts. Ultimately, he gravitated to the most familiar form, which was contained in the second edition published by the Grimms in 1819.[30] Stylistically, the art takes its inspiration from late Mediæval and Renaissance sources. The landscapes in the book suggest the work of Pieter Brueghel the Elder while the castle emulates the chateau in the month of *October* from *Les Très Riches Heures du Duc de Berry*, 1413–16, by the Limbourg Brothers. In the scene where Rumplestiltskin first spins the straw into gold for the miller's daughter [cat. no. 198], the composition conjures up the monumental peasant types in late sixteenth-century Flemish paintings by Pieter Aertsen and Joachim Beuckelaer. These earlier artists, who juxtaposed figures engaged in secular activities in the foreground with appropriate religious parallels, such as Christ in the house of Mary and Martha in the background, forged the way for pure genre painting or scenes of everyday life at the end of the sixteenth century.

Although Zelinsky was not specifically aware of these artists, he nevertheless captured their spirit. He recalled being intrigued by an image of the Virgin by Adriaen Ysenbrandt, which was formative in his vision for the miller's daughter. With the exception of Rumpelstiltskin, however, he worked from the live model, and a young woman whom he encountered in a restaurant in Chinatown posed for the miller's daughter.[31] Zelinsky endowed her with a beauty and refinement of features that deviates from the plainness of the Flemish models, but this departure is in the service of the story. Rumpelstiltskin, on the other hand, is positively repulsive with his bug-eyes, elongated misshapen hands, and spindly legs.

If the story of "Rumpelstiltskin," with its diminutive equivalent of a beast, offers a variant on the theme of "Beauty and the Beast," then Tomi Ungerer's *Zeralda's Ogre* constitutes a deliciously full-blown modern adaptation. The artist-author creates a whimsical tale in which a horrific child-devouring ogre's tastebuds are re-programmed by the delectable cuisine of Zeralda, an innocent, young girl whose culinary efforts are exceptional [cat. no. 199b]. Ungerer, with unbridled intensity, brings to the narrative

198. Paul O. Zelinsky (born 1953). American. "Rumpelstiltskin spinning," from *Rumpelstiltskin* [New York: Dutton Children's Books, 1986]. © Paul O. Zelinsky, 1986; Used by permission of Dutton Children's Books, a division of Penguin Books USA Inc. Collection of Paul O. Zelinsky

199b. Tomi Ungerer (born 1931). Born in Strasbourg, France; Came to the U.S. in 1957. "Such was her pity for the hungry giant that she used up half of her market supplies," from *Zeralda's Ogre* [New York: Delacorte Press, 1967]. © Tomi Ungerer. Donation Tomi Ungerer, Musées de la Ville de Strasbourg

and its illustrations a Rabelaisian zest for life that sets the gastric juices as well as all the senses into high gear. Ungerer challenges the boundaries of conformity and brings a subversive element to his work; adult and child find that they are willing co-conspirators in Ungerer's imaginatively rendered visual and literary concoctions.

200. (left) Kay Nielsen (1886-1957). Born in Copenhagen, Denmark; Came to the U.S. in 1936. "The Lad in Battle," from *East of the Sun West of the Moon; Old Tales from the North* [London: Hodder & Stoughton, 1914]. Collection of Kendra Krienke and Allan Daniel, New York City
201. (right) Edmund Dulac (1882-1953). Born in France, settled in England in 1904. "As soon as he came in, she began to jeer at him," from *Stories from the Arabian Nights* [London: Hodder & Stoughton, 1907]. Collection of Ann Conolly Hughey

OTHER FOREIGN INFLUENCES

America's growth is inextricably connected with immigration, and this country witnessed an enormous influx from the latter half of the nineteenth century until well into our own. The increasingly diverse population expanded the range of literary possibilities which were satisfied through imported books as well as works created by immigrant artists. Kay Nielsen did not come to America until the late thirties, but his work was known in this country by the second decade of this century. Among his most celebrated accomplishments were the splendid watercolor illustrations for *East of the Sun and West of the Moon*, published in 1914 [cat. no. 200]. These Norwegian stories were legends passed down orally over hundreds of years before being recorded in the nineteenth century. Nielsen's exquisite renderings—such as this battle scene from "The Widow's Son," in which the lad of the story outwits a troll and, by doing what an enchanted horse tells him, gains a kingdom and a beautiful wife—reveal the influence of Asian art in the flat patterning of the composition and exhibits an Art Nouveau ele-

MYTH, MAGIC, AND MYSTERY

gance of line inspired by Aubrey Beardsley. From this formal springboard, Nielsen captures the haunting atmosphere of these Nordic legends.

Nielsen's artistic sources bring to mind another migratory artist, Edmund Dulac, who only got as far as England from his native France, but who developed a strong following in America. His *Stories from the Arabian Nights*, which appeared in 1907, put him on equal footing with Arthur Rackham, whose *Peter Pan in Kensington Gardens* was issued to great acclaim the previous year (see above, p. 146). Where Rackham was energetic and spontaneous, Dulac was restrained and methodical. "As soon as he came in, she began to jeer at him" [cat. no. 201] reveals Dulac's preference for creating visual harmony and synthesis by balancing color and form. His crepuscular palette reflected his concern for tonal issues, while he also built on the opulence of Persian miniatures. Indeed, Near and Far Eastern art informed his work and contributed to the praise it received on both sides of the Atlantic.[32]

By the third decade of the twentieth century, much foreign material was being published on these shores. May Massee, the renowned children's book editor at Doubleday and later Viking, was instrumental in nurturing artists and writers from abroad. Among her earliest discoveries was Miska Petersham, who was born in Hungary and came to America in 1912. Here he met his future wife Maud Fuller. Initially, they collaborated on illustrations for other authors' books such as Carl Sandburg's *Rootabaga Stories* (1922) (see below) or Margery Clark's *Poppy Seed Cakes* (1924) (see above, p. 116); in 1929 they wrote and illustrated *MIKI: The Book of Maud and Miska Petersham*, which was about their young son's visit to Hungary.

Another artist whom Massee befriended was the Russian emigré Boris Artzybasheff, who had served with the White Army in 1918 and left Russia the following year. Initially engaged in a variety of undertakings, he illustrated his first book in 1922. Massee brought him with her from Doubleday to Viking and encouraged his desire to write as well as illustrate. One of his most successful creations was the retelling and artwork for *Seven Simeons: A Russian Tale*, published in 1937. It is a charming story of seven peasant brothers who aid their monarch find a bride and then selflessly return to their lands before the happy wedding between King Douda and Princess Helena [cat. no. 202]. The linear precision of the drawing reflects Artzybasheff's early training in ornamental design as well as lettering, and the economy of means recalls his work as a caricaturist and stage designer. The extravagant architectural and costume motifs, as well as implausible cello, reinforce the storybook nature of his subject matter. Around 1940 Artzybasheff turned his attention to another form of commercial art. This facet of his career included over 200 hundred covers for *Time Magazine* and many important advertising designs for major corporations.

Since World War II, there has been a resurgence of interest in folk tales from Eastern Europe. In the vanguard of this movement were Uri Shulevitz's illustrations created in 1968 for Arthur Ransome's retelling of the charming Russian tale, *The Fool of the World and the Flying Ship*. Ransome had covered Russia during World War I and collected numerous Russian tales which he published in 1916 as *Old Peter's Russian Tales*, including the one Shulevitz illustrated over fifty years later. The depiction of the ship hov-

202. Boris Artzybasheff (1899-1965). Born in Kharkov, Ukraine; Came to the U.S. in 1919. "King Douda and Princess Helena at their Wedding Banquet," from *Seven Simeons; A Russian Tale Retold* [New York: The Viking Press, 1937]. May Massee Collection, William Allen White Library, Emporia State University

203a. (above) Uri Shulevitz (born 1935). Born in Warsaw, Poland; Came to the U.S. in 1959. "They flew over the faggot gatherer," from *The Fool of the World and the Flying Ship*. Retold by Arthur Ransome [New York: Farrar, Strauss & Giroux, Inc. 1968]. Collection of Uri Shulevitz. Copyright © 1968 by Uri Shulevitz. Reprinted by permission of Farrar, Strauss & Giroux, Inc.

204. (below) Uri Shulevitz (born 1935). Born in Warsaw, Poland; Came to the U.S. in 1959. "Feitel's Reign," from *Fools of Chelm and Their History* [New York: Farrar, Straus, and Giroux, 1973]. © Uri Shulevitz, 1973; Collection of Uri Shulevitz

ering behind the old man who carries the fagot of wood, which later magically turns into an army of soldiers, demonstrates Shulevitz's fine draftsmanship and deft touch with watercolor [cat. no. 203a]. While complying with the demands of the text, the artist infuses the scene with a grand panoramic sweep that is punctuated with elegantly rendered details.

Shulevitz's versatility is apparent in subsequent works, notably *The Fools of Chelm and Their History* (1973), written by Isaac Bashevis Singer. The author builds on the folk tales about the city in Poland that has been identified as a city of fools in which the "wise men" are, in truth, the most foolish. "Feitel's Reign" deals with the overthrow of the government by Feitel the Thief and the anarchic laws and oppressive policies that he institutes. Shulevitz's illustration depicts the army mobilizing to conquer the neighboring city of Gorshkov [cat. no. 204]. His rendering of this ragtag bunch, wearing pots and pans for helmets and carrying the most unlikely weapons, masterfully captures Singer's satire. The extremely fine cross-hatching and controlled line emulates engraving or etching and gives us a rich array of blacks that are by no means monotonous.

In a recent compilation of Jewish tales from around the world, *The Diamond Tree* (1991), Shulevitz contributed ten exquisite watercolors, including another which considers the foolish citizenry of Chelm. "Moving a Mountain" tells of how the "wise men" counsel the townsfolk on how to deal with the heat of summer. One of the solutions is to try and fool the sun by dressing warmly and make it think it is winter. Shulevitz depicts this moment and presents an array of miserable peasants colorfully dressed in stifling winter garb [cat. no. 205]. The intense yellows and oranges of the sun and sky are picked up in the architecture and costumes, and the artist convincingly suggests the searing heat which these peasants endure with resignation. Their passive expressions further signify the eternally hopeless fate of the downtrodden. Formally, Shulevitz has balanced the diaphanous washes of color with a loose grid of interlocking diagonals, which anchors and structures the composition. This talented artist works in a broad range of technique often at the service of interpreting tales from Eastern Europe.

205. Uri Shulevitz (born 1935). Born in Warsaw, Poland; Came to the U.S. in 1959. "Moving a Mountain" from *The Diamond Tree: Jewish Tales from Around the World* [New York: HarperCollins Publishers, 1991]. © Uri Shulevitz, 1991. Collection of Uri Shulevitz

Charles Mikolaycak was of Polish and Ukrainian descent and enjoyed recrafting folk tales from these sources, but he also ventured much further afield in his fascination with legends, ranging from Japanese to Mediterranean stories. One of his most powerful achievements was the retelling and depiction of the Orpheus myth for which he probed not only literary sources but also musical ones. Mikolaycak believed, like many other artists illustrating children's books, that one should not "draw down" to an audience and that children can meet the challenge of a complex subject and instinctively

206. Charles Mikolaycak (1937-1993). American. Cover, for *Orpheus* [San Diego: Harcourt Brace Jovanovich, Publishers, 1992]. Copyright © Carole Kismaric Mikolaycak, 1995; Reprinted with the permission of Harcourt Brace & Company. From the Collection of Mr. and Mrs. Edward E. Wilson

understand a sophisticated drawing. In *Orpheus* (1992), the artist avowed his love of drawing and design, and in the image for the cover of Orpheus grieving between two columns of an ancient Greek temple [cat. no. 206], he created a powerful composition reinforced by an emphatic and controlled draftsmanship worthy of the great French Neoclassical artist Jean-Auguste Dominique Ingres with a tinge of Maxfield Parrish in the palette.

The dissolution of the Soviet Union has brought a recent influx of immigration to this country, and several eminent artists have been part of that wave. Gennady Spirin was born near Moscow in 1948 and trained at both the Moscow Academy of Art and the School of Industrial Art and Design. He published his first children's book illustrations in 1979 and has enjoyed international acclaim since then. In 1991 he illustrated Nikolai Gogol's *Sorotchintzy Fair*, a fanciful tale of the writer's native Ukraine. This story of the misadventures of a peasant family at the tumultuous annual fair, promulgated in great measure by a large and mischievous creature in a red coat, pulsates with the peaks and valleys of Russian emotion. Spirin, in the cover design [cat. no. 207],

207. Gennady Spirin (born 1948). Born in Russia; Came to the U.S. in 1991. Cover, for *Der Jahrmarkt von Sorotchinzy* [Esslingen: Esslinger Verlag J. F. Schreiber GmbH, 1990]. © Gennady Spirin, 1990; Reprinted with the permission of Esslinger Verlag J. F. Schreiber GmbH. From the Collection of Rose Sarkisian

combines the delicate touch of miniatures with an imagery that bursts with a vitality redolent of the sixteenth-century peasant scenes of Pieter Brueghel the Elder. The towering central figure possesses the gusto and monumentality of the proverbial Russian bear.

FOLKLORE

America, too, boasts some highly regarded and influential folktales which are epitomized in the stories of Uncle Remus as gathered and retold by Joel Chandler Harris. Harris set these stories down out of respect for their verve and content while acknowledging their cultural heritage.[33] Much has been made of their social and political function, and many of these divergent points of view have been nicely summed up and refined by Julius Lester, who eloquently concludes that the stories transcend race, servitude, and age and contain "the vital voice of our humanity."[34]

Although Harris' stories first appeared in 1880 with illustrations by Frederick S. Church and James H. Moser, the edition that garnered the greatest acclaim was published in 1895 with the legendary pen and ink drawings of Arthur Burdett Frost. Frost executed the frontispiece of *Uncle Remus: His Songs and His Sayings* in a monochromatic gouache and watercolor [cat. no. 208] similar to his illustrations for *The Story of a Bad Boy* (see above, p. 135). The artist objectively attempts to imbue the scene with elements of dignity and sensitivity which may be a legacy of his tutelage under Thomas Eakins. The facial features of Uncle Remus are not caricatured or stereotyped, which was so prevalent in the depiction of the African American at this time. The physiognomy is individualized, and the expression imparts a seriousness and sense of purpose. Uncle Remus sits on a workbench with several tools in his simple and well-ordered room, conveying a humble dignity. Thus, there is an atmosphere of industry and organization that runs contrary to the "patterned disordering" of these Trickster tales.[35]

The young child, identified only as "Miss Sally's seven–year–old boy," sits on an early nineteenth-century bamboo-turned Windsor chair and listens intently to the unfolding narrative. His Prince Valiant haircut, frilly shirt, breeches, and polished shoes allude not only to his class but also to the adult taste for emulating Little Lord Fauntleroy (see above, p. 136). While this introductory image may anchor the stories in a plantation setting of bondage, the tales themselves, when divorced from this context, are universally compelling because, once again, they proclaim the ability of the underdog to prevail through cunning and guile.

Among the most beloved of the tales is "The Wonderful Tar-Baby Story," in which Brer Fox is able to trap Brer Rabbit by means of sculpting an infant figure in sticky tar. Ultimately Brer Rabbit outwits Brer Fox, using reverse psychology to convince his captor that the briar patch will prove his most excruciating demise when in truth it is a haven. Frost selects the moment of Brer Fox's triumph for his culminating image where Brer Fox is rolling on the ground while Brer Rabbit is inextricably attached to the Tar-

208. Arthur Burdett Frost (1851-1928). American. "Uncle Remus Telling Stories," Frontispiece for *Uncle Remus: His Songs and His Sayings* [New York: D. Appleton & Co., 1895]. Collection of Mr. and Mrs. Henry M. Reed.

MYTH, MAGIC, AND MYSTERY

209. Arthur Burdett Frost (1851-1928). American. "He Laffed en laffed," from "The Tar Baby," in *Uncle Remus: His Songs and His Sayings* [New York: D. Appleton & Co., 1895]. Print Collection, Miriam and Ira D. Wallach Division of Art, Prints and Photographs. The New York Public Library. Astor, Lenox and Tilden Foundations

Baby [cat. no. 209]. The uncontrolled mirth is infectious as we witness the moment when Brer Fox "laughed en laughed twel he couldn't laugh no mo'." The vibrancy of Frost's pen stroke echoes the vitality of the story as he masterfully captures the gummy fusion of rabbit and Tar-Baby contrasted with the unbridled exuberance of Brer Fox who gleefully kicks his legs and holds his sides.

The popularity of these stories suffered as much from their extremely difficult, though faithful, use of dialect as they did from their sociopolitical frame of reference. Attempts to reinterpret them were welcomed with gratitude, and one of the early efforts to meet with approval was the South Carolina poet Ennis Rees' versification of three of his favorite stories in 1967.[36] Edward Gorey created the drawings. He achieves an acrobatic interpretation of Brer Rabbit wrestling with the Tar-Baby as they seem to float in midair while progressing through a series of increasingly sticky maneuvers [cat. no. 210a]. Gorey's consummate sense of design and draftsmanship brings a complete visual experience to what at first glance are five understated vignettes set within a single framework. The humorous body language he infuses into both rabbit and Tar-Baby provides an effective complement to Rees' spirited verse.

While Rees' efforts were commendable, they did not fully satisfy the need for a modern reading of the tales. Finally, in 1987, the eminent author Julius Lester published the first of a series of retellings of the Uncle Remus stories in collaboration with

210a. (right) Edward Gorey (born 1925). American. "The Tar Baby," from *Brer Rabbit and His Tricks* [New York: Young Scott Books, 1967]. © Edward Gorey, 1967; Published with the permission of Edward Gorey. Collection of Edward Gorey, Courtesy of Gotham Book Mart Gallery, New York City
212. (below) Barry Moser (born 1940). American. "Brer Rabbit," from *Jump! The Adventures of Brer Rabbit* [San Diego: Harcourt, Brace and Jovanovich, 1986]. ©Barry Moser, 1986; Reprinted with the permission of Harcourt Brace & Company. Justin G. Schiller (Personal Collection)

the equally accomplished artist Jerry Pinkney. Augusta Baker, a prominent figure in the world of children's literature and storytelling, heralded this cooperative venture and praised Lester's efforts to bring these stories into a modern vernacular, while preserving the rhythm and melody of the original language.[37]

Pinkney, for his part, has consolidated his visualization of the story into a double-page spread of four episodes, which proceed from Brer Fox putting the finishing touches on the Tar-Baby to Brer Rabbit's initial encounter and escalating entanglement with the doll to his final entrapment replete with Brer Fox's riotous laughter [cat. no. 211]. The drawings, deftly executed in graphite and watercolor, have a finish and particularity not evident in the versions already discussed. This objectivity reinforces the vivid voice of Lester's text, while the range of expressions and placement of the figures, such as Brer Fox peering from behind the bushes, captures the essential wit these stories impart. In the final vignette, where Brer Rabbit is joined to the Tar-Baby and Brer Fox explodes with laughter, Pinkney recognizes an important visual precedent. He acknowledges Frost's hallmark composition, by means of a similar positioning of the two characters, but through the subtle balance of detail and delicate washes of color the artist establishes a distinct vision.

Another recent characterization of Brer Rabbit which owes a debt to Frost comes from the hand of Barry Moser. This work also comprised part of a published series

211. Jerry Pinkney (born 1939). American. "The Tar Baby," from *The Tales of Uncle Remus* [New York: Dial Books, 1987]. © Jerry Pinkney, 1987. Collection of Jerry Pinkney

which initially appeared in 1986. Moser recognizes the influence of Frost as well as nineteenth– and twentieth-century American photographs and informs the reader of his conscious use of anachronism.[38] Thus in this portrait of Brer Rabbit [cat. no. 212], adroitly executed in watercolor, the striped coat, wide-eyed expression, and "stogie" dangling from the lips gives the subject an aura which blends back-room politician and used-car salesman—"tricksters" in their own right. In this entertaining record, Moser has conjured up a visual concoction that connects the past and present, reiterating the unceasing freshness of these stories.

From folklore of the rural South we move to the prairies of the Midwest and the inventive stories of the great poet and author, Carl Sandburg. These yarns, which Sandburg described as "nonsense tales with American fooling in them,"[39] do not carry the lineage of other works discussed. Sandburg wrote them for his daughters, nicknamed "Spink" and

213. (left) Robert Lawson (1892-1957). American. "Two Stories Above the Potato Face Blind Man," ca. 1922, from *The Rootabaga Stories* for *The Designer*, 1922-23. May Massee Collection, William Allen White Library, Emporia State University
214. (right) Maud Petersham (1890-1971) and Miska Petersham (1888-1960). Born in Hungary; Came to the U.S. in 1912. "There on a high stool in a high tower, on a high hill sits the Head Spotter of the Weather Makers," from *The Rootabaga Stories* [New York: Harcourt, Brace & Company, 1922]. Reprinted with the permission of Harcourt Brace & Company. de Grummond Children's Literature Collection, University of Southern Mississippi

"Skabootch." These whimsical stories beg to be read aloud so that the sound of the words can lend a special sonority to the experience. They have furnished a rich vein of material for the artist's pen or brush, and early on such notable figures as Robert Lawson, Maud and Miska Petersham, and Peggy Bacon brought their own special response to the text. In recent years, Harriet Pincus, Michael Hague, and Paul Zelinsky have affirmed the sustained interest in these zany narratives through their artistic efforts.

The drawings by Robert Lawson to accompany the serialization of the stories in *The Designer* in 1922/23 rank among his finest early work. "Two Stories Above the Potato Face Blind Man" [cat. no. 213] reflects his apprenticeship in magazine illustration and his commitment from the outset to bring a potent clarity to his art. He succeeded in the latter by means of highly accomplished draftsmanship. Lawson was not averse to humor, as he

215a. Peggy Bacon (1895-1987). American. "How the Animals Lost Their Tails and Got Them Back Traveling from Philadelphia to Medicine Hat," ca. 1922/28, from *Rootabaga Country: Selections from 'Rootabaga Stories' and Rootabaga Pigeons* [New York: Harcourt, Brace and Company, 1922; 1929 edition]. © Peggy Bacon, 1929, ren. 1957; Reprinted with the permission of Harcourt, Brace and Company. Courtesy of Kraushaar Galleries

provides a visual pun in the form of the two-storied dwelling that rises behind the blind man who plays his omnipresent accordion in his accustomed spot on the street corner near the Post Office in the Village of Liver-and-Onions. The round mirrored glasses and patched trousers add a special dimension to his character, while the architecture, with its half-timbered construction and tile roof, imparts a distinctly Mediæval flavor. This structure echoes the buildings found in the work of Howard Pyle and Maxfield Parrish, and they all seem to find a common source in the work of Albrecht Dürer.

Lawson's tightly controlled and precise line provides an interesting counterpoint to the almost simultaneous illustrations by Maud and Miska Petersham, which appeared in the first published volume, *Rootabaga Stories,* issued in 1922. Their pen and ink drawing, "There on a high stool in a high tower, on a high hill sits the Head Spotter of the Weather Makers" [cat. no. 214] from "How the Animals Lost their Tails and Got Them Back Traveling From Philadelphia to Medicine Hat," has a much heavier line than the Lawson, and the patterned stylization and two-dimensional emphasis—whether clouds, castle, mountain, wizard, or weathervane—brings the work closer to the realm of fantasy inherent in the stories themselves. The Petershams in their own concise manner have wittily captured the surreal and nonsensical aspect of Sandburg's prose but not with American imagery.

If the Petershams followed the text for their invention, then Peggy Bacon used it as a point of departure for her association with the unfolding regionalist style codified by such artists as Grant Wood, John Steuart Curry, and Thomas Hart Benton. Her training at the Art Students League under John Sloan, George Bellows, and Kenneth Hayes Miller, among others, predisposed her to subjects of daily life. In her 1928 illustrations of Sandburg's stories compiled in *Rootabaga Country*, Bacon's drawing for the same story pictured by the Petershams uses the extreme meteorological conditions described to depict a violent wind, whether tornado or cyclone, which blows a house (as well as everything around it) cleanly off its foundation, while the family huddles in the basement [cat. no. 215a]. One cannot help but think of the cyclone in *The Wonderful Wizard of Oz*, and in her own way, Bacon gives us an equally solid dose of the improbable. Her draftsmanship is sure, but there is a pulsating energy to the line which infuses a greater dynamism into the drawing. If this picture anticipates the rural imagery of regionalism then a second example looks back to the urban bias of Bacon's training.

"Hot Balloons Used to Open the Window in the Morning" [cat. no. 215b; see p. 33] interprets the opening scene from "How Hot Balloons and His Pigeon Daughters Crossed Over into the Rootabaga Country," originally published in *Rootabaga Pigeons* in 1923. Once again, in contrast to the literal yet imaginative creations of the Petershams, Bacon opted to root her depiction in the teeming squalor and vitality of a city's immigrant neighborhood. The drawing explodes with the street activity of what could be lower Manhattan as chronicled by John Sloan or George Luks, and Bacon assembles a rich inventory of humor tempered with pathos. Her incisive eye benefits from her quick and capable draftsmanship. Thus Bacon takes the playful inventions of Carl Sandburg and transforms them into equally imaginative scenarios that are grounded in the American landscape and cityscape. Even in her illustrative work, Bacon would not let go of that central American ingredient—objectivity.

Rachel Field continued the fascination with who and what was America in *Miss Hitty: Her First Hundred Years*. These "memoirs" of a doll named Mehitable, better known as Hitty, chronicle her experiences from being carved out of a piece of white ash by an itinerant peddler in Maine to her ending up in an antique shop on Eighth Street in New York. In its own way, the book communicates the growth and urbanization of America and alludes to the yearning for earlier, simpler times that was emerging by the third decade of the twentieth century. The illustrations by Dorothy P. Lathrop provide an appropriate visualization of the unfolding taste for Americana. The frontispiece [cat. no. 216] simulates an elaborately framed hand-colored photograph, while the profusion of detail in the patterned dress and potted plant suggest the needlework sampler which constituted an integral part of a young woman's education in the nineteenth century. Lathrop's art offers a middle ground between the fanciful stylization of the Petershams and the dynamic energy of Peggy Bacon. Yet, they all, in their own way, furnish a distinctly American essence.

Although non-European subject matter formed part of the roster of children's books and their illustrations, it was too often created by a Eurocentric ethos that did not bring a full measure of sensitivity to the undertaking.[40] Among the first to bring an understanding and insight to such subject matter was Ezra Jack Keats with *The Snowy Day* published in 1962 (see above, p. 86). It was not long, however, before there were voices coming from within, and John Steptoe's *Stevie*, which appeared in 1969, ranks among

216. Dorothy Pulls Lathrop (1891-1980). American. Frontispiece, for *Hitty: Her First Hundred Years* [New York: Macmillan Co., 1929]. From the Collection of the Central Children's Room, Donnell Library Center, The New York Public Library

MYTH, MAGIC, AND MYSTERY

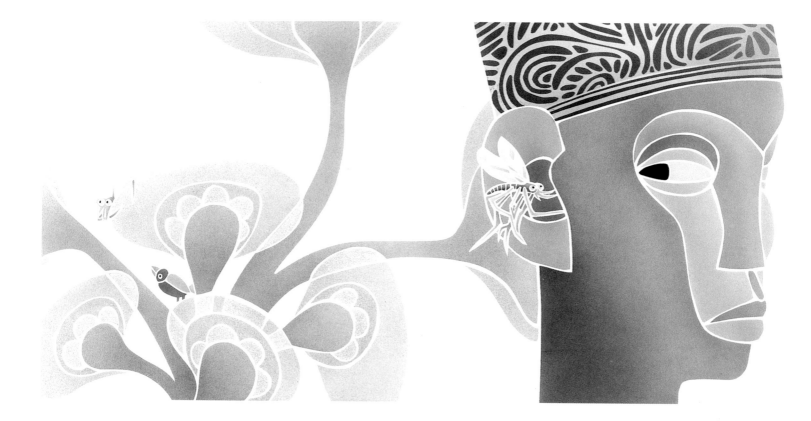

the earliest works in which young urban African Americans could enjoy a story set squarely within their frame of reference. While these stories explored the sociological realities of contemporary life—and *Stevie* appeared in the same year that The Metropolitan Museum of Art mounted its controversial exhibition, *Harlem on My Mind*—there also evolved an interest in African and African-American folklore.

One of the pioneering publications in this genre, which garnered widespread accolades, was *Why Mosquitoes Buzz in People's Ears* (1975). A collaborative effort of the distinguished author Verna Aardema and Leo and Diane Dillon, the book retold a West African tale about the dire consequences of spreading a "tall tale." The perpetrator, a mosquito, learns its lesson, but adopts a far more pernicious habit—buzzing in human's ears—with often fatal consequences. The artwork, such as the image of the mosquito buzzing into an ear [cat. no. 217], is a rich combination of sprayed watercolor and rubbed pastel that produces brilliantly colored and subtly textured patterns which evoke a sense of African textile design. The bold outline and planarity of the figure's features, especially the nose, recall the reductive geometry of African sculpture.

Also among the earliest disseminators of African folkore is Ashley Bryan who grew up in a rough neighborhood in the Bronx in New York, yet persevered with his interest in art to enjoy a celebrated career as an author and artist. In 1967 he created illustrations for *Moon For What Do You Want?*, and four years later he wrote and illustrated *The Ox of Wonderful Horns and Other African Folktales*, which extrapolated sources from

217. Leo (born 1933) and Diane Dillon (born 1933). American. "Mosquito Buzzing in Ear," from *Why Mosquitoes Buzz in People's Ears* [New York: Dial Books for Young Readers, 1975]. © Leo and Diane Dillon, 1975. Collection of Leo & Diane Dillon

218. Ashley Bryan (born 1923). American. "The husband Who Counted Spoonfuls," from *Beat the Story Drum, Pum-Pum* [New York: Atheneum, 1980]. © Ashley Bryan, 1980; Reprinted with the permission of Atheneum Books for Young Readers, an imprint of Simon & Schuster Children's Publishing Division. Collection of Ashley Bryan **219.** Ashley Bryan (born 1923). American. "The Foolish Boy," from The Lion and the Ostrich Chicks [New York: Atheneum, 1986]. Copyright © 1986 by Ashley Bryan. Reprinted with the permission of Atheneum Books for Young Readers, an imprint of Simon & Schuster Children's Publishing Division. Collection of Ashley Bryan

South Africa to Angola. In 1980 he published *Beat the Story-Drum, Pum-Pum*, which included the Hausa tale "The Husband that Counted Spoonfuls." It is a story of a man who, like the Count in *Sesame Street*, was obsessed with counting, which made it impossible for him to keep a wife. Bryan visualizes the moment when Tagwayi returns through the forest by moonlight with his penultimate wife, while a hornbill perches in a tree and offers encouragement [cat. no. 218]. This brightly colored tempera painting reduces the figures and surrounding landscape to a complex system of curvilinear shapes and patterns. The overall design echoes the decorative aspect of the authentic costumes and alludes to indigenous sources. The bold arrangement of colors contributes a visual vigor that perfectly supplements the lively text.

Another acclaimed book was Bryan's *The Lion and the Ostrich Chicks*, published in 1986. This compendium contains another Hausa tale titled "The Foolish Boy," which tells of a slow-witted youth, born to parents after many years of trying, who outwits the trickster spider Ananse. Here Bryan illustrates the episode in which Ananse arrives at

194   MYTH, MAGIC, AND MYSTERY

Jumoke's hut to con him out of some gazelle meat, but his ruse ultimately fails [cat. no. 219].

Also painted in spirited colors, the artist creates a far more intricate composition. He divides the image into a series of vignettes that relate to the central episode. The densely composed design imparts a visual intensity, as branches of trees and other elements of nature take on a tendril-like quality. Again, the forceful arrangement of forms and their jagged edges simulate woodblocks created at the beginning of this century by the German Expressionists, who, in turn, had been influenced by African and Oceanic art. Thus, Bryan reiterates the cross-fertilization of non-European and European artistic traditions and returns it to an African context.

In addition to exploring African folklore, writers and artists began to consider stories that transmitted an African-American heritage. *The Talking Eggs*, illustrated by Jerry Pinkney in 1989, is adapted from a Creole folk tale published in the late nineteenth century and probably has roots in European fairy tales, such as Perrault's *Diamonds and Toads*, brought to Louisiana by French émigrés.[41] The plot centers around a lazy mother who aligns herself with the bad and mean daughter (Rose) while the good and kind daughter (Blanche) does all the work. Through her good deeds, Blanche is befriended by an enchanted old witch-woman, who endows her with great wealth. With the exception of a Prince Charming, the story contains all the requisite ingredients of the universal fairy tale. Pinkney, again, brings his own special powers of artistic interpretation

220. Jerry Pinkney (born 1939). American. Cover, for *The Talking Eggs* [New York: Dial Books for Young Readers, 1989]. © Jerry Pinkney, 1989. Collection of Jerry Pinkney

to the book, and the combination of pencil, colored pencil, and watercolor imbue the pictures with a clarity tempered by suggestion in the shimmering, delicate touches of wash.

The cover [cat. no. 220] depicts Blanche walking hand in hand with the enchantress away from her cabin and carrying a basket of eggs all of which are animated by smiling faces. Blanche shows no fear as she passes through the dense growth of trees and underbrush, all the more unsettling as they, too, assume human expressions. This debt to Arthur Rackham is entirely apt, since Pinkney confirms that *The Wind in the Willows* with Rackham's illustrations was a pivotal book of his youth.[42] In making these visual references, also evident in the bulbous root (by Blanche's right leg) that looks like a Jurassic gargoyle, Pinkney encourages viewers to see what they want to see and infuses an important subjective element into the viewing process. Whatever is extracted from the image, Pinkney has given us a lush visual experience in drawings that are, at times, unsettling in their spectral quality.

From the bayous of Louisiana we move to the Sea Islands of South Carolina and the tale of a mermaid, a rare figure in African-American folk tales.[43] Brian Pinkney, who is Jerry Pinkney's son, created the artwork for *Sukey and the Mermaid*. This story tells of a young girl, Sukey, who is mistreated by her step-father and seeks refuge on the beach; there she unwittingly conjures up a beautiful black mermaid who radically alters her life.[44]

For the art, Pinkney employs the old-fashioned technique of scratchboard: a white board is covered in black ink, the ink is scratched off to reveal the white, and color is then added. The artist prefers this method because it allows him to sculpt as well as to draw.[45] In the scene where the mermaid first appears to Sukey [cat. no. 221], we witness the beginnings of their friendship as she looks tentatively at the apparition rising from a wave. Through the deft manipulation of line, Pinkney endows the scene with

221. Brian Pinkney (born 1961). American. "Sukey Meets the Mermaid on the Beach," from *Sukey and the Mermaid* [New York: Four Winds Press, 1992]. © Brian Pinkney, 1992; Reprinted with the permission of Simon & Schuster Books for Young Readers, an imprint of Simon & Schuster Children's Publishing Division. Collection of Brian Pinkney

MYTH, MAGIC, AND MYSTERY

a spontaneity and emotional force, as he handles this challenging technique with great dexterity, rendering detail with great skill. Sukey wears a floral print dress, while the mermaid is bedecked with jewelry, including an impressive breastplate which recalls African ornaments. Although the composition is dictated by the placement of the text, the artist establishes a nice rhythm of curve and countercurve, which animates and structures the scene.

MYTHICAL CREATURES

As well as mermaids, there are numerous other mythical creatures that have fascinated young and old people since time immemorial. We have already seen the dragon and can now turn our attention to a relative, the griffin. This legendary creature is usually represented in literature and art as having the head, beak, and wings of an eagle, the body and legs of a lion, and occasionally a serpent's tail. It has a long history of embellishing architecture which goes back to Assyrian, Persian, Greek, and Roman times. Frank R. Stockton, however, opted to utilize the Mediæval context in *The Griffin and the Minor Canon*. This wonderful tale of enchantment epitomizes Stockton's creative genius. It relates the story of the last griffin who encounters his likeness adorning a church and who subsequently befriends its self-effacing but brave canon to the horror and consternation of the townsfolk. Frederick Richardson's vigorous interpretation shows the moment at the end of the story when the griffin returns the sleeping canon from his exile [cat. no. 222]. The griffin, which the artist makes more like a dragon than anything else, virtually fills the entire sheet, and his exuberance is reinforced by the way his wings and tail burst beyond the limits of the frame. Richardson endows him with a friendly expression, while that of the canon approaches the beatific. Consequently, the drawing takes on a reassuringly benign quality. Richardson was a versatile artist, and the energy of this drawing differs enormously from his more controlled work such as "Little Bo–Peep" (see above, p. 67).

Just as the griffin was intrigued by his stone likeness, these effigies in turn have held a long-standing fascination for worshippers in and visitors to innumerable late Mediæval and Gothic churches, which frequently feature those other stone creatures that terrify and spellbind—gargoyles. Gargoyle derives from the Latin word "to swallow" and the creature became identified with the carved termination to a spout that conveys water from gutters. Although dating from Egyptian, Greek, and Roman times, this architectural element is best known in its late Mediæval grotesque form. Always of great appeal to artists recording architecture—most notably the nineteenth-century French Romantic, Charles Meryon—gargoyles have continued to hold our attention.

And Leonard Baskin has produced a stirring image for a book of scary monsters, *Did You Say Ghosts?* (1994), on which he collaborated with the poet Richard Michelson. The text graphically lists the "boils, warts, and scaly snakeskin coils" that make up the gargoyle before it turns to stone, and Baskin creates a strong visual corollary to this description [cat. no. 223]. The olive-green color of the skin refers not only to the scales but

222. Frederick Richardson (1862-1937). American. "The Griffin and the Minor Canon," from *The Queen's Museum and Other Fanciful Tales* [New York: Charles Scribner's Sons, 1906]. Reprinted with the permission of Scribner, an imprint of Simon & Schuster. Anonymous Loan

223. Leonard Baskin (born 1922). American. "Gargoyle," from *Did You Say Ghosts?* [New York: Macmillan Publishing Co., Inc., 1994]. © Leonard Baskin, 1994; Reprinted with the permission of Simon & Schuster Books for Young Readers, an imprint of Simon & Schuster Children's Publishing Division. Courtesy of R. Michelson Galleries, Northampton, Mass.

also to the mossy texture that the stone incarnation can assume, while the flecks of red and pink may signify blood or some other sinister association. Baskin challenges the viewer with chilling ambiguities that are continually defused by reassuring couplets at the end of each page of text.

Fables

While children have demonstrated a great capacity to tolerate scary images, much of their early visual vocabulary is formed from less threatening sources, among which number fables. Like fairy tales, fables have a long and rich history that extends back to Greek and Roman antiquity. In contrast, however, they assumed a literary form at a much earlier date, thanks to such authors as Aesop and Phaedrus. The fable, like folktales, also extends to all corners of the world, and important sources may be found in the Far East as well as India. One such exotic story that received important recognition is Marcia Brown's retelling and illustration of *Once A Mouse . . .* (1961), an ancient fable from India. The tale revolves around a hermit who transforms a vulnerable mouse into a mighty tiger in several stages. Once he is a tiger, the now proud and vain creature forgets his humble origins and experiences the inevitable fall from grace as he is turned back into a mouse. Brown's woodcuts, such as the early episode of the mouse being chased by a predatory crow, suggest a Far Eastern aesthetic in the use of rice paper and the bold two-dimensional pattern [cat. no. 224]. The artist effectively uses the patterns for double purposes so that the olive area representing the ground can also be read as the head of the bird straining to swallow the mouse. This element of abstraction also emulates a non-Western vision. The balance of the book's illustrations inject great credibility and personality into the animals, so that they come very much alive for the reader, which makes their transformations even more magical.

In *Seven Blind Mice* (1992), Ed Young has also adapted an ancient fable from India, "The Blind Men and the Elephant," substituting mice for the human arguers. Employing paper collage and bright colors, he offers the young reader a wide variety

224. Marcia Brown (born 1918). American. "Mouse Running from Crow," from *Once a Mouse* [New York: Charles Scribner's Sons, 1961]. © Marcia Brown, 1961; Reprinted with the permission of Atheneum Books for Young Readers, an imprint of Simon & Schuster Children's Publishing Division. de Grummond Children's Literature Collection, University of Southern Mississippi

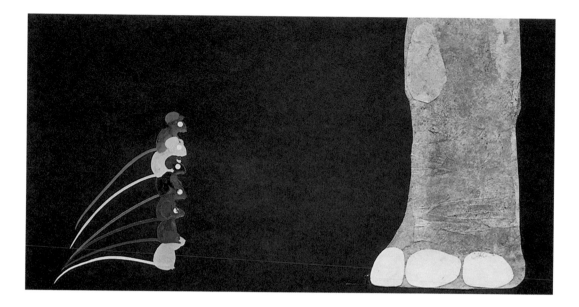

225. Ed Young (born 1931). Born in Tianjin, China; Came to the U.S. in 1951. "On Monday, Red Mouse went first to find out," from *Seven Blind Mice* [New York: Philomel Books, 1992]. © Ed Young, 1992; Reprinted with the permission of Philomel Books, an imprint of the Putnam & Grosset Group. Collection of Ed Young

of learning paths from the property of shapes and colors to the days of the week [cat. no. 225]. Overriding these elements is the important message that it is best to base one's opinion on all the information available rather than just on isolated parts. Like Marcia Brown, Young employs a non-Western compositional arrangement and two-dimensional pattern in highly reductive images and brings a clarity and harmony to his work, recalling the fables of Leo Lionni (see below).

In the Western idiom, *Aesop's Fables*, which date from the early sixth century B.C., form part of almost every child's lexicon. They provide the primary basis for animals that take on human attributes, such as speech, to render their didactic and moralizing stories. Anyone who has witnessed children's animated conversation and play with their stuffed animals easily recognizes the profound impact such stories have. Among the most endearing of *Aesop's Fables* is the story of "The Tortoise and the Hare." It teaches the lesson that slow but steady in the race of life will always prevail over fast and careless. Eric Carle and Charles Santore have created examples which offer a rich visual range of interpretation.

Carle employs his hallmark technique of richly colored collage to provide a profusion of color and shape. He aligns the plodding turtle with a snail while the slick rabbit, replete with dress shoes and spats, reclines against a kilometric distance marker and reads a book which bears the artist's initials [cat. no. 226]. While this last detail indicates that the overconfident hare is occupied in a worthwhile diversion and is not simply napping, the "E.C." may be read as "easy," which alludes to his misguided cockiness. Thus, in simple yet painterly terms, Carle generates a visually engaging rendition.

Where Carle shows the race in progress, Charles Santore chronicles the finish, which permits him to depict an opulently rendered panoply of the animal kingdom [cat. no. 227]. The tortoise has just crossed the tape, while the hare, aghast, comes up a few yards short. Meticulously rendered in watercolor, the animals convey a broad

226. (right) Eric Carle (born 1929). American. "The Rabbit and The Turtle," 1980, from *Eric Carle's Treasury of Classic Stories* [New York: Orchard Books, 1988]. © Eric Carle, 1980; Published with the permission of Eric Carle. Collection of the artist; Loan arranged by R. Michelson Galleries, Northampton, Mass.

227. (above) Charles Santore (born 1935). American. "The Hare and the Tortoise," from *Aesop's Fables* [New York: JellyBean Press, 1988]. © Charles Santore, 1988; Published with the permission of Charles Santore. Collection of Olenka and Charles Santore

228. (above) Leo Lionni (born 1910). Born in Amsterdam, The Netherlands; Came to the U.S. in 1939. "Alexander and the Wind-up Mouse," from *Alexander and the Wind-up Mouse* [New York: Pantheon Books, 1969]. © Leo Lionni, 1969; Reprinted with the permission of Random House, Inc. Collection of Leo Lionni

229. (below) Leo Lionni (born 1910). Born in Amsterdam, The Netherlands; Came to the U.S. in 1939. "The fish lay there dreaming," from *Fish is Fish* [New York: Pantheon Books, 1970]. © Leo Lionni, 1970; Reprinted with the permission of Random House, Inc. Collection of Leo Lionni

range of human expressions which eloquently impart the humor as well as the wisdom of the story. By interpreting this fable in this manner, Santore connects the animals to their own narratives and offers the equivalent of a curtain call. He also sets this culminating image in a full landscape, whose Greek architecture connects it to Aesop's time and country. Consequently, Santore pays homage to one of the earliest proponents of this literary genre.

Happily, the fable has endured as a literary form and benefited from the talents of gifted authors and artists in this century. Since the late 1950s, Leo Lionni has provided readers of all ages with memorable stories and images, among which number *Alexander and the Wind-Up Mouse* (1969) and *Fish is Fish* (1970). Remarkably, Lionni did not create his first children's book until the age of fifty, derived from an attempt to appease two restless grandchildren. From this episode evolved these wonderful animal fables. *Alexander and the Wind-Up Mouse* tells of a mouse's love for a wind-up toy which is transformed into a real mouse through Alexander's devotion, comprising a delicate balance between fantasy and reality [cat. no. 228]. Artistically, Lionni combines watercolor and collage to create images that are as much dictated by shape and texture as they are by detail. The artist stretches the ranges of the watercolor medium to the fullest and provides the viewer with a picture that is subtle and evanescent.

For *Fish is Fish*, Lionni elected to use colored pencil [cat. no. 229]. The images are rendered with a control and precision inherent in the medium yet reaffirm the artist's rich sense of color. The fanciful array of birds, cow, and people envisioned as fish is as provocatively imaginative in its hard-edged execution as the artist's lyrical watercolors. In both instances he has struck a careful balance between text and depiction in the service of good picture books which, in his words, "ha[ve] the power and hence the mission to reveal beauty and meaning."

Arnold Lobel has been more traditional in his approach to fables and embraces the literary format of Aesop and La Fontaine. In "The Elephant and his Son" (1980), Lobel crafts a story about an elephant, who, in his desire to appear wise, does not heed the warnings of his son and ends up with his left slipper aflame [cat. no. 230]. Lobel's illustration captures perfectly the elder elephant's oblivion as his son stares intently at the burning slipper, and the artist's confident draftsmanship gives visual substance to the text.

230. Arnold Lobel (1933-1987). American. "The Elephant and his Son," from *Fables* [New York: Harper & Row Publishers, 1980]. © Arnold Lobel, 1980. The Estate of Arnold Lobel

HEROES AND HEROINES

As well as central characters from fairy tales and fables, children's literature has gravitated to legendary characters who have taken on truly heroic proportions. In the American idiom, folk such as Paul Bunyan, Johnny Appleseed, and Pecos Bill come to mind. Significantly, a traditional hero and a newly minted heroine were the basis of books recognized by the Caldecott committee in 1994. Both Jerry Pinkney's watercolors for *John Henry* and Paul O. Zelinsky's paintings for *The Swamp Angel* were deservedly named Honor Caldecott Books.

Jerry Pinkney, again collaborating with Julius Lester, retells the story of John Henry, that fabled African-American railroad worker who raced against a steam drill to cut a tunnel through a mountain. His victory, however, cost him his life, as his heart gave out from the enormous exertion. Pinkney's jacket illustration [cat. no. 231] shows John Henry sitting in the foreground on some railroad ties just at a point where the track ends, indicated by the pile of rubble next to him. He holds two prodigious hammers, and directly behind him looms a mountain that has already been cut through, since a steam locomotive emerges from it to cross a trestle bridge. Once again, Pinkney's extraordinary

MYTH, MAGIC, AND MYSTERY

facility with the demanding medium of watercolor comes to the fore, as he achieves a masterful balance between detail and atmosphere. He imbues his central figure with the distinction that befits John Henry's Herculean achievement, but the artist also signifies the constricting nature of the railroad man's existence through the way in which the landscape envelops him. There is little hope for escape, and this inevitablity brings to mind Gustave Courbet's iconic *Stonebreakers* (1849, formerly Dresden; destroyed 1945) in terms of celebrating the heroic dignity of the common laborer. In the rich litany of interpretations of John Henry ranging from James Daugherty to Ezra Jack Keats, that of Lester and Pinkney is truly transcendent.

While there have also been extraordinary women, such as Betsy Ross, Clara Barton, or Annie Oakley, who have achieved legendary status, an emerging author invented an American woman with mythic proportions in *Swamp Angel*. Angelica Longrider is a female equivalent of Davy Crockett and then some. "Swamp Angel," as Angelica came to be known, was big in size, heart, and humor. She earned recognition as the greatest woodswoman in Tennessee, when she saved settlers from "Thundering Tarnation," a fearsome bear whom no man could tame. In the scene where Angel uses a tornado to

231. Jerry Pinkney (born 1939). American. Cover, for *John Henry* [New York: Dial Books for Young Readers, 1994]. © Jerry Pinkney, 1994; Collection of Jerry Pinkney

232. Paul O. Zelinksy (born 1953). American. "Angel Wrestled Tarnation," from *Swamp Angel* [New York: Dutton Children's Books, 1994]. © Paul O. Zelinsky, 1994; Used by permission of Dutton Signet, a division of Penguin Books USA Inc. Collection of Paul O. Zelinsky

lasso Tarnation, the outline and large areas of local color evoke the legacy of the well-intentioned yet untutored limners who were asked to fill the artistic void in remote regions of this developing nation more than a century and a half ago [cat. no. 232].

Paul Zelinsky's masterful compositions on cherry and maple veneers exude an American naive style that salutes the efforts of such nineteenth-century figures as Edward Hicks and the most prevalent artist in this "folk art" category, "Anonymous." The artist, through the use of bold curves and countercurves, achieves a level of compositional sophistication that would have been rare in his nineteenth-century models. Thus, Zelinsky brings to his task a narrative clarity and simple homespun charm indelibly associated with this early artistic tradition, but amplifies it with his own skilled touch.

In this wide-ranging discussion, we have considered a broad panorama of classic fairy tales, folk tales, and fables from an equally diverse spectrum of sources that have touched virtually all points of the globe. Understandably, the artistic response has been as varied as the stories themselves; yet, there is a loose connective tissue within the artistic arena. Regardless of whether the story has a European, American, African, or Asian source, the artist has not only tried to honor the source but also attempted to blend indigenous imagery with universal ingredients to provide their audience with a more resonant vision. As the base of literary source and artistic background continues to expand, this point of reference becomes more diverse, and we begin to read with global minds and see with global eyes.

Notes

I. Discover, Explore, Enjoy

1. "Familiar Themes and Variations," The New York *Herald-Tribune Book Week*, November 1, 1964.
2. Caldecott Acceptance Speech reprinted in Lee Kingman's *Newbery and Caldecott Medal Books, 1966–1975* (Boston: The Horn Book, Inc.), 211–212.
3. "A Lesson in Illustration," *Imprint*, vol. 2 (1941), 2.
4. "An Illustrator's View," *The Horn Book*, February 1961.
5. *Of the Decorative Illustration of Books Old and New* (London: G. Bell & Sons, 1896), 130.
6. "And So Madeline was Born," in Bertha Mahony Miller and Elinot Whitney Field's *Caldecott Medal Books: 1938–1957* (Boston: The Horn Book, Inc., 1957), 256.
7. "Ducklings at Home and Abroad," in *Caldecott Medal Books: 1938–1957*, 80 and 82.
8. "Caldecott Acceptance Speech," in *Newbery and Caldecott Medal Books, 1966–1975*, 219.
9. "The Book Artist: Yesterday and Today," Bertha Mahony and others, *Illustrators of Children's Books, 1744–1945* (Boston: The Horn Book Inc., 1947), 251.
10. "The Turning of the Page," in *Caldecott Medal Books: 1938–1957*, 248.
11. Quoted by Esther Averill in "What Is a Picture Book?," *Caldecott Medal Books: 1938–1957*, 313.
12. "Make Me A Child Again," *The Horn Book*, November 1940, 448.
13. *Of the Decorative Illustration of Books Old and New*, 128–30.
14. "The Work of Walter Crane," *The Art Journal* (Easter Art Annual 1898), 4.
15. Quoted in Bertha Mahony and others, *Illustrators of Children's Books, 1744–1945* (Boston: The Horn Book 1947), 69.
16. "The Art of Caldecott and Greenaway," *The New York Times Book Review*, March 17, 1946.
17. Michael Hutchins, ed., *Yours Pictorially: Letters of Randolph Caldecott* (London: Frederick Warne, 1976), 109.
18. "Notes on My Own Books for Children," *The Junior Bookshelf*, October 1940, 14.
19. Jane Crowell Morse, ed., *Beatrix Potter's Americans* (Boston: The Horn Book, 1982), 181.
20. *Of the Decorative Illustration of Books Old and New*, 137.
21. Preface, *Uncle Remus: His Songs and Sayings* (New York: D. Appleton & Co., 1895).
22. Quoted by Henry C. Pitz, *Howard Pyle* (New York: Clarkson N. Potter, 1975), 179.
23. Harris, however, did not care for Kemble's pictures for his stories. "For a man who has no conception whatever of human nature," he groused, "Kemble does very well. But he is too dog-flip to suit me." See Beverly R. David, "Visions of the South: Joel Chandler Harris and His Illustrators," *American Literary Realism* (Summer 1976), 198–199.
24. "Some Books I've Illustrated," *Publishers Weekly*, October 19, 1935.
25. Quoted by Henry C. Pitz, *Howard Pyle*, 68.
26. Quoted by Henry C. Pitz, *Illustrating Children's Books* (New York: Watson-Guptill, 1963), 70.
27. "Howard Pyle and His Times," in Bertha E. Mahony and others, *Illustrators of Children's Books, 1744–1945*, 105.
28. Quoted by Henry C. Pitz, *The Brandywine Tradition* (Boston: Houghton Mifflin, 1969), 149.
29. Quoted by Anne Carroll Moore, *Nicholas and the Golden Goose* (New York: Macmillan, 1932), 125–126.
30. Quoted by Ernest W. Watson, "N.C. Wyeth, Giant on a Hilltop," *American Artist*, January 1945, 17.
31. Martin Birnbaum, *The Last Romantic* (New York: Twayne Publishers, 1960), 103.
32. "The Illustration of Children's Books As a Fine Art," *Publishers' Weekly*, October 16, 1926, 1580.
33. *Books in Search of Children* (New York: Macmillan, 1969), 190.
34. Quoted by Rowe Wright, "Women in Publishing: May Massee," *Publishers' Weekly*, September 29, 1928, 1335.
35. "Perhaps Even Cheerful," *The Retail Bookseller*, August 1948, 70.
36. May Massee, "Publishing Children's Books the Public Wants," *Publishers' Weekely*, July 24, 1954, 310.
37. "The Art of Illustration," *The Horn Book*, December 1962.
38. Ingri and Edgar d'Aulaire, "Working Together on Books for Children," in *Caldecott Medal Books: 1938–1957*, 46.
39. "Illustration in Children's Books," *Children's Literature in Education*, No. 1, 41.
40. Lynd Ward, "Modern Picture Books," in Anne Carroll Moore, *The Three Owls* (New York: Macmillan, 1925), 398.
41. "Make Me a Child Again," 450.
42. "The Language of Color and Form," in *Caldecott Medal Winners: 1938–1957*, 155.
43. "Make Me a Child Again," 452.
44. "A Few Men and Women," *The Horn Book*, February 1962, 32.
45. "The Art of Illustration."
46. "The Book Artist: Yesterday and Tomorrow,"

In Bertha Mahony and others, *Illustrators of Children's Books, 1744–1945*, 249.

47. *Books in Search of Children*, 27.

48. "Make Me a Child Again, 452.

49. Caldecott Medal Acceptance Speech in Lee Kingman, *Newbery and Caldecott Medal Books, 1976–1985* (Boston: The Horn Book, Inc., 1986), 256.

50. Caldecott Acceptance Speech in Kingman, *Newbery and Caldecott Medal Books, 1976–1985*, 170–171.

II. AND THE DISH RAN AWAY WITH THE SPOON

1. Rita Dove, "The First Book." © 1994 by Rita Dove. Used by permission of the author.

2. Maria Montessori, *The Absorbent Mind* (translated from the Italian by Claude A. Claremont) [Madras, India: 1949; New York: A Delta Book, 1967], 122. I would like to thank Suzanne Pugin, from the Ghent Montessori School, Norfolk, Virginia, for providing me with her insight, expertise, and library.

3. John Locke, "Some Thoughts Concerning Education" [written in 1693], as found in *John Locke: On Politics and Education* (Rosyln, NY: Walter J. Black, Inc., Published for the Classics Club ©, 1947), 333.

4. Ibid., 336.

5. Selma G. Lanes, *The Art of Maurice Sendak* (New York: Harry N. Abrams, Inc., 1980), 71–72.

6. Maria Montessori, *The Absorbent Mind*, 120.

7. Bruno Bettelheim, *A Good Enough Parent* (New York: Alfred A. Knopf, Inc., 1987/Vintage Books-Random House, 1988), 252.

8. Mother Goose, *The Only True Mother Goose Melodies*, (reprinted by Lothrop, Lee and Shepard Co., Boston, 1905, from the Munroe and Francis edition, Boston, 1833), as found in May Hill Arbuthnot, *Children and Books*, 3rd ed. (Chicago: Scott, Foresman and Company, 1964), 77.

9. Even the existence of a "Mother Goose" is questioned. For a comprehensive and scholarly examination of the sources of nursery rhymes, see Iona and Peter Opie, *The Oxford Dictionary of Nursery Rhymes*, 1991 ed. (Oxford [England]/New York: Oxford University Press, 1951). For a specific discussion on the existence of Mother Goose, see 37–38. Other sources on the subject include: James O. Halliwell, *The Nursery Rhymes of England* (London: Published for the Percy Society by T. Richards, 1842); James O. Halliwell, *Popular Rhymes and Nursery Tales* (London: John Russell Smith, 1849); *The Annotated Mother Goose: Nursery Rhymes Old and New, Arranged and Explained By William S. Baring-Gould and Ceil Baring-Gould* (New York: The World Publishing Company, 1967).

10. The Opies, *The Oxford Dictionary of Nursery Rhymes*, 3–4.

11. Paul-Gustave-Marie-Camille Hazard, *Books, Children and Men*, trans. from the French by Marguerite Mitchell (Boston: Horn Book, Inc., 1947), as found in Arbuthnot, *Children and Books*, 36.

12. The Opies, *The Oxford Dictionary of Nursery Rhymes*, 7. Certainly, specific nursery rhymes are attached to various members of the royal family and court in England: some sources cite "Old King Cole" as referring to a king in the third century; other sources believe "Humpty Dumpty" could allude to Richard III. But the real seeds for nursery rhymes are sown during the reign of Henry VIII. See Katherine Elwes Thomas, *The Real Personages of Mother Goose* (London: Lothrop, Lee & Shepard Co., 1930), for specific historic references. Also see Halliwell, *The Nursery Rhymes of England*.

13. The term "ma mère l'oye" had been in use before 1697. The Opies, *The Oxford Dictionary of Nursery Rhymes*, 39.

14. Judy L. Larson, *Enchanted Images: American Children's Illustration, 1850-1925* (Santa Barbara: Santa Barbara Museum of Art, 1980), 23.

15. The Opies, *The Oxford Dictionary of Nursery Rhymes*, 37–38.

16. William and Ceil Baring-Gould, *Mother Goose*, 333 (bibliography).

17. As found in Arbuthnot, *Children and Books*, 37. She notes, the Thomas edition was reproduced in 1944 by F. G. Melcher.

18. See The Opies, *The Oxford Dictionary of Nursery Rhymes*, 33 and 40, for a more exhaustive discussion. It should be noted that John Newbery was the first publisher to recognize that there was a "market" for books specifically written and illustrated for children. From this time on, many publishers began to focus more attention on this particular audience. And, indeed, it is a fitting tribute that the much sought-after Newbery awards for the best children's literature were named in honor of John Newbery.

19. This version was reproduced in Barchilon, Jacques, and Henry Pettit, *The Authentic Mother Goose Fairy Tales and Nursery Rhymes* (Denver, Colorado: Alan Swallow, 1960).

20. Arbuthnot, *Children and Books*, 78.

21. See Betsy Beinecke Shirley, *Read Me a Story—Show Me a Book: American Children's Literature, 1690-1988, from the Collection of Betsy Beinecke Shirley* (New Haven, Connecticut: Yale University [an exhibition at the Beinecke Rare Book and Manuscript Library], 1991), 26-31. She refers to both *A Continuation of the Comic Adventures of Old Mother Hubbard and her Dog* (Boston: N. Coverly, 1813) and *Continuation of*

Old Mother Hubbard and Her Dog (Philadelphia: Morgan & Yeager, ca. 1825).

22. A cracker, or "cracker bonbon," is a paper holder filled with candies and trinkets and used as a party favor. When the ends are pulled, the cracker pops. These were particularly popular in Victorian England and have long been used in that country at Christmas celebrations.

23. The more traditional wording is "sport" (see The Opies, *The Oxford Dictionary of Nursery Rhymes*, 203). However, Caldecott changed the text to read "fun," a liberty he was known to take periodically when illustrating nursery rhymes (conversation with Michael Patrick Hearn, 21 June 1995).

24. As Pyle is not represented in this section of the exhibition, refer to the chapter, "High Adventure and Fantasy: Art for All Ages".

25. L. Frank Baum, *Mother Goose in Prose* (Chicago: Way and Williams, 1897).

26. Coy Ludwig, *Maxfield Parrish* (New York: Watson-Guptill Publications, 1973), 25.

27. Rossboard was a commercially prepared board used to make ruled or shaded surfaces for printing halftones before the Ben Day shading machine was invented. Named for its inventor, Rossboard was known for its assortment of surface textures which varied from coarse to fine and could be stippled or patterned. Charles W. Hackleman, *Commercial Engraving and Printing* (Indianapolis: Commercial Engraving Publishing Company, 1921), 59, 68.

28. First appeared as *Little Bo-Peep*, one of *Leslie Brooke's Little Books* which were issued between 1904 and 1922, and again in *Ring O' Roses: A Nursery Rhyme Picture Book* (London: Frederick Warne, 1922; reprinted New York: Clarion Books, 1992).

29. *Mother Goose: The Classic Volland Edition* (Chicago: P.F. Volland & Company, 1915; reprinted New York, Chicago: Rand McNally & Company, 1971).

30. The Opies, *The Oxford Dictionary of Nursery Rhymes*, 93–94.

31. Barbara Bader, *American Picturebooks from Noah's Ark to the Beast Within* (New York: Macmillan Publishing Co., Inc., 1976), 128–129.

32. Bader, *American Picturebooks from Noah's Ark to the Beast Within*, 130.

33. See Christian Zervos, *Pablo Picasso*, 33 vols. (Paris: Cahiers d'Art, 1932-1978), Vol. XIV, 167. [Collection of Ms. Françoise Gilot]

III. HERE AND NOW, THEN AND THERE

1. Johan Comenius, *Orbis sensualium pictus* (1658); cited in Selma G. Lanes, *Down the Rabbit Hole* (New York: Atheneum, 1971), 45.

2. Bruno Bettelheim, "Introduction," in *Frederick's Fables: A Leo Lionni Treasury of Favorite Stories* (New York: Pantheon Books, 1985), ix.

3. Lanes, *Down the Rabbit Hole*, 22.

4. Gail Stavitsky, "The Artful Life of Esphyr Slobodkina," in *Esphyr Slobodkina*, exhibition catalogue (Medford, Mass.: Tufts University Art Gallery, 1992), 15ff.

5. Brian Alderson, *Ezra Jack Keats: Artist and Picture-Book Maker* (Gretna, La.: Pelican Publishing Company, 1994), 185. Taken from an article by Keats, "The Right to be Real," *Saturday Review* 9 (Nov. 1963), 56.

6. Alderson, *Keats*, 183–185.

7. Ann White, executor of the Steptoe Estate, conversation with author, 5 May 1995.

8. Stavitsky, *Esphyr Slobodkina*, 22, cites the artist's autobiography.

9. See Joyce Irene Whalley and Anne Stevenson Hobbs, "Fantasy, Rhymes, Fairy Tales and Fables," in *Beatrix Potter 1866–1943: The Artist and Her World* (London: Frederick Warne with The National Trust, 1987), 66–69.

10. For a thorough discussion of the genesis, production and history of this book, see Leonard Marcus, *Margaret Wise Brown: Awakened by the Moon* (Boston: Beacon Press, 1992), 183–219.

11. Roger Angell, "Onward and Upward with the Arts: 'The Minstrel Steig,'" *The New Yorker*, 70 (Feb. 20 and 27, 1995), 252–261.

12. See Selma G. Lanes, *The Art of Maurice Sendak* (New York: Harry N. Abrams, Inc., 1980); Lanes' chapters on *Where the Wild Things Are* and *In the Night Kitchen* were seminal to my own observations.

13. Conversation with the artist, 16 May 1995. The full title of the print is, "Poisson Aerostatique enlevé à Plazentia Ville d'Espagne . . . et dirigé par Dom Joseph Patinho jusqu'a la Ville de Coria au bord de la Rivière d'Arragon, éloigné de 12 lieues de Plazentia le 10 mars 1784." I am indebted to Sue Welsh Reed for identifying this print.

14. This observation was confirmed in conversation with the artist, 15 February 1995.

15. Judith L. Larson, *Enchanted Images: American Children's Illustration, 1850–1925* (Santa Barbara, Calif.: Santa Barbara Museum of Art, 1980), 31–32.

IV. HIGH ADVENTURE

1. Susan Danly, "Daniel Huntington, *Mercy's Dream*," *Telling Tales: Nineteenth-Century Narrative Painting from the Collection of the Pennsylvania Academy of the Fine Arts*, exhibition catalogue (Philadelphia: Pennsylvania Academy of the Fine Arts, 1991), 35.

2. Neil Harris, *The Artist in American Society: The Formative Years, 1790–1860* (New York: George Braziller, 1966), 20–21.

3. James Callow, *Kindred Spirits: Knickerbocker*

Writers and American Artists, 1807–1855 (Chapel Hill, N.C.: The University of North Carolina Press, 1967), 183ff.

4. William H. Gerdts, "The Painting of Washington Allston," in William H. Gerdts and Theodore E. Stebbins, Jr., *"A Man of Genius:" The Art of Washington Allston (1779–1843)*, exhibition catalogue (Boston: Museum of Fine Arts Boston, 1979), 96.

5. Joshua C. Taylor, "The Creation of an American Mythology," in *America as Art*, exhibition catalogue (Washington, D.C.: Smithsonian Institution Press, 1976), 77.

6. Donald G. Hoffman, *Form and Fable in American Fiction* (New York: Oxford University Press, 1961), 84ff.

7. Taylor, *America as Art*, 71.

8. Sinclair Hamilton, *Early American Book Illustrators and Wood Engravers, 1670–1870* (Princeton, N.J.: Princeton University Press, 1958), xxxviii. See also, Theodore Bolton, *The Book Illustrations of Felix Octavius Carr Darley* (Worcester, Mass.: American Antiquarian Society, 1952) and Christine Hahler, "... illustrated by Darley," exhibition catalogue (Wilmington, Del.: The Delaware Art Museum, 1978).

9. For a discussion of the American Art-Union, see Maybelle Mann, *The American Art-Union*, exhibition catalogue (Otisville, N.Y.: ALM Associates, Inc., 1977).

10. Hoffman, *Form and Fable*, 95–96.

11. George L. McKay, "Artists Who Have Illustrated Irving's Works," *American Collector* 16 (Oct. 1947), 38–40.

12. Conversation with the author, 7 February 1995.

13. Taylor, *America as Art*, 90.

14. Judith L. Larson, "Storybook Characters," in *Enchanted Images: American Children's Illustration, 1850–1925*, (Santa Barbara, Calif.: Santa Barbara Museum of Art, 1980), 20.

15. Thomas Hart Benton, "A Note by the Illustrator," for Mark Twain, *Adventures of Huckleberry Finn*, ed. and intro. Bernard de Voto; illus. Thomas Hart Benton (New York: Limited Editions Club, 1942), lxxii.

16. Eric Gugler and James Daugherty, "Homer Price," *The Horn Book* 19 (Nov. 1943), 424–426.

17. Catherine C. Stryker, "Jessie Willcox Smith," in *A Small School of Art: The Students of Howard Pyle*, exhibition catalogue (Wilmington, Del.: The Delaware Art Museum, 1980), 180.

18. Edward D. Nudelman, *Jessie Willcox Smith: American Illustrator* (Gretna, La.: Pelican Publishing Company, 1990), 42.

19. For a consideration of the book, the recent movie starring Susan Sarandon and Winona Ryder as well as the book based on the movie, see Alison Lurie, "She Had It All," (*Little Women*, by Louisa May Alcott), *The New York Review of Books* 42 (2 March 1995), 3–5.

20. Howard P. Brokaw, "Howard Pyle and the Art of Illustration," in *Howard Pyle and the Wyeths: Four Generations of American Imagination*, exhibition catalogue (Memphis, Tenn.: The Memphis Brooks Museum of Art, 1983), 14.

21. Douglas K. S. Hyland, "The Wyeths: Tradition in Transition," in *Howard Pyle and the Wyeths*, 41.

22. See Brigid Peppin, *Fantasy: The Golden Age of Fantastic Illustration* (New York: Watson-Guptill Publications, 1975) and Diana L. Johnson, *Fantastic Illustration and Design in Britain, 1850–1950*, exhibition catalogue (Providence, R.I.: Museum of Art Rhode Island School of Design, 1979) for good overviews of this subject.

23. Nudelman, *Jessie Willcox Smith*, 42.

24. Ann Percy, "Jessie Willcox Smith (1863–1935)," in *Philadelphia: Three Centuries Of American Art*, exhibition catalogue (Philadelphia, Pa.: Philadelphia Museum of Art, 1976), 505.

25. Michael Patrick Hearn, "Preface," to L. Frank Baum, *The Wizard of Oz*, ed. Michael Patrick Hearn, (New York: Schocken Books, 1983), ix.

26. Author's conversation with the artist, 6 April 1995.

27. Michael Danoff, "Introduction," in David Larkin, ed., *The Art of Nancy Ekholm Burkert* (New York: Peacock Press/Bantam Book, 1977), n.p.

V. Happily Ever after

1. Iona and Peter Opie, *The Classic Fairy Tales* (London and New York: Oxford University Press, 1974), 5.

2. The seminal works that can lead the reader into deeper discussions of these issues are: Bruno Bettelheim, *The Uses of Enchantment: The Meaning and Importance of Fairy Tales* (New York: Alfred A. Knopf, Inc., 1976); Ruth B. Bottigheimer, *Grimms' Bad Girls and Bold Boys: The Moral and Social Vision of the Tales* (New Haven: Yale University Press, 1987); Jack Zipes, ed., *The Trials and Tribulations of Little Red Riding Hood*, 2nd ed. (New York: Routledge, 1993); Michael Patrick Hearn, ed., *The Victorian Fairy Tale Book* (New York: Pantheon Books, 1988); Jack Zipes, ed., *Spells of Enchantment: The Wondrous Fairy Tales of Western Culture* (New York: Viking, 1991); Jason Heda and Dmitri Segal, eds., *Patterns in Oral Literature* (The Hague: Mouton, 1977); and Alison Lurie, *Don't Tell the Grown-ups: Subversive Children's Literature* (Boston: Little Brown & Company, 1990).

3. Opie, *Classic Fairy Tales*, 6.

4. Zipes, *Spells of Enchantment*, xiff.

5. Opie, *Classic Fairy Tales*, 18–20.

6. John Hayes, "Introduction," in *A History of Children's Book Illustrations 1750–1940*, exhibition catalogue (Stratford, Ontario: The Gallery of Stratford, ca. 1978) n.p.

7. Opie, *Classic Fairy Tales*, 25–27.

8. Richard Dalby, *The Golden Age of Children's Book Illustration* (London: Michael O'Mara Books Limited 1991), 9.

9. Opie, *Classic Fairy Tales*, 121.

10. Ai-Ling Louie, *Yeh Shen: A Cinderella Story from China* (New York: Philomel Books, 1982), illustrated by Ed Young. For an extensive discussion of the Cinderella story in the Far East, see Nai-Tung Ting, *The Cinderella Cycle in China and Indo-China* (Helsinki: Suomalainen Tiedeakatemia, 1974).

11. Sinclair Hamilton, *Early American Book Illustrators and Wood Engravers, 1670–1870* (Princeton, N.J.: Princeton University Press, 1958), xxxviii. See also, Theodore Bolton, *The Book Illustrations of Felix Octavius Carr Darley* (Worcester, Mass.: American Antiquarian Society, 1952) and Christine Hahler, ". . . illustrated by Darley," exhibition catalogue (Wilmington, Del.: Delaware Art Museum, 1978).

12. Author's note, *Mufaro's Beautiful Daughters* (New York: Lothrop, Lee & Shepard Books, 1987), n.p.

13. Zipes, *Trials and Tribulations of "Little Red Riding Hood,"* 31ff.

14. Ibid., 66ff.

15. Beatrice Schenk de Regniers, *Red Riding Hood, Retold in Verse for Boys and Girls to Read Themselves* (New York: Atheneum, 1972).

16. Sylvia and Kenneth Marantz, *Artists of the Page: Interviews with Children's Book Illustrators* (Jefferson, N.C.: McFarland & Company, Inc. Publishers, 1992), 227–40.

17. Opie, *Classic Fairy Tales*, 175.

18. Bettelheim, *The Uses of Enchantment*, 194–215.

19. Diana L. Johnson, *Fantastic Illustration and Design in Britain, 1850–1930*, exhibition catalogue (Providence, R.I.: Museum of Art Rhode Island School of Design, 1979), 78.

20. Helmut Brackert, "Introduction," in Helmut Brackert and Volkmar Sander, eds., *Jakob and Wilhem Grimm and Others: German Fairy Tales* (New York: Continuum, 1985), xxv.

21. Michael Danoff, "Introduction," in David Larkin, ed., *The Art of Nancy Ekholm Burkert* (New York: Peacock Press/Bantam Book, 1977), n.p.

22. Conversation with the artist, 5 April 1995. For the iconography of the various elements, see George Ferguson, *Signs and Symbols in Christian Art* (New York: Oxford University Press, 1961), 29, 36.

23. Hellmut Baumann, trans. and aug. William T. and Eldwyth Ruth Stearn, *The Greek Plant World in Myth, Art, and Literature* (Portland, Ore.: Timber Press, 1993), 108.

24. For a discussion of this project and many of the individual drawings, see Selma G. Lanes, *The Art of Maurice Sendak* (New York: Harry N. Abrams, Inc., 1980), 191–207.

25. Ibid., 196.

26. Mary T. Swanson, *From Swedish Fairy Tales to American Fantasy: Gustaf Tenggren's Illustrations 1920–1970*, exhibition catalogue (Minneapolis, Minn.: University of Minnesota Art Museum, 1986), 6.

27. Ibid., 14.

28. Ibid., 11–12.

29. For a discussion of this aspect of the artist's career, see Jane P. Davidson, *David Teniers the Younger* (Boulder, Colo.: Westview Press, 1979), 33–34, 38–43.

30. Paul O. Zelinsky, "A Note on the Text," in Paul Zelinsky, *Rumpelstiltskin* (New York: E. P. Dutton, 1986), n.p.

31. Conversation with the artist, 7 April 1995. Re model from Chinatown

32. Ann Conolly Hughey, *Edmund Dulac: His Book Illustrations* (Potomac, Md.: Buttonwood Press, Inc., 1995), n.p.

33. Joel Chandler Harris, "Introduction," in *Uncle Remus: His Songs and His Sayings* (New York: D. Appleton and Company, 1895), viiff.

34. Julius Lester, "Introduction," in *More Tales of Uncle Remus: Further Adventures of Brer Rabbit, His Friends, Enemies, and Others* (New York: Dial Books, 1988), xiv.

35. Lester, *More Tales of Uncle Remus*, xi, refers to the analysis of Roger D. Abrahams in *Afro-American Folktales: Stories from Black Traditions in the New World* (New York: Pantheon Books, 1985).

36. Ennis Rees, *Brer Rabbit and His Tricks* (New York: Young Scott Books, 1967). Selma G. Lanes, in *Down the Rabbit Hole*, (New York: Atheneum, 1971), 164, accords both his Brer Rabbit picture books high praise.

37. Augusta Baker, "Introduction," in Julius Lester, *Tales of Uncle Remus*, (New York: Dial Books, 1987), x.

38. Barry Moser, "Illustrator's Note," in Van Dyke Parks, *Jump! The Adventures of Brer Rabbit* (San Diego: Harcourt Brace Johanovich, 1986), vii.

39. Cited in Barbara Elleman, "Sandburg, Rootabagas, and the Midwest," *Book Links 3* (Mar. 1994), 19.

40. Lanes, *Down the Rabbit Hole* (New York: Atheneum, 1971), 162ff.

41. Author's note, *The Talking Eggs* (New York: Dial Books for Young Readers, 1989), n.p.

42. Author's conversation with the artist, 13 April 1995.

43. Author's note, *Sukey and the Mermaid* (New York: Four Winds Press, 1992), n.p.

44. Ibid.

45. Artist's note, *Sukey and the Mermaid*, n.p.

CHECKLIST OF ILLUSTRATIONS

I: DISCOVER, EXPLORE, ENJOY

125. Hans Augusto Rey (1898-1977). Born in Hamburg, Germany; Came to the U.S. in 1940. "George Sees Yellow Hat," from *Curious George* [Boston: Houghton Mifflin Company, 1940]. Colored pencil on paper; 10-1/2 x 8-7/8". de Grummond Children's Literature Collection, University of Southern Mississippi. ©1940 by Margret E. Rey. Reprinted with permission of Houghton Mifflin Company.

176a. George Cruikshank (1792-1878). British. "Cinderella and the Glass Slipper," from *The Fairy Library* [London: David Bogue, 1854]. Graphite and watercolor on paper; 5-7/8 x 4-5/16". Bequest of John T. Spaulding, Courtesy, Museum of Fine Arts, Boston.

176b. George Cruikshank (1792-1878). British. "Cinderella and the Glass Slipper," from *The Fairy Library* [London: David Bogue, 1854]. India proof etching on china paper; 7-5/16 x 4-7/8". Department of Rare Books and Special Collections, Princeton University Libraries.

158a. John Tenniel (1820-1914). British. "The Mad Hatter's Tea Party," from *Alice's Adventures in Wonderland*. By Lewis Carroll [London: Macmillan and Company, 1865]. Graphite on paper; 5-15/16 x 8-15/16". Gift of Mrs. Harcourt Amory, 1927, Houghton Library, Harvard University. Norfolk only.

183. Walter Crane (1845-1915). British. "Puss Kills the Ogre," from *Puss in Boots* [London: George Routledge and Sons, 1873]. Pen, black ink, and watercolor over graphite on paper; 8-5/8 x 6-9/16". Gift of Mrs. John L. Gardner, Courtesy, Museum of Fine Arts, Boston.

151. Walter Crane (1845-1915). British. Cover from *Household Stories from the Collection of the Bros. Grimm* [London: Macmillan and Company, 1882]. Gouache over graphite on paper; 7-7/8 x 6-7/8". Justin G. Schiller (Personal Collection).

55a. Kate Greenaway (1846-1901). British. "Where the waters rushed and fruit trees grew," Frontispiece from *The Pied Piper of Hamelin*. By Robert Browning [London: George Routledge and Sons, 1888]. Pen, black ink, and watercolor on paper; 8-5/8 x 7-5/8". The Pierpont Morgan Library, New York. Gift of Mrs. George Nichols. ©1995 by The Pierpont Morgan Library. Norfolk only.

54a. Randolph Caldecott (1846-1886). British. "His neighbour in such trim,/Laid down his pipe, flew to the gate,/And thus accosted him," from *The Diverting History of John Gilpin*. By William Cowper [London: George Routledge and Sons, 1878]. Pen, ink, and watercolor on paper mounted on board; 6-15/16 x 4-3/8". Private Collection.

54b. Randolph Caldecott (1846-1886). British. "The youth did ride, and soon did meet/John coming back amain," from *The Diverting History of John Gilpin*. By William Cowper [London: George Routledge and Sons, 1878]. Pen, ink, and watercolor on paper mounted on board; 4-3/8 x 6-13/16". Private Collection.

57a. Maurice Boutet de Monvel (1851-1913). French. "Jeanne before the Dauphin," from *Jeanne d'Arc* [Paris: Plon, Nourrit & Co., 1896]. Watercolor on paper, 9-1/4 x 12-1/4". Memorial Art Gallery, University of Rochester. Gift of Mr. Simon N. Stein. Norfolk only.

177a. Felix O. C. Darley, (1822-1888). American. "Cinderella with Fairy Godmother" from *Grandfather Lovechild's Nursery Stories*. By Fred Fearnought [Philadelphia: George B. Zieber, 1847]. Graphite on paper; 5-13/16 x 4-9/16". Department of Rare Books and Special Collections, Princeton University Libraries.

32a. Henry Louis Stephens (1824-1882). American. "Froggie Dressing," from *Froggie Would A-Wooing Go* [New York: Hurd & Houghton, 1865]. Graphite over red chalk tracing on illustration board, 6-11/16 x 4-11/16". Frances Hofer Bequest, Department of Printing & Graphic Arts, Houghton Library, Harvard University. Norfolk only.

208. Arthur Burdett Frost (1851-1928). American. "Uncle Remus Telling Stories," Frontispiece from *Uncle Remus: His Songs and His Sayings*. By Joel Chandler Harris [New York D. Appleton & Co., 1895]. Gouache on paper; 18 x 11". Collection of Mr. and Mrs. Henry M. Reed.

139. E. W. Kemble (1861-1933). American. Frontispiece from *Adventures of Huckleberry Finn*. By Mark Twain [New York: Charles L. Webster & Co., 1884]. Pen and ink on paper; 15-1/4 x 11-1/4". The Mark Twain House, Hartford, Connecticut.

97a. Peter Newell (1862-1924). American. "Pet Shop with Mice Escaping," from *The Hole Book* [New York: Harper Brothers, 1908]. Gouache over graphite on illustration board; 8-1/4 x 6-3/8". Philip Hofer Bequest, Department of Printing & Graphic Arts, Houghton Library, Harvard University. Norfolk only.

119a. Palmer Cox (1840-1924). Born in Granby, Quebec, Canada; Came to the U.S. in 1863. "The Brownies in Automobiles," n.d. [unpublished]. Pen and ink on light illustration board; 7 x 7-1/2". Rare Book Department, The Free Library of Philadelphia. Norfolk only.

120a. Gelett Burgess (1866-1951). American. "Patience," from *Goops and How to Be Them* [New York: Frederick A. Stokes, 1900]. Pen and ink on illustration board with text pasted on; 9-3/8 x 7-1/4". Betsy B. Shirley Collection of American Children's Literature, The Beinecke Library of Yale University.

147a. Howard Pyle (1853-1911). American. "Yankee Doodle by the Cannon," from *Yankee Doodle, an Old Friend in a New Dress* [New York: Dodd, Mead and Company, 1881]. Watercolor on illustration board; 9 x 8-1/2". Delaware Art Museum, Bequest of Joseph Bancroft, 1940.2704.

147b. Howard Pyle (1853-1911). American. "Washington Reviewing the Citizenry," from *Yankee Doodle, an Old Friend in a New Dress* [New York: Dodd, Mead and Company, 1881]. Watercolor on illustration board; 9 x 8-1/2". Delaware Art Museum, Bequest of Joseph Bancroft, 1940.2705.

115. Will H. Bradley (1868-1962). American. "Peter Poodle," Frontispiece from *Peter Poodle, Toy Maker to the King* [New York: Dodd, Mead & Company, 1906]. Chromolithograph; 11-3/16 x 14-3/16". Lent by The Metropolitan Museum of Art, Gift of Fern Bradley Dufner, 1952. ©The Metropolitan Museum of Art, 1995.

163. W. W. Denslow (1865-1915). American. "The soldier with the green whiskers led them through the streets," from *The Wonderful Wizard of Oz*. By L. Frank Baum [Chicago: George M. Hill Company, 1900]. Pen and ink on paper; 14-7/16 x 10-13/16". Print Collection, The Miriam and Ira D. Wallach Division of Art, Prints and Photographs, The New York Public Library, Astor, Lenox and Tilden Foundations.

21. Sir William Nicholson (1872-1949). English. "U is for Urchin," from *An Alphabet* [London: William Heinemann, 1898]. Hand-colored woodcut; 9-3/4 x 7-3/4". Courtesy of the Fogg Art Museum, Harvard University Art Museums, Anonymous loan in honor of Daniel Bell.

160. Arthur Rackham (1867-1939). British. "A Hundred flew off with the String and Peter clung to the tail" from *Peter Pan in Kensington Gardens*. By J. M. Barrie [London: Hodder & Stoughton, 1906]. Pen, ink, and watercolor on paper; 8-1/4 x 10". Collection of Kendra Krienke and Allan Daniel, New York City.

81a. Beatrix Potter (1866-1943). British. "Mice tailoring with cat looking through window," from first version of *The Tailor of Gloucester*, 1901 [unpublished]. Watercolor on paper; 6-1/4 x 8-7/8". Rare Book Department, The Free Library of Philadelphia. ©1986 Frederick Warne & Co. Norfolk only.

153. N. C. Wyeth (1882-1945). American. "One more step, Mr. Hands," said I, "and I'll blow your brains out!," from *Treasure Island*. By Robert Louis Stevenson [New York: Charles Scribner's Sons, 1911]. Oil on canvas; 47-1/2 x 38-1/2". Lent by the New Britain Museum of American Art, Harriet Russell Stanley Fund. Reprinted with the permission of Atheneum Books for Young Readers, an imprint of Simon & Schuster Children's Publishing Division. Photo by Michael Agee.

84. Harrison Cady (1877-1970). American. "Peter Rabbit with Uncle Billy Possum," from *The Adventures of Peter Cottontail* [Boston: Little, Brown & Company, 1914]. Pen and ink and wash on illustration board; 9-7/16 x 13". Kendra Krienke and Allan Daniel, New York City.

121. Johnny Gruelle (1880-1938). American. Cover from *Raggedy Ann in Cookie Land* [Chicago: P. F. Volland & Co., 1931]. Watercolor and ink on illustration board; 19-3/4 x 12-3/4". Kendra Krienke and Allan Daniel, New York City.

89a. Clement Hurd (1908-1988). American. "Goodnight room," from *Goodnight Moon*. By Margaret Wise Brown [New York: Harper & Row Publishers, 1947]. Tempera on posterboard; 6-7/8 x 16-1/4". The Kerlan Collection, University of Minnesota. ©1947 by Clement Hurd, ren. 1975 by Edith T. Hurd, Clement Hurd, John Thacher Hurd, and George Hellyer, as Trustees of the Edith and Clement Hurd 1992 Trust. Used by permission of HarperCollins Publishers.

100. Wanda Gág (1893-1946). American. "Old Man Confronted by Cats in a Landscape," from *Millions of Cats* [New York: Coward, McCann & Geohegan, 1928]. Pen and ink on paper; 6-5/8 x 9-3/4". The Kerlan Collection, University of Minnesota. Reprinted with permission of Coward-McCann, an imprint of The Putnam & Grosset Group.

168. Feodor Rojankovsky (1891-1970). Born in Mitava, Russia; Came to the U.S. in 1941. "By the campfire at night he talked with a trader named Finley. . . ," from *Daniel Boone: Historic Adventure of an American Hunter among the Indians*. By Esther Averill and Lila Stanley [Paris: Domino Press, 1931]. Graphite, colored pencil, and gouache on paper; 8-3/8 x 5-3/4". The Kerlan Collection, University of Minnesota.

CHECKLIST OF ILLUSTRATIONS

215a. Peggy Bacon (1895-1987). American. "How the Animals Lost Their Tails and Got Them Back Traveling from Philadelphia to Medicine Hat," from *Rootabaga Country: Selections from Rootabaga Stories and Rootabaga Pigeons*. By Carl Sandburg [New York: Harcourt Brace and Company, 1922; 1929 edition]. Pen, ink, and graphite on paper; 7-1/2 x 7-1/2". Courtesy of Kraushaar Galleries. ©1922, 1923, 1929 by Harcourt Brace and Company, Inc.

61. Hardie Gramatky (1907-1979). American. "Little Toot with Reflection in the Water," from *Little Toot* [New York: G. P. Putnam's Sons, 1939]. Pen, ink, and watercolor on paper; 10-1/2 x 10-1/2". Spencer Collection, The New York Public Library, Astor, Lenox and Tilden Foundations. ©1939 by Hardie Gramatky. Reprinted with permission of The Putnam & Grosset Group.

63. Virginia Lee Burton (1909-1968). American. "Country," "Growing Suburbia," "City," and "Moving out to the Country," from *The Little House* [Boston: Houghton Mifflin Company, 1942]. Crayon and gouache on paper; 8-3/8 x 10-1/4"; 8-7/8 x 10"; 7-3/8 x 10-3/4"; and 8-1/2 x 9-3/4". The Kerlan Collection, University of Minnesota. ©1942 by Virginia Lee Burton. Reprinted with permission of the Houghton Mifflin Company.

70. Robert McCloskey (born 1914). American. "Policeman Stopping Traffic," from *Make Way for Ducklings* [New York: The Viking Press, 1941]. Graphite and crayon on paper; 18 x 24". May Massee Collection, William Allen White Library, Emporia State University.©1941 by Robert McCloskey. ren. ©1969 by Robert McCloskey. Used by permission of Viking Penguin, a division of Viking Penguin, a division of Penguin Books USA Inc.

123a. Robert Lawson (1892-1957). American. "Ferdinand sitting in the bull ring," from The Story of *Ferdinand*. By Munro Leaf [New York: The Viking Press, 1936]. Pen and black and white ink on paper; 9-7/16 x 8". The Pierpont Morgan Library, New York. Gift of Mary Flagler Cary Charitable Trust. ©1936 by Munro Leaf and Robert Lawson, ren. ©1964 by Munro Leaf and John W. Boyd. Used by permission of Viking Penguin, a division of Penguin Books USA Inc. Norfolk only.

169. Ingri Parin d'Aulaire (1904-1980). Born in Konigsberg, Norway; Came to the U.S. in 1929 and Edgar Parin d'Aulaire (1898-1986) Born in Munich, Germany; Came to the U.S. in 1929. "Abe Reading by the Fire," from *Abraham Lincoln* [Garden City, L.I.: Doubleday, Doran and Company, 1939]. Lithograph; 11 x 8". The Kerlan Collection, University of Minnesota. ©1939, 1957 by Doubleday, a division of Bantam Doubleday Dell Publishing Group, Inc. Used by permission of Doubleday, a division of Bantam Doubleday Dell Publishing Group, Inc.

88. Gustaf Tenggren (1896-1970). Born in Magra, Sweden; Came to the U.S. in 1920. "There he was, running around with his nose to the ground," from *The Poky Little Puppy*. By Janette S. Lowrey [New York: The Golden Press, 1942]. Tempera on posterboard; 7-1/2 x 13-1/2". The Kerlan Collection, University of Minnesota. ©1942 by Western Publishing Company, Inc., renewed 1970. Used by permission.

67. John Steptoe (1950-1989). American. "Naw, my momma said he can't go in the park cause the last time. . . ," from *Stevie* [New York: Harper & Row Publishers, 1969]. Studio marker with pastel overpainting on paper; 8-3/4 x 6-3/4". The John Steptoe Collection. ©1969 by John Steptoe. Reprinted with the approval of the Estate of John Steptoe and used by permission of HarperCollins Publishers.

95. William Steig (born 1907). American. "Dr. De Soto fastened his extractor to the bad tooth," from *Dr. De Soto* [New York: Farrar, Straus & Giroux, Inc. 1982]. Pen and ink, graphite, and watercolor on paper; 12-1/8 x 9". Collection of Melinda Franceschini. ©1982 by William Steig. Reprinted by permission of Farrar, Straus & Giroux, Inc.

104. Maurice Sendak (born 1928). American. "And they put that batter up to Bake a Delicious Mickey-cake," from *In the Night Kitchen* [New York: Harper & Row Publishers, 1970]. Watercolor on paper; 11-5/8 x 17-3/8". ©1970 by Maurice Sendak. Courtesy, Maurice Sendak and The Rosenbach Museum & Library. Used by permission of HarperCollins Publishers.

190a. Nancy Ekholm Burkert (born 1933). American. ". . . in the evening they came back. . . ," from *Snow White and the Seven Dwarfs*. By the Brothers Grimm. Translated by Randall Jarrell [New York: Farrar, Straus & Giroux, Inc., 1972]. Colored inks and watercolor on paper; 12 x 18". Lent by the Artist. ©1972 by Nancy Ekholm Burkert. Reprinted by permission of Farrar, Straus & Giroux, Inc.

110. Peter Sís (born 1949). Born in Brünn, Czechoslovakia; Came to the U.S. in 1982. "I follow the determined cat back across the ancient bridge," from *The Three Golden Keys* [New York: Doubleday, 1994]. Oil pastel on gesso with gold border; 12 x 18". Collection of Peter Sís. ©1994 by Peter Sís. Used by permission of Doubleday, a division of Bantam Doubleday Dell Publishing Group, Inc.

228. Leo Lionni (born 1910). Born in Amsterdam, The Netherlands; Came to the U.S. in 1939. "Alexander and the Wind-up Mouse," from *Alexander and the Wind-up Mouse.* [New York: Pantheon Books, 1969]. Watercolor and collage on illustration board; 11 x 18-3/8". Collection of Leo Lionni. ©1969 by Leo Lionni. Reprinted with permission of Random House, Inc.

196. Leo Dillon (born 1933) and Diane Dillon (born 1933). American. Cover from *The Porcelain Cat.* By Michael Patrick Hearn [Little, Brown and Company, 1987]. Airbrushed watercolor on paper; 11-3/16 x 15-3/16". Private Collection. ©1987 by Leo and Diane Dillon. Reprinted by permission of Little, Brown and Company.

133. James Marshall (1942-1992). American. "The Guests Arrive," from *The Stupids Have a Ball.* By Harry Allard [Boston: Houghton Mifflin Company, 1978]. Pen and ink on paper; 7 x 8-1/2". de Grummond Children's Literature Collection, University of Southern Mississippi. ©1978 by James Marshall. Reprinted with permission of the Houghton Mifflin Company.

II. AND THE DISH RAN AWAY WITH THE SPOON

1. Maurice Sendak (born 1928). American. "A FOR ALLIGATORS/B...BURSTING BAL-LOONS," from *Alligators All Around* from the *Nutshell Library* series [New York: Harper & Row, 1962]. Pen and ink on paper; 4-3/8 x 6". ©1962 by Maurice Sendak. Courtesy, Maurice Sendak and The Rosenbach Museum & Library. Used by permission of HarperCollins Publishers.

2. Edward Gorey (born 1925). American. "B is for Basil assaulted by Bears," from *The Gashlycrumb Tinies* [New York: Peter Weed Books, 1962]. Pen and ink on paper; 3-3/16 x 4-1/2". Collection of Edward Gorey. Courtesy of Gotham Book Mart Gallery, New York City. ©1962 by Edward Gorey. Published with the permission of Edward Gorey.

3. Wanda Gág (1893-1946). American. "C is for Crash/D is for Dash," from *The ABC Bunny* [New York: Coward-McCann, 1933]. Graphite on paper; 10 x 9-3/4". The Kerlan Collection, University of Minnesota. Reprinted with permission of Coward-McCann, an imprint of the Putnam & Grosset Group.

4. Roger Duvoisin (1904-1980). Born in Geneva, Switzerland; Came to the U.S. in 1925. "D/E," from *A is for the Ark* [New York: Lothrop, Lee & Shepard Company, 1952]. Gouache, graphite, and ink on paper with text pasted on; 12-1/8 x 18-1/4". Jane Voorhees Zimmerli Art Museum, Rutgers, The State University of New Jersey, Gift of

Louise Fatio Duvoisin, Transfer from the Alexander Library. Photo by Jack Abraham. Reprinted with the permission of Lothrop, Lee & Shepard, an imprint of William Morrow and Company, Inc.

5. Stefano Vitale (born 1958). Born in Padova, Italy; Came to the U.S. in 1982. "E," from *The Folks in the Valley: A Pennsylvania Dutch ABC.* By Jim Aylesworth [New York: HarperCollins Publishers, 1992]. Oil on panel; 7 3/4 x 6-5/8". Collection of Stefano Vitale. ©1992 by Stefano Vitale. Use by permission of HarperCollins Publishers.

6. Esphyr Slobodkina (born 1908). Born in Siberia; Came to the U.S. in 1928. "F is for Feet that won't fall asleep," 1995, from *The Sleepy ABC.* By Margaret Wise Brown [New York: Lothrop, Lee & Shepard Company, 1953]. Collage on paper [reconstruction of original image]; 9-1/2 x 7-3/4". Collection of Esphyr Slobodkina. ©1995 by Esther Slobodkina. Used by permission of HarperCollins Publishers.

7. Edmund Dulac (1882-1953). French. "'G' was a Giddy Young Girl," 1906, from *Lyrics Pathetic & Humorous from A to Z* [London: Frederick Warne & Co., 1908]. Watercolor and ink on paper; 7 x 7". Collection of Ann Conolly Hughey.

8. Leo Dillon (born 1933) and Diane Dillon (born 1933). American. "'H' is for Hausa," from *Ashanti to Zulu: African Traditions.* By Margaret Musgrove [New York: The Dial Press, 1976]. Watercolor on paper; 6-1/2 x 6-1/2". Collection of Leo and Diane Dillon. ©1976 by Leo and Diane Dillon. Used by permission of Dial Books for Young Readers, a division of Penguin Books USA Inc.

9. Anita Lobel (born 1934). Born in Cracow, Poland; Came to the U.S. in 1952. "Ice Cream," from *On Market Street.* By Arnold Lobel [New York: Greenwillow Books, 1981]. Black penline and full color separation in watercolor on paper; 8-1/4 x 9-5/8". Collection of Anita Lobel. ©1981 by Anita Lobel. Reprinted with the permission of Greenwillow Books, a division of William Morrow and Company, Inc.

10. Charles B. Falls (1874-1960). American. "J is for Jazz," from *The Modern ABC Book* [New York: John Day, 1930]. Black, red, blue inks and white bodycolor over pencil on illustration board; 20 x 15". Chapin Library of Rare Books, Williams College, Gift of Bedelia C. Falls.

11. Charles B. Falls (1874-1960). American. "K is for Kangaroo," from *ABC Book* [Garden City: Doubleday, Page and Company, 1923]. Colored woodblocks; 15-7/8 x 11-1/2". May Massee

Collection, William Allen White Library, Emporia State University. ©1923 by Doubleday. Used by permission of Doubleday, a division of Bantam Doubleday Dell Publishing Group, Inc.

12. Hans Augusto Rey (1898-1977). Born in Germany; Came to the U.S. in 1940. "L = Lion Blows out the Candle," from *Look for the Letters: A Hide and Seek Alphabet* [New York: Harper & Row Publishers, 1942]. Watercolor and charcoal on paper; 10 x 11-3/4". Lent by Margret E. Rey. ©1942 by Margret E. Rey. Used by permission of HarperCollins Publishers.

13. Wendy Watson (born 1942). American. "M for Magic," from *Applebet: An ABC*. By Clyde Watson [New York: Farrar, Straus & Giroux, Inc. 1982]. Watercolor on paper; 7 x 8-1/8" (sight). Lent by Hubert A. Scoble & Margaret A. Gruszka. ©1982 by Wendy Watson. Reprinted by permission of Farrar, Straus & Giroux, Inc.

14. Mary Shepard (born 1909). British. "N is for Nursery," from *Mary Poppins From A to Z*. By Pamela L. Travers [New York: Harcourt Brace & Company, 1962]. Pen and ink on paper; 7-1/4 x 5-13/16". The New York Public Library, Central Children's Room, Donnell Library Center. ©1962 by John Lyndon Ltd. and renewed 1990 by Mrs. Pamela Travers. Reproduced by permission of Harcourt Brace & Company.

15. John O'Brien (born 1953). American. "O," from *MacMillan Fairy Tale Alphabet Book*. By Nancy Christensen Hall [New York: Macmillan, 1983]. Pen, ink, and watercolor on paper; 12 x 18". Collection of John O'Brien. ©1983 by John O'Brien. Reprinted with the permission of Simon & Schuster Books for Young Readers, an imprint of Simon & Schuster Children's Publishing Division.

16. Chris Van Allsburg (born 1949). American. "P was repeatedly Pecked," from *The 'Z' was Zapped* [Boston: Houghton Mifflin Company, 1987]. Graphite on paper; 10 x 12" (sight). Collection of Mr. and Mrs. David Lord Porter. ©1987 by Chris Van Allsburg. Reprinted with the permission of Houghton Mifflin Company.

17. Cathi Hepworth (born 1964). American. "QuarANtine," from ANTICS! *An Alphabetical ANThology* [New York: G. P. Putnam's Sons, 1992]. Colored pencil and pastel on paper; 6-1/2 x 5-1/4". Collection of Cathi Hepworth. ©1992 by Cathi Hepworth. Reprinted with permission of G. P. Putnam's Sons, an imprint of The Putnam & Grosset Group.

18. Anne Rockwell (born 1934). American. "Rr," from *Albert B. Cub & Zebra: An Alphabet Storybook* [New York: Thomas Y. Crowell, 1977]. Pen, ink,

and watercolor on paper; 12-3/4 x 11-3/4". The Kerlan Collection, University of Minnesota. ©1977 by Anne Rockwell. Used by permission of HarperCollins Publishers.

19. Leonard Baskin (born 1922). American. "S is for Self-Portrait," 1996, from [forthcoming alphabet book]. Watercolor on paper; 11-1/2 x 8-1/4". Courtesy of R. Michelson Galleries, Northampton and Amherst, Massachusetts. ©1996 by Leonard Baskin.

20. Marcia Brown (born 1918). American. "Tip-Toe Tommy turned a Turk for a Two-pence," from *Peter Piper's Alphabet: Peter Piper's Practical Principles of Plain and Perfect Pronunciation* [New York: Charles Scribner's Sons, 1959]. Pen, ink, gouache, and watercolor on paper; 8-1/8 x 19-5/8". From the Marcia J. Brown Papers, 1942-1994. The M. E. Grenander Department of Special Collections and Archives, University Libraries, University at Albany, State University of New York. ©1958 by Marcia Brown. Reprinted with permission of Marcia Brown.

21. Sir William Nicholson (1872-1949). British. "U is for Urchin," from *An Alphabet* [London: William Heinemann, 1898]. Hand-colored woodcut; 9-3/4 x 7-3/4". Courtesy of the Fogg Art Museum, Harvard University Art Museums, Anonymous loan in honor of Daniel Bell.

22. Richard Scarry (1919-1994). American. "Vinny and Vicki," from *Richard Scarry's Find Your ABCs* [New York: Random House, Inc., 1973]. Pen, ink, and watercolor on illustration board; 9-3/8 x 18-3/4". Richard Scarry Estate. ©1973 by Richard Scarry. Reprinted with permission of Random House, Inc.

23. William Steig (born 1907). American. "Worry Wart," from *Alpha Beta Chowder*. By Jeanne and William Steig [New York: HarperCollins Publishers, 1992]. Watercolor on paper; 8 x 10". Collection of Jeanne Steig. ©1992 by William Steig. Used by permission of HarperCollins Publishers.

24. Scott Gustafson (born 1956). American. "Ox and Xylopia Extract," from *Alphabet Soup: A Feast of Letters* [Shelton, Connecticut: The Greenwich Workshop Press, 1994]. Acrylic on paper; 11-1/2 x 15-1/4". Collection of Scott Gustafson. ©1994 by Scott Gustafson. Reprinted with permission of The Greenwich Workshop Press.

25. Maud Petersham (1890-1971) American, and Miska Petersham (1888-1960); Born in Hungary; Came to the U.S. in 1912. "Y is for Yankee Doodle," from *An American ABC* [New York: Macmillan, 1941]. Lithographic proof; 10-9/16 x 8-1/2".

Department of Special Collections, University of Oregon Library. Reprinted with the permission of Simon & Schuster Books for Young Readers, an imprint of Simon & Schuster Children's Publishing Division.

26. Edward R. Emberley (born 1931). American. "Z," from *Ed Emberley's ABC* [Boston: Little, Brown and Company, 1978]. Pen, ink, and watercolor on paper; 4 sheets, each 10-11/16 x 7". Collection of Ed Emberley. ©1978 by Ed Emberley.

27. Dr. Seuss (1904-1991). American. "When you go beyond Zebra <u>Who Knows</u>? . . . Like Quan is for quandary," from *On Beyond Zebra!* [New York: Random House, Inc., 1955]. Pen, ink, chinese white, and collage on illustration board; 12-3/4 x 19". Dr. Seuss Collection, Mandeville Special Collections Library, University of California, San Diego. ©1955 Dr. Seuss Enterprises, L.P., ren. 1983.

28a. Antonio Frasconi (born 1919). Born in Uruguay; Came to the U.S. in 1945. "Wind, whale, fishermen, sea, anchor," from *See and Say* [New York: Harcourt, Brace & World, 1955]. Woodblock and collage on paper; 10-7/8 x 16-9/16". Collection of Antonio Frasconi ©1955 by Antonio Frasconi.

28b. Antonio Frasconi (born 1919). Born in Uruguay; Came to the U.S. in 1945. "Pig, grass, Farmer, turkey," from *See and Say* [New York: Harcourt, Brace & World, 1955]. Woodblock and collage on paper; 10-1/4 x 16-5/8". Collection of Antonio Frasconi. ©1955 by Antonio Frasconi. [not illus.]

29. Antonio Frasconi (born 1919). Born in Uruguay; Came to the U.S. in 1945. "Alphabet," 1965 [unpublished]. 4-color woodblock; 16-1/4 x 10-1/16". Collection of Antonio Frasconi. ©1996 by Antonio Frasconi.

30. Richard Scarry (1919-1994). American. Cover from *Find Your ABCs* [New York: Random House, Inc., 1973]. Pen, ink, and watercolor on illustration board; 7-15/16 x 7-15/16". Richard Scarry Estate. ©1973 by Richard Scarry. Reprinted with permission of Random House, Inc.

31. Roger Duvoisin (1904-1980). Born in Geneva, Switzerland; Came to the U.S. in 1925. Endpapers from *A is for the Ark* [New York: Lothrop, Lee & Shepard Company, 1952]. Pen, ink, graphite, and gouache on paper with typeset text; 10-13/16 x 16-13/16". Jane Voorhees Zimmerli Art Museum, Rutgers, The State University of New Jersey, Gift of Louise Fatio Duvoisin, Transfer from the Alexander Library. Photo by Jack Abraham.

Reprinted with the permission of Lothrop, Lee & Shepard, an imprint of William Morrow and Company, Inc.

32a. Henry Louis Stephens (1824-1882). American. "Froggie Dressing," from *Froggie Would A-Wooing Go* [New York: Hurd & Houghton, 1865]. Graphite over red chalk tracing on illustration board; 6-11/16 x 4-11/16". Frances Hofer Bequest, Department of Printing & Graphic Arts, Houghton Library, Harvard University. Norfolk only.

32b. Henry Louis Stephens (1824-1882). American. "Froggie Visiting Mrs. Mouse," from *Froggie Would A-Wooing Go* [New York: Hurd & Houghton, 1865]. Graphite over red chalk tracing on illustration board; 6-11/16 x 4-7/8". Frances Hofer Bequest, Department of Printing & Graphic Arts, Houghton Library, Harvard University. Memphis only [not illus.]

32c. Henry Louis Stephens (1824-1882). American. "Froggie Listening to Mrs. Mouse Play the Piano," from *Froggie Would A-Wooing Go* [New York: Hurd & Houghton, 1865]. Graphite over red chalk tracing on illustration board; 6-11/16 x 4-7/8". Frances Hofer Bequest, Department of Printing & Graphic Arts, Houghton Library, Harvard University. Wilmington only [not illus.].

33. Walter Crane (1845-1915). British. "Old Mother Hubbard Went to the Cupboard," from *For Old Mother Hubbard* [London: George Routledge and Sons, 1874]. Pen, black ink, and watercolor over graphite on paper; 8 x 6-3/8". Museum of Fine Arts, Boston. William A. Sargent Fund, 1964.1556.

34a. Randolph Caldecott (1846-1886). British. "And the Dish Ran Away with the Spoon," from *Hey Diddle Diddle, and Bye, Baby Bunting* [London: George Routledge and Sons, 1882]. Pen and ink, gouache, and watercolor on paper; 6-5/16 x 7-3/4". Parker Fund, Houghton Library, Harvard University. Norfolk only.

34b. Randolph Caldecott (1846-1886). British. "Hey Diddle Diddle," from *Hey Diddle Diddle, and Bye, Baby Bunting* [London: George Routledge and Sons, 1882]. Pen and ink, gouache, and watercolor on paper; 6-7/16 x 7-7/16". Parker Fund, Houghton Library, Harvard University. Memphis only [not illus.].

34c. Randolph Caldecott (1846-1886). British. "The Cow Jumped Over the Moon," from *Hey Diddle Diddle, and Bye, Baby Bunting* [London: George Routledge and Sons, 1882]. Pen and ink, gouache, and watercolor on paper; 6-3/8 x 7-1/2". Parker Fund, Houghton Library, Harvard University. Wilmington only [not illus.].

35. Arthur Rackham (1867-1939). British. "The Old Woman Who lived in a Shoe," from *Mother Goose. The Old Nursery Rhymes* [New York: The Century Company, 1913]. Pen, ink, and watercolor on paper; 10-5/8 x 8-3/8". Courtesy of The Boston Public Library, Print Department.

36. Maxfield Parrish (1870-1966). American. "Humpty Dumpty," from *Mother Goose in Prose*. By L. Frank Baum [Chicago: Way and Williams, 1897]. Pen, ink, and wash on wove paper mounted on board; 16-3/4 x 12-3/4". Courtesy of the Syracuse University Art Collection.

37. Peter Newell (1862-1924). American. "I'm Old Mother Hubbard's Dog," from *Mother Goose's Menagerie*. By Caroline Wells [Boston: Noyes, Platt and Co., 1901]. Pen, ink, watercolor, and gouache on paper; 10-15/16 x 8-5/16". Courtesy of The Boston Public Library Print Department, John D. Merriam Collection.

38. Jessie Willcox Smith (1863-1935). American. "Peter, Peter, Pumpkin Eater," from *Good Housekeeping*, November 1913; subsequently published in *The Jessie Willcox Smith Mother Goose* [New York: Dodd, Mead & Company, 1914]. Mixed media on illustration board; 18-1/2 x 24-1/2". Collection of Mr. and Mrs. Benjamin Eisenstat.

39. L. Leslie Brooke (1862-1941). British. "Little Bo-Peep," ca. 1904; first appeared as *Little Bo-Peep*, one of Leslie *Brooke's Little Books*, issued between 1904-1922; and in *Ring O' Roses: A Nursery Rhyme Picture Book* [London: Frederick Warne, 1922]. Pen, ink, and watercolor on paper; 7-1/4 x 9-3/8". Courtesy of Jo Ann Reisler, Ltd.

40. Frederick Richardson (1862-1937). American. "Little Bo-Peep," from *Mother Goose: The Classic Volland Edition* [Chicago: P. F. Volland & Company, 1915]. Pen, ink, watercolor, and gouache on illustration board; 13-7/16 x 10-7/16". Collection of Kendra Krienke and Allan Daniel, New York City.

41. Charles B. Falls (1874-1960). American. "Old Mother Hubbard," from *Mother Goose* [New York: Doubleday, 1924]. Black ink, watercolor, and white bodycolor over pencil on illustration board; 12-1/16 x 10-5/8". Chapin Library of Rare Books, Williams College, Gift of Bedelia C. Falls. ©1924 by Doubleday. Used by permission of Doubleday, a division of Bantam Doubleday Dell Publishing Group, Inc.

42. Roger Duvoisin (1904-1980). Born in Geneva, Switzerland; Came to the U.S. in 1925. "Dickery, Dickery Dare/The Jolly Miller," from *Mother Goose: A Comprehensive Collection of the Rhymes*. Edited by William Rose Benét [New York: The

Heritage Press, 1936]. Pen, ink, graphite, watercolor, and collage on paper; 13 x 9-3/4". Jane Voorhees Zimmerli Art Museum, Rutgers, The State University of New Jersey, Gift of Louise Fatio Duvoisin. Photo by Jack Abraham.

43a. Antonio Frasconi (born 1919). Born in Uruguay; Came to the U.S. in 1945. Title page from *The House that Jack Built* [New York: Harcourt, Brace & World, 1958]. Woodblock and collage on paper; 10-1/2 x 16-5/16". Collection of Antonio Frasconi. ©1958 by Antonio Frasconi.

43b. Antonio Frasconi (born 1919). Born in Uruguay; Came to the U.S. in 1945. "This is the cow with the crumpled horn . . . ," from *The House that Jack Built* [New York: Harcourt, Brace & World, 1958]. Woodblock and collage on paper; 10-1/4 x 16-9/16". Collection of Antonio Frasconi. ©1958 by Antonio Frasconi.

44a. Dr. Seuss (1904-1991). American. "We looked! Then, we saw him step in on the mat!," from *The Cat in the Hat* [New York: Random House, 1957]. Pen and ink on illustration board with tissue overlays—color and typescript; 12-7/16 x 18". Dr. Seuss Collection, Mandeville Special Collections Library, University of California, San Diego. ©™1957 Dr. Seuss Enterprises, L.P., ren. 1985.

44b. Dr. Seuss (1904-1991). American. "We looked! Then, we saw him step in on the mat!," from *The Cat in the Hat* [New York: Random House, 1957]. Color pencil rough, with typescript on paper; 8-1/2 x 11". Dr. Seuss Collection, Mandeville Special Collections Library, University of California, San Diego. ©™1957 Dr. Seuss Enterprises, L.P., ren. 1985.

45. Nancy Ekholm Burkert (born 1933). American. "Chippetty Tip, Chippetty Tip," from *The Scroobious Pip*. By Edward Lear [New York: Harper & Row, Publishers, 1968]. Watercolor, brush, and colored inks on paper; 10-1/4 x 16-3/4". Lent by the Artist. ©1968 by Nancy Ekholm Burkert. Used by permission of HarperCollins Publishers.

46. Alice Provensen (born 1918) and Martin Provensen (1916-1987). "Sing a Song of Sixpence," from *Mother Goose* [New York: Random House, 1976]. Pen, ink, and watercolor on paper; 8-1/2 x 6-3/8". The Kerlan Collection, University of Minnesota. ©1976 by Alice Provensen. Reprinted with the permission of Random House, Inc.

47. Hilary Knight (born 1926). American. "Owl and Pussycat out to Sea," from *The Owl and the Pussycat* [New York: Macmillan, 1983]. Watercolor, graphite, and tempera on paper; 12-

7/16 x 19-1/8". Collection of Mr. Hilary Knight. ©1983 by Hilary Knight. Reprinted with the permission of Simon & Schuster Books for Young Readers, an imprint of Simon & Schuster Children's Publishing Division.

48. Arnold Lobel (1933-1987). American. "Mary, Mary, Quite Contrary," from *The Random House Book of Mother Goose* [New York: Random House, 1986]. Pen, ink, and watercolor on paper; 7-9/16 x 15-7/8". The Estate of Arnold Lobel. ©1986 by Arnold Lobel. Reprinted with the permission of Random House, Inc.

49. Wendy Watson (born 1942). American. "Old Mother Hubbard," from *Wendy Watson's Mother Goose* [New York: Lothrop, Lee & Shepard Books, 1989]. Pen, ink, and watercolor on board; 5-3/4 x 5-13/16". Collection of Wendy Watson. ©1989 by Wendy Watson. Reprinted by permission of Lothrop, Lee & Shepard Books, an imprint of William Morrow.

50a. Eric Carle (born 1929). American. Cover from *Brown Bear, Brown Bear, What Do You See?* By Bill Martin Jr [New York: Henry Holt and Company, 1992]. Collage on paper; 12-1/4 x 19-1/4". Collection of the Artist. Loan arranged courtesy of R. Michelson Galleries, Northampton and Amherst, Massachusetts. ©1992 by Eric Carle. Published with the permission of Eric Carle and Henry Holt & Company.

50b. Eric Carle (born 1929). American. Cover from *Brown Bear, Brown Bear, What Do You See?* By Bill Martin Jr [New York: Henry Holt and Company, 1983]. Collage on paper. ID: 18 x 23-1/2". Collection of the Artist. Loan arranged courtesy of R. Michelson Galleries, Northampton and Amherst, Massachusetts.

51. Edward R. Emberley (born 1931). American. "The Drummer," from *Drummer Hoff*. Adapted by Barbara Emberley [New York: Simon & Schuster Books for Young Readers, 1967]. Woodcut; 7-7/8 x 4". Collection of the Artist. ©1967 by Ed Emberley. Reprinted with the permission of Simon & Schuster Books for Young Readers, an imprint of Simon & Schuster Children's Publishing Division.

52. Edward R. Emberley (born 1931). American. "The Cannon," from *Drummer Hoff*. Adapted by Barbara Emberley [New York: Simon & Schuster Books for Young Readers, 1967]. Woodcut; 7-11/16 x 13-1/8". Collection of the Artist. ©1967 by Ed Emberley. Reprinted with the permission of Simon & Schuster Books for Young Readers, an imprint of Simon & Schuster Children's Publishing Division.

53. Edward R. Emberley (born 1931). American. "The General," from *Drummer Hoff*. Adapted by Barbara Emberley [New York: Simon & Schuster Books for Young Readers, 1967]. Woodcut; 8-1/16 x 7-1/16". Collection of the Artist. ©1967 by Ed Emberley. Reprinted with the permission of Simon & Schuster Books for Young Readers, an imprint of Simon & Schuster Children's Publishing Division.

III. HERE AND NOW, THEN AND THERE

54a. Randolph Caldecott (1846-1886). British. "His neighbour in such trim,/Laid down his pipe, flew to the gate,/And thus accosted him," from *The Diverting History of John Gilpin*. By William Cowper [London: George Routledge and Sons, 1878]. Pen, ink, and watercolor on paper mounted on board; 6-15/16 x 4-3/8". Private Collection.

54b. Randolph Caldecott (1846-1886). British. "The youth did ride, and soon did meet/John coming back amain," from *The Diverting History of John Gilpin*. By William Cowper [London: George Routledge and Sons, 1878]. Pen, ink, and watercolor on paper mounted on board; 4-3/8 x 6-13/16". Private Collection.

55a. Kate Greenaway (1846-1901). British. "Where waters rushed and fruit trees grew," Frontispiece from *The Pied Piper of Hamelin*. By Robert Browning [London: George Routledge and Sons, 1888]. Pen, black ink, and watercolor on paper; 8-5/8 x 7-5/8". The Pierpont Morgan Library, New York. Gift of Mrs. George Nichols. ©1995 by The Pierpont Morgan Library. Norfolk only.

55b. Kate Greenaway (1846-1901). British. "There was a rustling," from *The Pied Piper of Hamelin*. By Robert Browning [London: George Routledge and Sons, 1888]. Pen, black ink, and watercolor on paper; 9-7/16" x 8". The Pierpont Morgan Library, New York. Gift of Miss Jane Page and Mr. Mark Page. Memphis and Wilmington [not illus.].

56. Elmer Boyd Smith (1860-1943). American. "The Pig Family," from *The Country Book* [Boston: Houghton Mifflin Company, 1924]. Watercolor, pen, and ink on paper; 8-7/8 x 12-9/16". Kendra Krienke and Allan Daniel, New York City.

57a. Louis-Maurice Boutet de Monvel (1851-1913). French. "Jeanne before the Dauphin," from *Jeanne d'Arc*. [Paris: Plon, Nourrit & Co., 1896]. Watercolor on paper; 9-1/4 x 12-1/4". Memorial Art Gallery of the University of Rochester. Gift of Mr. Simon N. Stein. Norfolk only.

57b. Louis-Maurice Boutet de Monvel (1851-1913). French. "Saint Michel," from *Jeanne d'Arc*.

[Paris: Plon, Nourrit & Co., 1896]. Watercolor on paper; 9-1/2 x 12-1/2". Memorial Art Gallery of the University of Rochester. Gift of Mr. Simon N. Stein. Memphis only [not illus.].

57c. Louis-Maurice Boutet de Monvel (1851-1913). French. "The Consultation," from *Jeanne d'Arc* [Paris: Plon, Nourrit & Co., 1896]. Watercolor on paper; 9-1/4 x 12-1/2". Memorial Art Gallery of the University of Rochester. Gift of Mr. Simon N. Stein. Wilmington only [not illus.].

58. Esphyr Slobodkina (born 1908). American. "Nanny Goat and Horse," 1938, from *The Wonderful Feast* [New York: Lothrop, Lee & Shepard Company, 1955]. Collage on cardboard; 9 x 18-3/8". Northeast Children's Literature Collections, Archives and Special Collections Department, Senator Thomas J. Dodd Research Center, University Libraries, University of Connecticut, Storrs. ©1955 by Esphyr Slobodkina. Reprinted with the permission of Lothrop, Lee & Shepard Company, an imprint of William Morrow.

59. Barbara Cooney (born 1917). American. "He packed the candles the family made," from *Ox-Cart Man*. By Donald Hall [New York: The Viking Press, 1979]. Acrylic on paper; 10 x 15". de Grummond Children's Literature Collection, University of Southern Mississippi. ©1979 by Barbara Cooney Porter. Porter illustrations. Used by permission of Viking Penguin, a division of Penguin Books USA Inc.

60. Barbara Cooney (born 1917). American. "Miss Rumphius Watching Children Gather Lupine," from *Miss Rumphius* [New York: Viking Penguin, 1982]. Acrylic, colored pencil, and pastel on gesso-coated percale, mounted on acid-free illustration board; 8-1/4 x 20-1/4". Lent by the artist; courtesy of the Bowdoin College Museum of Art, Brunswick, Maine. ©1982 by Barbara Cooney Porter. Porter illustrations. Used by permission of Viking Penguin, a division of Penguin Books USA Inc.

61. Hardie Gramatky (1907-1979). American. "Little Toot with Reflection in the Water," from *Little Toot* [New York: G. P. Putnam's Sons, 1939]. Pen, ink, and watercolor on paper; 10-1/2 x 10-1/2". Spencer Collection, The New York Public Library, Astor, Lenox and Tilden Foundations. ©1939 by Hardie Gramatky. Reprinted with permission of The Putnam & Grosset Group.

62. Virginia Lee Burton (1909-1968). American. "No Steam Shovels Wanted," from *Mike Mulligan and his Steam Shovel*. [Boston: Houghton Mifflin Company, 1939]. Lithograph; 11 x 14-3/8". Department of Special Collections, University of Oregon Library. ©1939 by Virginia Lee Burton.

Reprinted with permission of the Houghton Mifflin Company.

63. Virginia Lee Burton (1909-1968). American. "Country," "Growing Suburbia," "City," and "Moving out to the Country," from *The Little House* [Boston: Houghton Mifflin Company, 1942]. Crayon and gouache on paper; 8-3/8 x 10-1/4"; 8-7/8 x 10"; 7-3/8 x 10-3/4"; and 8-1/2 x 9-3/4". The Kerlan Collection, University of Minnesota. ©1942 by Virginia Lee Burton. Reprinted with permission of the Houghton Mifflin Company.

64. Ezra Jack Keats (1916-1983). American. "Crunch, crunch, crunch, his feet sank into the snow," from *The Snowy Day* [New York: The Viking Press, 1962]. Collage and tempera on board; 9-7/8 x 20". de Grummond Children's Literature Collection, University of Southern Mississippi. ©1962 by Ezra Jack Keats, ren. ©1990 by Martin Pope. Used by permission of Viking Penguin, a division of Penguin Books USA Inc.

65. Ezra Jack Keats (1916-1983). American. "Jennie's Hat Being Decorated by Birds," from *Jennie's Hat* [New York: Harper & Row Publishers, 1966]. Collage and tempera on board; 10 x 20". de Grummond Children's Literature Collection, University of Southern Mississippi. ©1966 by Ezra Jack Keats. Used by permission of HarperCollins Publishers.

66. Ezra Jack Keats (1916-1983). American. "Peter chasing Letter," from *A Letter to Amy* [New York: Harper & Row Publishers, 1968]. Collage and tempera on board; 10 x 20-1/8". de Grummond Children's Literature Collection, University of Southern Mississippi. ©1968 by Ezra Jack Keats. Used by permission of HarperCollins Publishers.

67. John Steptoe (1950-1989). American. "Naw, my momma said he can't go in the park cause the last time . . . ," from *Stevie* [New York: Harper & Row Publishers, 1969]. Studio marker with pastel overpainting on paper; 8-3/4 x 6-3/4". The John Steptoe Collection. ©1969 by John Steptoe. Reprinted with the approval of the Estate of John Steptoe and HarperCollins Publishers. Used by permission of HarperCollins Publishers.

68. James Daugherty (1889-1974). American. "Andy Pulling Thorn from Lion's Paw," from *Andy and the Lion* [New York: The Viking Press, 1938]. Pen and ink on paper; 20-1/2 x 15-1/4". Spencer Collection, The New York Public Library, Astor, Lenox and Tilden Foundations. ©1938 by James Daugherty, renewed 1966 by James Daugherty. Used by permission of Viking Penguin, a division of Penguin Books USA Inc.

69a. Esphyr Slobodkina (born 1908). Born in Siberia; Came to the U.S. in 1928. "Man Under Tree with Caps," 1940-47, from *Caps For Sale* [New York: William R. Scott, Inc., 1940]. Pen, ink, and watercolor on paper; 14 x 12". The Kerlan Collection, University of Minnesota. ©1947 by Esphyr Slobodkina. Used by permission of HarperCollins Publishers.

69b. Esphyr Slobodkina (born 1908). Born in Siberia; Came to the U.S. in 1928. "Monkeys in Tree with Caps," 1940-47, from *Caps for Sale* [New York: William R. Scott, Inc., 1940]. Pen, ink, and watercolor on paper; 11-1/2 x 16". The Kerlan Collection, University of Minnesota. ©1947 by Esphyr Slobodkina. Used by permission of HarperCollins Publishers.

70. Robert McCloskey (born 1914). American. "Policeman Stopping Traffic," from *Make Way for Ducklings* [New York: The Viking Press, 1941]. Graphite and crayon on paper; 18 x 24". May Massee Collection, William Allen White Library, Emporia State University. ©1941 by Robert McCloskey, renewed ©1969 by Robert McCloskey. Used by permission of Viking Penguin, a division of Penguin Books USA Inc.

71. Robert McCloskey (born 1914). American. Sketch for "Louisburg Square from Above," ca. 1940, from *Make Way for Ducklings* [New York: The Viking Press, 1941]. Graphite and charcoal on paper; 13-1/8 x 16-7/16". Courtesy of The Boston Public Library Print Department. ©1941 by Robert McCloskey.

72. Robert McCloskey (born 1914). American. "Out of Whale's Mouth," from *Burt Dow, Deepwater Man* [New York: The Viking Press, 1963]. Tempera on paper; 17 x 26". May Massee Collection, William Allen White Library, Emporia State University. ©1963 by Robert McCloskey, renewed ©1991 by Robert McCloskey. Used by permission of Viking Penguin, a division of Penguin Books USA Inc.

73. Charles Mikolaycak (1937-1993). American. "Jim waked. He clutched the bedclothes up to his chin . . . ," from *Shipwreck*. By Vera Cumberlege [Chicago: Follett Publishing Co., 1974]. Graphite with colored oil glaze overlays on paper; 8-3/4 x 12-1/2". The Kerlan Collection, University of Minnesota. ©1995 by Carole Kismaric Mikolaycak.

74. Laurent de Brunhoff (born 1925). Born in Paris, France; Came to the U.S. in 1985. "Babar Crosses the Rockies," from *Babar Comes to America* [New York: Random House, Inc., 1965]. Watercolor on paper; 10-1/2 x 16-1/2". Courtesy of Norfolk Southern Corporation. Reprinted with the permission of Random House, Inc.

75. Donald Crews (born 1938). American. "Moving Freight Train," ca. 1986, variant of a drawing from *Freight Train* [New York: Greenwillow, 1986]. Watercolor on paper; 10 x 16". Mazza Collection Galleria, The University of Findlay.

76a. Tomi Ungerer (born 1931). Born in Strasbourg, France; Came to the U.S. in 1957. "Their arrival in Paris was a triumph," from *The Beast of Monsieur Racine* [New York: Farrar, Straus & Giroux, Inc., 1971]. Chinese ink on tracing paper; 18-29/32 x 23-5/8". ©1971 Tomi Ungerer. Donation Tomi Ungerer, Musées de la Ville de Strasbourg.

76b. Tomi Ungerer (born 1931). Born in Strasbourg, France; Came to the U.S. in 1957. "Their arrival in Paris was a triumph," from *The Beast of Monsieur Racine* [New York: Farrar, Straus & Giroux, Inc., 1971]. Wash drawing of colored inks on paper; 12-13/16 x 22-7/16". Donation Tomi Ungerer, Musées de la Ville de Strasbourg [not illus.].

77. Vladimir Radunsky (born 1954). Born in Russia; Came to the U.S. in 1982. "A lady came to the station with a pan, a divan . . . ," from *The Pup Grew Up!* By Samuel Marshak [New York: Henry Holt & Co., 1989]. Acrylic on paper; 15-3/8 x 11". Collection of Brenda Bowen. ©1989 by Vladimir Radunsky. Reprinted with permission of Henry Holt & Company.

78. Chris Van Allsburg (born 1949). American. "The Polar Express Entering the North Pole," from *The Polar Express* [Boston: Houghton Mifflin Company, 1985]. Gouache on paper; 9 x 22". Justin G. Schiller (Personal Collection). ©1985 by Chris Van Allsburg. Reprinted with permission of the Houghton Mifflin Company.

79. Dr. Seuss (1904-1991). American. "Then he slid down the chimney," from *How the Grinch Stole Christmas* [New York: Random House, 1957]. Pencil and ink, with typescript; 13-3/8 x 19-1/8". Dr. Seuss Collection, Mandeville Special Collections Library, University of California, San Diego. ©™1957 Dr. Seuss Enterprises, L.P., ren. 1985.

80. William Joyce (born 1957). American. "Mrs. Claus Led Them into an Enormous Room," from *Santa Calls* [New York: HarperCollins Publishers, 1993]. Acrylic on bristol board; 10 x 28". Collection of William Joyce. ©1993 by William Joyce. Used by permission of HarperCollins Publishers.

81a. Beatrix Potter (1866-1943). British. "Mice tailoring with cat looking through window," from first version of *The Tailor of Gloucester*, 1901 [unpublished]. Watercolor on paper; 6-1/4 x 8-7/8". Rare Book Department, The Free Library of Philadelphia. ©1986 by Frederick Warne & Co. Norfolk only.

81b. Beatrix Potter (1866-1943). British. Frontispiece from first version of *The Tailor of Gloucester*, 1901 [unpublished]. Watercolor, pen, and ink on paper; 4 x 3-1/4". Rare Book Department, The Free Library, Philadelphia. Memphis only [not illus.].

81c. Beatrix Potter (1866-1943). British. "Lady Mouse," from first version of *The Tailor of Gloucester*, 1901 [unpublished]. Watercolor on paper; 9 x 7". Rare Book Department, The Free Library, Philadelphia. Wilmington only [not illus.].

82a. Ernest H. Shepard (1879-1976). British. "Winnie the Pooh Marooned with Ten Jars of Honey," from *Winnie the Pooh*. By A. A. Milne [New York: E. P. Dutton, 1926]. Pen and black ink, scratched, some corrections in white lead, on white drawing board; 5-1/2 x 10-3/8". The Pierpont Morgan Library, New York. Gift of Mr. and Mrs. Malcolm P. Aldrich. ©1926 by E. P. Dutton, renewed ©1954 by A. A. Milne. Used by permission of Dutton Children's Books, a division of Penguin Books USA Inc. Norfolk only.

82b. Ernest H. Shepard (1879-1976). British. "Kanga preparing the bath," from *Winnie the Pooh*. By A. A. Milne [New York: E. P. Dutton, 1926]. Pen and black ink on white drawing board, scratched in white lead; 5-1/2 x 7-3/8". The Pierpont Morgan Library, New York. Gift of Mr. and Mrs. Malcolm P. Aldrich. Memphis and Wilmington [not illus.].

83. Ernest H. Shepard (1879-1976). British. "Christopher Robin's Party for Pooh," from *Winnie the Pooh*. By A. A. Milne [New York: E. P. Dutton, 1926]. Graphite, pen, and black ink on paper; 9-1/2 x 14". Collection of Lynda J. Robb. Norfolk only [not illus.].

84. Harrison Cady (1877-1970). American. "Peter Rabbit with Uncle Billy Possum," from *The Adventures of Peter Cottontail* [Boston: Little, Brown & Company, 1914]. Pen and ink and wash on illustration board; 9-7/16 x 13". Kendra Krienke and Allan Daniel, New York City.

85. Harrison Cady (1877-1970). American. "Woodland Serenade," from *St. Nicholas Magazine*, 1907. Pen, ink, and gouache on paper; 26 x 18-1/2". Prints and Photographs Division, The Library of Congress.

86. Boris Artzybasheff (1899-1965). Born in Kharkov, Ukraine; Came to the U.S. in 1919. "The Jack Daw," from *Creatures*. By Padraic Colum [New York: Macmillan, 1927]. Watercolor and gouache on paper; 17 x 12". Courtesy of The Boston Public Library Print Department, John D. Merriam Collection. Reprinted with the permission of Simon & Schuster Books for Young Readers, an imprint of Simon & Schuster Children's Publishing Division.

87. Dr. Seuss (1904-1991). American. "They laughed and they laughed," from *Horton Hatches the Egg* [New York: Random House, Inc., 1940]. Graphite and watercolor on paper; 10-13/16 x 17". Dr. Seuss Collection, Mandeville Special Collections Library, University of California, San Diego. ©™1940 Dr. Seuss Enterprises, L.P., ren. 1968.

88. Gustaf Tenggren (1896-1970). Born in Magra, Sweden; Came to the U.S. in 1920. "There he was, running around with his nose to the ground," from *The Poky Little Puppy*. By Janette S. Lowrey [New York: The Golden Press, 1942]. Tempera on posterboard; 7-1/2 x 13-1/2". The Kerlan Collection, University of Minnesota. ©1942 by Western Publishing Company, Inc., renewed 1970. Used by permission.

89a. Clement Hurd (1908-1988). American. "Goodnight room," from *Goodnight Moon*. By Margaret Wise Brown [New York: Harper & Row Publishers, 1947]. Tempera on posterboard; 6-7/8 x 16-1/4". The Kerlan Collection, University of Minnesota. ©1947 by Clement Hurd, ren. 1975 by Edith T. Hurd, Clement Hurd, John Thacher Hurd, and George Hellyer, as Trustees of the Edith and Clement Hurd 1982 Trust. Used by permission of HarperCollins Publishers.

89b. Clement Hurd (1908-1988). American. "Goodnight noises everywhere," from *Goodnight Moon*. By Margaret Wise Brown [New York: Harper & Row Publishers, 1947]. Tempera on posterboard; 6-7/8 x 16-1/4". The Kerlan Collection, University of Minnesota. ©1947 by Clement Hurd, ren. 1975 by Edith T. Hurd, Clement Hurd, John Thacher Hurd, and George Hellyer, as Trustees of the Edith and Clement Hurd 1982 Trust. Used by permission of HarperCollins Publishers.

90. Garth Williams (born 1912). American. Alternate cover for *Charlotte's Web*, ca. 1952. By E. B. White [New York: Harper & Row Publishers, 1952]. Pen, ink, and watercolor on paper; 8-1/4 x 7". Estate of Ursula Nordstrom.

91. Lillian Hoban (n.d.). American. "Family Eating Bread and Jam," from *Bread and Jam for Frances*. By Russell Hoban [New York: Harper &

Row Publishers, 1964]. Graphite on paper; 10 x 8-3/8". Northeast Children's Literature Collections, Archives and Special Collections Department, Senator Thomas J. Dodd Research Center, University Libraries, University of Connecticut, Storrs. ©1964 by Lillian Hoban. Used by permission of HarperCollins Publishers.

92. Tasha Tudor (born 1915). American. "There was the Big Tent . . . ," from *Corgiville Fair*, 1970 [New York: Thomas Y. Crowell Company, 1971]. Watercolor on paper; 7-1/4 x 20-15/16" (sight). Collection of Colonel Thomas Tudor, Courtesy of The Pierpont Morgan Library, New York. ©1971 Tasha Tudor.

93. Don Freeman (1908-1978). American. Preliminary sketch for "Norman Lecturing to Guests at the Majestic Museum," ca. 1959, for *Norman the Doorman* [New York: The Viking Press, 1959]. Colored pencil and crayon on paper; 8-7/8 x 11-13/16". May Massee Collection, William Allen White Library, Emporia State University.

94. Petra Mathers (born 1945). Born in Germany; Came to the U.S. in 1968. " 'Yes,' she said and flung the covers back. Victor's heart jumped and his knees gave way," from *Victor and Christabel* [New York: Alfred A. Knopf, Inc., 1993]. Watercolor on paper; 11 x 13-1/2". Collection of Petra Mathers. ©1993 by Petra Mathers. Reprinted with permission of Alfred A. Knopf, Inc., an imprint of Random House, Inc.

95. William Steig (born 1907). American. "Dr. De Soto fastened his extractor to the bad tooth," from *Dr. De Soto* [New York: Farrar, Straus & Giroux, Inc. 1982]. Pen and ink, graphite, and watercolor on paper; 12-1/8 x 9". Collection of Melinda Franceschini. ©1982 by William Steig. Reprinted by permission of Farrar, Straus & Giroux, Inc.

96. William Steig (born 1907). American. "Zeke leaving the family living room having put them to sleep with his harmonica playing," from *Zeke Pippin* [New York: HarperCollins Publishers, 1994]. Pen, ink, and watercolor on paper; 7-3/4 x 15-1/2". Collection of Holly M. McGhee. Used by permission of HarperCollins Publishers.

97a. Peter Newell (1862-1924). American. "Pet Shop with Mice Escaping," from *The Hole Book* [New York: Harper Brothers, 1908]. Gouache over graphite on illustration board; 8-1/4 x 6-3/8". Philip Hofer Bequest, Department of Printing & Graphic Arts, Houghton Library, Harvard University. Norfolk only.

97b. Peter Newell (1862-1924). American. "Sister Sue on the Swing," from *The Hole Book* [New York: Harper Brothers, 1908]. Gouache over graphite on illustration board; 8-1/4 x 6-7/16". Philip Hofer Bequest, Department of Printing & Graphic Arts, Houghton Library, Harvard University. Memphis only [not illus.].

97c. Peter Newell (1862-1924). American. "Cook Running from Gushing Boiler," from *The Hole Book* [New York: Harper Brothers, 1908]. Gouache over graphite on illustration board; 8-3/8 x 6-7/16". Philip Hofer Bequest, Department of Printing & Graphic Arts, Houghton Library, Harvard University. Wilmington only [not illus.].

98. Richard Egielski (born 1952). American. "I fancy that he shrank/Because of all the India ink that Mr. Master drank," from *The Little Father*. By Gelett Burgess [New York: Farrar, Straus & Giroux, Inc., 1985]. Watercolor on paper; 5 x 6-1/2". Collection of Richard Egielski. ©1985 by Richard Egielski. Reprinted by permission of Farrar, Straus & Giroux, Inc.

99. Richard Egielski (born 1952). American. "Louis attacked by hamburgers, salamis, roast beefs, etc.," from *Louis the Fish*. By Arthur Yorinks [New York: Farrar, Straus & Giroux, Inc., 1980]. Watercolor on paper; 6-1/2 x 12". Collection of Richard Egielski. ©1980 by Richard Egielski. Reprinted by permission of Farrar, Straus & Giroux, Inc.

100. Wanda Gág (1893-1946). American. "Old Man Confronted by Cats in a Landscape," from *Millions of Cats* [New York: Coward, McCann & Geohegan, 1928]. Pen and ink on paper; 6-5/8 x 9-3/4". The Kerlan Collection, University of Minnesota. Reprinted with permission of Coward-McCann, an imprint of The Putnam & Grosset Group.

101. Dr. Seuss (1904-1991). American. "And he flung out his arms to push Bartholomew off" [Bartholomew on parapet with magnificent hat], from *The 500 Hats of Bartholomew Cubbins* [New York: Vanguard Press, 1938]. Crayon, graphite, and chinese white on illustration board; 15-3/16 x 11-7/8". Dr. Seuss Collection, Mandeville Special Collections Library, University of California, San Diego. ©1938 Dr. Seuss Enterprises, L.P., ren. 1965.

102. Crockett Johnson (1906-1975). American. "He made lots of buildings full of windows," from *Harold and the Purple Crayon* [New York: Harper & Row Publishers, 1955]. Pen, black ink, and gouache on paper; 6-1/8 x 9-3/4". Northeast Children's Literature Collections, Archives and Special Collections Department, Senator Thomas J. Dodd Research Center, University Libraries, University of Connecticut, Storrs. ©1955 by

Crockett Johnson. Used by permission of HarperCollins Publishers.

103. Maurice Sendak (born 1928). American. ". . . and made him King of all wild things," from *Where the Wild Things Are* [New York: Harper & Row Publishers, 1963]. Pen, ink, and watercolor on paper; 9-3/4 x 22". ©1962 by Maurice Sendak. Courtesy, Maurice Sendak and The Rosenbach Museum & Library. Used by permission of HarperCollins Publishers.

104. Maurice Sendak (born 1928). American. "And they put that batter up to Bake a Delicious Mickey-cake," from *In the Night Kitchen*. [New York: Harper & Row Publishers, 1970]. Watercolor on paper; 11-5/8 x 17-3/8". ©1970 by Maurice Sendak. Courtesy, Maurice Sendak and The Rosenbach Museum & Library. Used by permission of HarperCollins Publishers.

105. Chris Van Allsburg (born 1949). American. "Monkeys Steal food, Miss one turn," from *Jumanji* [Boston: Houghton Mifflin Company, 1981]. Graphite on paper; 19 x 21". Lent by Chris and Lisa Van Allsburg. ©1981 by Chris Van Allsburg. Reprinted with permission of Houghton Mifflin Company.

106. David Wiesner (born 1956). American. "Frogs Flying on Lilypads," from *Tuesday* [New York: Clarion Books, 1991]. Watercolor on paper; 8 x 20-1/2". Collection of David Wiesner. ©1991 by David Wiesner. Reprinted with permission of Clarion Books, an imprint of Houghton Mifflin Company.

107. David Wiesner (born 1956). American. "At last, the blue ribbon at the state fair is mine!," from *June 29, 1999* [New York: Clarion Books, 1992]. Watercolor on paper; 10-1/2 x 20-1/2". Collection of David Wiesner. ©1992 by David Wiesner. Reprinted with permission of Clarion Books, an imprint of Houghton Mifflin Company.

108. William Joyce (born 1957). American. "'Hooray!' yelled the Lazardos and they launched into the Hokey Pokey," from *Dinosaur Bob and His Adventures with the Family Lazardo*, rev. ed. [New York: HarperCollins Publishers, 1995]. Oil on bristol board; 13-3/8 x 27". Collection of William Joyce. ©1995 by William Joyce. Used by permission of HarperCollins Publishers.

109. Peter Sís (born 1949). Born in Brünn, Czechoslovakia; Came to the U.S. in 1982. "I Made a Mechanical Dragon," from *The Dragons Are Singing Tonight*. By Jack Prelutsky [New York: Greenwillow Books, 1993]. Oil and mixed media on bristol board; 12 x 18". Collection of Peter Sís. ©1993 by Peter Sís. Reprinted with the permission of Green-Willow Books, a division of William Morrow and Company, Inc.

110. Peter Sís (born 1949). Born in Brünn, Czechoslovakia; Came to the U.S. in 1982. "I follow the determined cat back across the ancient bridge," from *The Three Golden Keys* [New York: Doubleday, 1994]. Oil pastel on gesso with gold border; 12 x 18". Collection of Peter Sís. ©1994 by Peter Sís. Used by permission of Doubleday, a division of Bantam Doubleday Dell Publishing Group, Inc.

111. Petra Mathers (born 1945). Born in Germany; Came to the U.S. in 1968. "Suddenly a stray cat leaped onto the piano," from *Mrs. Merriwether's Musical Cat*. By Carol Purdy [New York: G. P. Putnam's Sons, 1994]. Watercolor on paper; 11 x 17". Private Collection. ©1994 by Petra Mathers. Reprinted with permission of G. P. Putnam's Sons, an imprint of The Putnam & Grosset Group.

112. Vladimir Radunsky ((born 1954). Born in Russia; Came to the U.S. in 1982. "But suddenly, he's playing wildly . . . he slaps the strings," from *The Maestro Plays*. By Bill Martin Jr [New York: Henry Holt & Co., 1993]. Acrylic and collage on paper; 10 x 10". Collection of Vladimir Radunsky ©1993 by Vladimir Radunsky. Reprinted with permission of Harcourt Brace and Company.

113. Emily Arnold McCully (born 1939). American. "The Family Arrives at the Ship," from *The Amazing Felix* [New York: G. P. Putnam's Sons, 1993]. Watercolor with pastel highlights on paper; 13-7/8 x 27-1/4". Collection of Emily Arnold McCully. ©1993 by Emily Arnold McCully. Reprinted with permission of G. P. Putnam's Sons, an imprint of The Putnam & Grosset Group.

114. Emily Arnold McCully (born 1939). American. "Mirette Raced into Bellini's Room," from *Mirette on the High Wire* [New York: G. P. Putnam's Sons, 1992]. Watercolor with pastel highlights on paper; 9 x 19". Collection of Emily Arnold McCully. ©1992 by Emily Arnold McCully. Reprinted with permission of G. P. Putnam's Sons, an imprint of the Putnam & Grosset Group.

115. Will H. Bradley (1868-1962). American. "Peter Poodle," Frontispiece from *Peter Poodle, Toy Maker to the King*. [New York: Dodd, Mead & Company, 1906]. Chromolithograph; 11-3/16 x 14-3/16". Lent by The Metropolitan Museum of Art, Gift of Fern Bradley Dufner, 1952. ©1995, The Metropolitan Museum of Art.

116. Maud Petersham (1890-1971) American, and Miska Petersham (1888-1960); Born in Hungary; Came to the U.S. in 1912. "The Goat Was Not Easy to Catch," from *The Poppy-Seed Cakes*. By

Margery Clark [Garden City, L.I.: Doubleday, Doran and Company, 1924]. Pen, ink, and gouache on paper; 6 x 4-1/4". Mazza Collection Galleria, The University of Findlay. ©1924 by Doubleday, a division of Bantam Doubleday Dell Publishing Group, Inc. Used by permission of Doubleday, a division of Bantam Doubleday Dell Publishing Group, Inc.

117. Ingri Parin d'Aulaire (1904-1980) Born in Konigsberg, Norway; Came to the U.S. in 1929 and Edgar Parin d'Aulaire (1898-1986) Born in Munich, Germany; Came to the U.S. in 1929. Cover proof of *Ola*, 1932 [Garden City, L.I.: Doubleday, Doran and Company, 1939]. Hand-pulled lithograph on paper; 13-9/16 x 18-13/16". Courtesy of The Boston Public Library, Print Department, John D. Merriam Collection.

118. Tasha Tudor (born 1915). American. "October," from *A Time to Keep: Tasha Tudor's Book of Holidays* [New York: Rand McNally & Company, 1977]. Pen, ink, and watercolor on paper; 12-11/16 x 18-3/4". Collection of Colonel Thomas Tudor. ©1977 Tasha Tudor. Reprinted with permission of Checkerboard Press.

119a. Palmer Cox (1840-1924). Born in Granby, Quebec, Canada; Came to the U.S. in 1863. "The Brownies and the Automobiles," n.d. [unpublished]. Pen and ink on light illustration board; 7 x 7-1/2". Rare Book Department, The Free Library of Philadelphia. Norfolk only.

119b. Palmer Cox (1840-1924). Born in Granby, Quebec, Canada; Came to the U.S. in 1863. "The Brownies at the Race Track," from *Another Brownie Book* [New York: The Century Co., 1890]. Pen and ink on light illustration board; 11-1/2 x 7-3/16". Rare Book Department, The Free Library of Philadelphia. Memphis only [not illus.].

119c. Palmer Cox (1840-1924). Born in Granby, Quebec, Canada; Came to the U.S. in 1863. "The Brownies in the Toy Shop," from *The Brownies: Their Book* [New York: The Century Co., 1887]. Pen and ink on light illustration board; 7 x 7-1/2". Rare Book Department, The Free Library of Philadelphia. Wilmington only [not illus.].

120a. Gelett Burgess (1866-1951). American. "Patience," from *Goops and How to Be Them* [New York: Frederick A. Stokes, 1900]. Pen and ink on illustration board with text pasted on; 9-3/8 x 7-1/4". Betsy B. Shirley Collection of American Children's Literature, The Beinecke Library of Yale University.

120b. Gelett Burgess (1866-1951). American. "Politeness," from *Goops and How to Be Them* [New York: Frederick A. Stokes, 1900]. Pen and ink on illustration board with text pasted on; 9-3/8 x 7-1/4". Betsy B. Shirley Collection of American Children's Literature, The Beinecke Library of Yale University.

120c. Gelett Burgess (1866-1951). American. "Helpfulness," from *Goops and How to Be Them* [New York: Frederick A. Stokes, 1900]. Pen and ink on illustration board with text pasted on; 9-3/8 x 7-1/4". Betsy B. Shirley Collection of American Children's Literature, The Beinecke Library of Yale University.

121. Johnny Gruelle (1880-1938). American. Cover from *Raggedy Ann in Cookie Land* [Chicago: P. F. Volland & Co., 1931]. Watercolor and ink on illustration board; 19-3/4 x 12-3/4". Kendra Krienke and Allan Daniel, New York City.

122. William Pène du Bois (1916-1993). American. Cover from *Giant Otto* [New York: The Viking Press, 1936]. Pen, ink, and watercolor on paper; 7-1/4 x 13-3/4". Private Collection. Courtesy of Illustration House. Used by permission of Viking Penguin, a division of Penguin Books USA Inc.

123a. Robert Lawson (1892-1957). American. "Ferdinand sitting in the bull ring," from *The Story of Ferdinand*. By Munro Leaf [New York: The Viking Press, 1936]. Pen and black and white ink on paper; 9-7/16 x 8". The Pierpont Morgan Library, New York. Gift of Mary Flagler Cary Charitable Trust. ©1936 by Munro Leaf and Robert Lawson, ren. ©1964 by Munro Leaf and John W. Boyd. Used by permission of Viking Penguin, a division of Penguin Books USA Inc.

123b. Robert Lawson (1892-1957). American. "Stung!," from *The Story of Ferdinand*. By Munro Leaf [New York: The Viking Press, 1936]. Pen and black and white ink on paper; 9-7/16 x 8-1/16". The Pierpont Morgan Library, New York. Gift of Mary Flagler Cary Charitable Trust Memphis and Wilmington [not illus.].

124. Palmer Cox (1840-1924). Born in Granby, Quebec, Canada; Came to the U.S. in 1863. "The Bull Broke Through the Gate," from *The Brownies Around the World* [New York: The Century Co., 1894]. Pen and ink on paper; 9-7/16 x 9-9/16". Prints and Photographs Division, The Library of Congress.

125. Hans Augusto Rey (1898-1977). Born in Hamburg, Germany; Came to the U.S. in 1940. "George Sees Yellow Hat," from *Curious George* [Boston: Houghton Mifflin Company, 1940]. Colored pencil on paper; 10-1/2 x 8-7/8". de Grummond Children's Literature Collection, University of Southern Mississippi. ©1940 by Margret E. Rey. Reprinted with permission of Houghton Mifflin Company.

126. Hans Augusto Rey (1898-1977). Born in Hamburg, Germany; Came to the U.S. in 1940. "George Floating Over City with Balloon," from *Curious George* [Boston: Houghton Mifflin Company, 1940]. Pen, ink, and watercolor on paper (mounted on stiff paper); 12-3/8 x 9-3/8". Department of Special Collections, University of Oregon Library. ©1940 by Margret E. Rey. Reprinted with permission of Houghton Mifflin Company.

127. Dr. Seuss (1904-1991). American. "Then Yertle the Turtle was perched up so high," from *Yertle the Turtle and Other Stories* [New York: Random House, 1950]. Pen, ink, and chinese white on illustration board; 17-1/2 x 13-7/8". Dr. Seuss Collection, Mandeville Special Collections Library, University of California, San Diego. ©™ 1950 Dr. Seuss Enterprises, L.P., ren. 1977.

128. James Marshall (1942-1992). American. Cover from *George and Martha Back in Town* [Boston: Houghton Mifflin Company, 1972]. Blue ink and watercolor on paper; 7 x 7". Northeast Children's Literature Collections, Archives and Special Collections Department, Senator Thomas J. Dodd Research Center, University Libraries, University of Connecticut, Storrs. ©1972 by James Marshall. Reprinted with permission of Houghton Mifflin Company.

129. Roger Duvoisin (1904-1980). Born in Geneva, Switzerland; Came to the U.S. in 1925 "Then suddenly she stumbled on something she had never seen before . . . ," from *Petunia* [New York: Alfred A. Knopf, Inc., 1950]. Pen, ink, watercolor, tempera, acetate, and gouache on paper with text added; 10-3/16 x 16-11/16". Jane Voorhees Zimmerli Art Museum, Rutgers, the State University of New Jersey, Gift of Louise Fatio Duvoisin. Photo by: Jack Abraham. Reprinted by permission of Alfred A. Knopf, Inc., an imprint of Random House, Inc.

130. Ludwig Bemelmans (1898-1962). Born in Meran, Tyrol, Austria, Came to the U.S. in 1914. "They left at half past nine in two straight lines," from *Madeline* [New York: The Viking Press, 1939]. Pen, ink, and watercolor on paper; 15-1/4 x 13". Collection of Mr. and Mrs. Benjamin Eisenstat. ©1939 by Ludwig Bemelmans, renewed ©1987 by Madeleine Bemelmans and Barbara Bemelmans Marciano. Used by permission of Viking Penguin, a division of Penguin Books USA Inc.

131. Hilary Knight (born 1926). American "Eloise with Skibberdee," 1954, unpublished drawing from *Eloise*. By Kay Thompson [New York: Simon and Schuster, 1955]. Pen and ink on paper; 7 x 9-5/16". Collection of Mr. Hilary Knight. ©1996 by Hilary Knight.

132. Hilary Knight (born 1926). American. Alternate cover from *Eloise in Paris*. By Kay Thompson [New York: Simon and Schuster, 1957]. Graphite and watercolor on paper; 11-1/4 x 7-7/8". Collection of Mr. Hilary Knight. ©1996 by Hilary Knight.

133. James Marshall (1942-1992). American. "The Guests Arrive," from *The Stupids Have a Ball*. By Harry Allard [Boston: Houghton Mifflin Company, 1978]. Pen and ink on paper; 7 x 8-1/2". de Grummond Children's Literature Collection, University of Southern Mississippi. ©1978 by James Marshall. Reprinted with permission of the Houghton Mifflin Company.

IV. HIGH ADVENTURE

134. Gennady Spirin (born 1948). Born in Russia; Came to the U. S. in 1991. "I must have slept a long time," from *Gulliver's Adventures in Lilliput*. By Jonathan Swift, retold by Ann Keay Beneduce [New York: Philomel Books, 1993]. Watercolor on paper; 14 x 20". Collection of Sara Jane Kasperzak ©1993 by Gennady Spirin. Reprinted with permission of Philomel Books, an imprint of The Putnam & Grosset Group.

135. Felix O. C. Darley (1822-1888). American. "Rip Amusing Children," from *Rip Van Winkle*. By Washington Irving [New York: n.p., 1848]. Pen and ink on paper; 8-3/4 x 11-1/8". Munson-Williams-Proctor Institute, Utica, New York.

136. N. C. Wyeth (1882-1945). American. "It was with some difficulty that he found his way to his own house," from *Rip Van Winkle*. By Washington Irving [Philadelphia: David McKay Company, 1921]. Oil on canvas; 48 x 38". Millport Conservancy.

137. Maud Petersham (1890-1971) American, and Miska Petersham (1888-1960) Born in Hungary; Came to the U.S. in 1912. "He Found His House Gone to Decay," from *Rip Van Winkle*. By Washington Irving [New York: Macmillan, 1951]. Pen and ink on paper with acetate overlay; 9-3/4 x 8-1/2". Department of Special Collections, University of Oregon Library. Reprinted with the permission of Simon & Schuster Books for Young Readers, an imprint of Simon & Schuster Children's Publishing Division.

138. Thomas Locker (born 1937). American. "Rip Returns Home," from *Rip Van Winkle*. By Washington Irving [New York: Dial Books, 1988]. Oil on canvas; 32 x 40". Collection of Thomas Locker, Courtesy of Elizabeth Stone Gallery. ©1988 by Thomas Locker. Used by permission of Dial Books for Young Readers, a division of Penguin Books USA Inc.

139. E. W. Kemble (1861-1933). American. Frontispiece from *Adventures of Huckleberry Finn*. By Mark Twain [New York: Charles L. Webster & Co., 1884]. Pen and ink on paper; 15-1/4 x 11-1/4". The Mark Twain House, Hartford, Connecticut.

140. Barry Moser (born 1940). American. "Never Saying a Word," from *Adventures of Huckleberry Finn*. By Mark Twain [West Hatfield, Mass.: Pennyroyal Press, 1985]. Wood engraving; 11 x 8. Courtesy of R. Michelson Galleries, Northampton and Amherst, Massachusetts. ©1984 by Barry Moser. Published with the permission of Barry Moser.

141. Arthur Burdett Frost (1851-1928). American. "The Initiation," from *The Story of a Bad Boy*. By T. B. Aldrich [Boston: Houghton Mifflin Company, 1894]. Pen, ink, watercolor, and gouache on paper; 16-3/4 x 10-3/8". Courtesy of The Boston Public Library Print Department, John D. Merriam Collection.

142. Robert McCloskey (born 1914). American. "Homer Building a Radio," from *Homer Price* [New York: The Viking Press, 1943]. Graphite, brush, and ink on grained tracing paper; 7-1/2 x 5-13/16". May Massee Collection, William Allen White Library, Emporia State University. ©1943 by Robert McCloskey, renewed ©1971 by Robert McCloskey. Used by permission of Viking Penguin, a division of Penguin Books USA Inc.

143. Reginald Bathurst Birch (1856-1943). Born in England; Came to the U.S. in 1880. "Mr.Mordaunt Held the Small Hand as he Looked Down at the Child's Face" from *Little Lord Fauntleroy*. By Frances Hodgson Burnett [New York: Charles Scribner's Sons, 1916]. Watercolor and ink on paper; 13-1/2 x 10". Betsy B. Shirley Collection of American Children's Literature, The Beinecke Library of Yale University. Reprinted with the permission of Atheneum Books for Young Readers, an imprint of Simon & Schuster Children's Publishing Division.

144. Reginald Bathurst Birch (1856-1943). Born in England; Came to the U.S. in 1880. "Gaily the troubador touched the guitar," from *Little Men*. By Louisa May Alcott [Boston: Little Brown & Co., 1901]. Pen, ink, and gouache on paper; 20-5/8 x 12-3/8". Courtesy of The Boston Public Library Print Department.

145. Jessie Willcox Smith (1863-1935). American. "Little Women" ca. 1915, from *Boys and Girls of Bookland* [New York: Cosmopolitan Book Corporation, 1923]. Mixed media on illustration board; 19-3/4 x 18". Collection of the Brandywine

River Museum. Gift of the Women's Club of Ardmore, Haverford, Pennsylvania.

146. Barbara Cooney (born 1917). American. "The Nightly Sing at the Piano," from *Little Women*. By Louisa May Alcott [New York: Crowell, 1955]. Scratchboard; 6-11/16 x 4-1/8". Courtesy of The Boston Public Library Print Department. ©1955 by Barbara Cooney. ©1940 by Margret E. Rey. Used by permission of HarperCollins Publishers.

147a. Howard Pyle (1853-1911). American. "Yankee Doodle by the Cannon," from *Yankee Doodle, an Old Friend in a New Dress* [New York: Dodd, Mead and Company, 1881]. Watercolor on illustration board; 9 x 8-1/2". Delaware Art Museum, Bequest of Joseph Bancroft, 1940.2704.

147b. Howard Pyle (1853-1911). American "Washington Reviewing the Citizenry," from *Yankee Doodle, an Old Friend in a New Dress*. [New York: Dodd, Mead and Company, 1881]. Watercolor on illustration board; 9 x 8-1/2". Delaware Art Museum, Bequest of Joseph Bancroft, 1940.2705.

148. Howard Pyle (1853-1911). American. "This is the way that one in Cap and Motley stops for awhile along the stony Path of Life to Make you laugh," ca. 1883 from *Pepper and Salt*. [New York: Harper & Brothers, 1886]. Pen and ink on paper; 14-7/8 x 10-5/8". Collection of the Brandywine River Museum, Museum Volunteers' Purchase Fund, 1985.

149. Howard Pyle (1853-1911). American. "Robin Shooteth His Last Shaft," from *The Merry Adventures of Robin Hood* [New York: Charles Scribner's Sons, 1883]. Pen and ink on paper; 6-3/4 x 9-1/2". The New York Public Library, Central Children's Room, Donnell Library Center. Reprinted with the permission of Scribner, an imprint of Simon & Schuster.

150. Walter Crane (1845-1915). British. "The Golden Bird," from *Household Stories from the Collection of the Bros. Grimm* [London: Macmillan and Company, 1882]. Pen and ink on paper; 9-1/2 x 6-1/4". Mazza Collection Galleria, The University of Findlay.

151. Walter Crane (1845-1915). British. Cover from *Household Stories from the Collection of the Bros. Grimm* [London: Macmillan and Company, 1882]. Gouache over graphite on paper; 7-7/8 x 6-7/8". Justin G. Schiller (Personal Collection).

152. N. C. Wyeth (1882-1945). American. "The Passing of Robin Hood," from *Robin Hood*. By Paul Creswick [Philadelphia: David McKay Company, 1917]. Oil on canvas; 40 x 32". The

New York Public Library, Central Children's Room, Donnell Library Center. Photography courtesy of the Brandywine River Museum.

153. N. C. Wyeth (1882-1945). American. "One more step, Mr. Hands," said I, "and I'll blow your brains out!," from *Treasure Island*. By Robert Louis Stevenson [New York: Charles Scribner's Sons, 1911] . Oil on canvas; 47-1/2 x 38-1/2". Lent by the New Britain Museum of American Art, Harriet Russell Stanley Fund. Photo Credit: Michael Agee. Reprinted with the permission of Atheneum Books for Young Readers, an imprint of Simon & Schuster Children's Publishing Division.

154. John R. Neill (1877-1943). American. *Treasure Island*, 1914, by Robert Louis Stevenson [unpublished]. Pen, ink, and watercolor on paper; 26 x 18". Collection of Natalie Neill Mather.

155. Frank Schoonover (1877-1972). American. "Siege of the Round-House," from *Kidnapped*. By Robert Louis Stevenson [New York: Harper & Brothers, 1921]. Oil on canvas; 43 x 35". Collection of General Edward R. Burka.

156. Frank Schoonover (1877-1972). American. "Fritz Striding with Flamingo," from *Swiss Family Robinson*. By Johann Wyss [New York: Harper & Brothers, 1921]. Oil on canvas; 42 x 34". Collection of General Edward R. Burka.

157. Trina Schart Hyman (born 1939). American. "Then they heard a hideous roaring that filled the air with terror," from *Saint George and the Dragon*. Adapted by Margaret Hodges from Edmund Spenser's *Faerie Queen* [Boston: Little, Brown and Company, 1984]. Acrylic and india ink on paper; 9-3/4 x 20-1/2". Collection of Trina Schart Hyman. ©1984 by Trina Schart Hyman. By permission of Little, Brown and Company.

158a. John Tenniel (1820-1914). British. "The Mad Hatter's Tea Party," from *Alice's Adventures in Wonderland*. By Lewis Carroll [London: Macmillan and Company, 1865]. Graphite on paper; 5-15/16 x 8-15/16". Gift of Mrs. Harcourt Amory, 1927, Houghton Library, Harvard University. Norfolk only.

158b. John Tenniel (1820-1914). British. "Alice with the Flamingo," from *Alice's Adventures in Wonderland*. By Lewis Carroll [London: Macmillan and Company, 1865]. Graphite, ink, and china white on paper; 4-1/16 x 2-15/16". Gift of Mrs. Harcourt Amory, 1927, Houghton Library, Harvard University. Memphis only [not illus.].

158c. John Tenniel (1820-1914). British. "Alice with Tweedledee and Tweedledum," from

Through the Looking-Glass and What Alice Found There. By Lewis Carroll [London: Macmillan and Company, 1871]. Graphite on illustration board; 5-1/8 x 7-1/8". Gift of Mrs. Harcourt Amory, 1927, Houghton Library, Harvard University. Wilmington only [not illus.].

159. Jessie Willcox Smith (1863-1935). American. "Mrs. Bedonebyasyoudid," from *The Water Babies*. By Charles Kingsley [New York: Dodd, Mead & Company, 1916]. Charcoal, watercolor, and oil on illustration board; 22-3/4 x 18-1/2". Prints and Photographs Division, The Library of Congress.

160. Arthur Rackham (1867-1939). British. "A Hundred flew off with the String and Peter clung to the tail," from *Peter Pan in Kensington Gardens*. By J. M. Barrie [London: Hodder & Stoughton, 1906]. Pen, ink, and watercolor on paper; 8-1/4 x 10". Collection of Kendra Krienke and Allan Daniel, New York City.

161. Arthur Rackham (1867-1939). British. "Butter is Got from the Roots of an Old Tree," from *Peter Pan in Kensington Gardens*. By J. M. Barrie [London: Hodder & Stoughton, 1906]. Pen, ink, watercolor, and gouache on paper; 11-3/16 x 7-3/16". Beinecke Rare Book and Manuscript Library, Yale University. Reprinted with the permission of Atheneum Books for Young Readers, an imprint of Simon & Schuster Children's Publishing Division. [Norfolk only].

162. Trina Schart Hyman (born 1939). American. "Up and down they went, and round and round," from *Peter Pan*. By J. M. Barrie [New York: Charles Scribner's Sons, 1980]. Acrylic and india ink on paper; 7-5/16 x 4-3/8". Collection of Trina Schart Hyman. ©1980 by Trina Schart Hyman. Reprinted with the permission of Atheneum Books for Young Readers, an imprint of Simon & Schuster Children's Publishing Division.

163. W. W. Denslow (1865-1915). American. "The soldier with the green whiskers led them through the streets," from *The Wonderful Wizard of Oz*. By L. Frank Baum [Chicago: George M. Hill Company, 1900]. Pen and ink on paper; 14-7/16 x 10-13/16". Print Collection, The Miriam and Ira D. Wallach Division of Art, Prints and Photographs, The New York Public Library, Astor, Lenox and Tilden Foundations.

164. Charles Santore (born 1935). American. "The soldier with the green whiskers led them through the streets," from *The Wizard of Oz*. By L. Frank Baum [New York: JellyBean Press, 1991]. Watercolor and ink on paper; 15-3/4 x 23-1/2". Collection of Olenka and Charles Santore. ©1991 by Charles Santore. Published with the permission of Charles Santore.

165. John R. Neill (1877-1943). American. "Drinking the Health of Princess Ozma of Oz," 1909, from *The Road to Oz*. By L. Frank Baum [Chicago: Reilly & Britton Company, 1909]. Pen and ink on illustration board; 18-1/2 x 13-1/4". Private Collection.

166. William Pène du Bois (1916-1993). American. "Jettisoning Ballast from 'The Globe'," from *The Twenty-one Balloons* [New York: The Viking Press, 1947]. Pen, ink, and wash on paper; 9 x 6-1/4". Mazza Collection Galleria, The University of Findlay. ©1947 by William Pène du Bois. ren. ©1975 by William Pène du Bois. Used by permission of Viking Penguin, a division of Penguin Books USA Inc.

167. Nancy Ekholm Burkert (born 1933). American. "Everyone can have some!," from *James and the Giant Peach*. By Roald Dahl [New York: Alfred A. Knopf, Inc., 1961]. India ink on paper; 11-1/2 x 8". Lent by the Artist. ©1961 by Nancy Ekholm Burkert. Reprinted with permission of Alfred A. Knopf, Inc., an imprint of Random House, Inc.

168. Feodor Rojankovsky (1891-1970). Born in Mitava, Russia; Came to the U.S. in 1941. "By the campfire at night he talked with a trader named Finley . . . ," from *Daniel Boone: Historic Adventure of an American Hunter among the Indians*. By Esther Averill and Lila Stanley [Paris: Domino Press, 1931]. Graphite, colored pencil, and gouache on paper; 8-3/8 x 5-3/4". The Kerlan Collection, University of Minnesota.

169. Ingri Parin d'Aulaire (1904-1980) Born in Konigsberg, Norway; Came to the U.S. in 1929 and Edgar Parin d'Aulaire (1898-1986) Born in Munich, Germany; Came to the U.S. in 1929. "Abe Reading by the Fire," from *Abraham Lincoln* [Garden City, L.I.: Doubleday, Doran and Company, 1939]. Lithograph; 11 x 8". The Kerlan Collection, University of Minnesota. ©1939, 1957 by Doubleday, a division of Bantam Doubleday Dell Publishing Group, Inc. Used by permission of Doubleday, a division of Bantam Doubleday Dell Publishing Group, Inc.

170. James Daugherty (1889-1974). American. "Lincoln Leading the Parade in the Wake of Emancipation," from *Abraham Lincoln* [New York: The Viking Press, 1943]. Lithographic proof; 9-1/2 x 6-3/4". May Massee Collection, William Allen White Library, Emporia State University. ©1943 by James Daugherty. Used by permission of Viking Penguin, a division of Penguin Books USA Inc.

171. Brian Pinkney (born 1961). American. "Benjamin Banneker riding along the shore of the Chesapeake," from *Dear Benjamin Banneker*. By

Andrea Davis Pinkney [New York: Gulliver Books, 1994]. Scratchboard and oil paint; 10 x 15". Collection of Brian Pinkney. ©1994 by Brian Pinkney. Reprinted with permission of Gulliver Books, an imprint of Harcourt Brace & Company.

172a. Robert Lawson (1892-1957). American. "Ben Flying Kite with Amos on his knee," from *Ben and Me* [New York: Dell Publishing Co., 1939]. Pen and ink on paper; 6-7/8 x 9-1/2". The Betsy Beinecke Shirley Collection of American Children's Literature in the Beinecke Rare Book and Manuscript Library at Yale University. ©1939 by Robert Lawson; ©renewed 1967 by John W. Boyd. By permission of Little, Brown and Company. Norfolk only.

172b. Robert Lawson (1892-1957). American. "Ben in Paris, fixing his cravat," from *Ben and Me* [New York: Dell Publishing Co., 1939]. Pen and ink on illustration board; 9-3/4 x 5-5/16". Rare Book Department, The Free Library of Philadelphia. Memphis only [not illus.].

172c. Robert Lawson (1892-1957). American. "Amos Riding in Ben's Hat with 'Stop' and 'Go' Sign," from *Ben and Me* [New York: Dell Publishing Co., 1939]. Pen and ink on illustration board; 14-1/2 x 11-1/2". Rare Book Department, The Free Library of Philadelphia. Wilmington only [not illus.].

173. Alice Provensen (born 1918) and Martin Provensen (1916-1987). American. "Bleriot V and VI," from *The Glorious Flight: Across the Channel with Louis Blériot July 25, 1909* [New York: The Viking Press, 1983]. Pen, ink, and acrylic on paper; 8 x 12-3/8". Mazza Collection Galleria, The University of Findlay. ©1983 by Alice and Martin Provensen. Used by permission of Viking Penguin, a division of Penguin Books USA Inc.

174. Allen Say (born 1937). Born in Yokohama, Japan; Came to the U.S. ca. 1953. "Sure enough, the first rancher I saw gave me the nod," from *El Chino* [Boston: Houghton Mifflin Company, 1990]. Watercolor on paper; 9-3/8 x 8-3/4". Collection of Allen Say. ©1990 by Allen Say. Reprinted with permission of Houghton Mifflin Company.

175. Allen Say (born 1937). Born in Yokohama, Japan; Came to the U.S. ca. 1953. "He met many people along the way," from *Grandfather's Journey* [Boston: Houghton Mifflin Company, 1993]. Watercolor on paper; 11 x 12-1/8". Collection of Allen Say. ©by Allen Say. Reprinted with permission of Houghton Mifflin Company.

V. AND THEY LIVED HAPPILY EVER AFTER

176a. George Cruikshank (1792-1878). British. "Cinderella and the Glass Slipper," from *The Fairy*

Library [London: David Bogue, 1854]. Graphite and watercolor on paper; 5-7/8 x 4-5/16". Bequest of John T. Spaulding, Courtesy, Museum of Fine Arts, Boston.

176b. George Cruikshank (1792-1878). British. "Cinderella and the Glass Slipper," from *The Fairy Library* [London: David Bogue, 1854]. India proof etching on china paper; 7-5/16 x 4-7/8". Department of Rare Books and Special Collections, Princeton University Libraries.

177a. Felix O. C. Darley (1822-1888). American. "Cinderella with Fairy Godmother" from *Grandfather Lovechild's Nursery. Stories.* By Fred Fearnought [Philadelphia: George B. Zieber, 1847]. Graphite on paper; 5-13/16 x 4-9/16". Department of Rare Books and Special Collections, Princeton University Libraries.

177b. Felix O. C. Darley (1822-1888). American. "Cinderella Trying on Slipper," from *Grandfather Lovechild's Nursery Stories.* By Fred Fearnought [Philadelphia: George B. Zieber, 1847]. Graphite on paper; 5-13/16 x 4-11/16". Department of Rare Books and Special Collections, Princeton University Libraries.

178. Leonard Weisgard (born 1916). American. "Cinderella Trying on Slipper," from *Cinderella* [Garden City, L. I.: Doubleday, 1938). Gouache over graphite on board; 11 x 15-1/8". Department of Special Collections, University of Oregon Library. ©1938 by Leonard Weisgard. Used by permission of Doubleday, a division of Bantam Doubleday Dell Publishing Group, Inc.

179. Marcia Brown (born 1918). American. "Cinderella Going to Ball," from *Cinderella* [New York: Charles Scribner's Sons, 1954). Pen, ink, and watercolor on paper; 9 x 15-5/8". Mazza Collection Galleria, The University of Findlay. ©1954 by Marcia Brown. Reprinted with the permission of Atheneum Books for Young Readers, an imprint of Simon & Schuster Children's Publishing Division.

180. James Marshall (1942-1992). American. "'My turn!,' cried the younger step-sister, thrusting her pudgy foot at the prince," from *Cinderella* [Boston: Little, Brown and Company, 1989]. Watercolor over graphite on paper; 12-3/8 x 9". Northeast Children's Literature Collections, Archives and Special Collections Department, Senator Thomas J. Dodd Research Center, University Libraries, University of Connecticut, Storrs. ©1989 by James Marshall. By permission of Little, Brown and Company.

181. Anita Lobel (born 1934). Born in Cracow, Poland; Came to the U.S. in 1952. "While they were dancing, he slipped a tiny gold ring on her finger," from *Princess Furball.* By Charlotte Huck [New York: Greenwillow Books, 1989]. Watercolor and gouache on paper; 8-3/4 x 10-7/8". Collection of Anita Lobel. ©1989 by Anita Lobel. By permission of Greenwillow Books, a division of William Morrow and Company, Inc.

182. John Steptoe (1950-1989). American. "On the seat of the great chief's stool lay the little garden snake," from *Mufaro's Beautiful Daughters* [New York: Lothrop, Lee & Shepard Books, 1987]. Colored ink, graphite, and watercolor on paper; 11-1/2 x 18-1/2". The John Steptoe Collection. ©1987 by John Steptoe. Reprinted with the approval of the Estate of John Steptoe and Lothrop, Lee & Shepard Books, an imprint of William Morrow.

183. Walter Crane (1845-1915). British. "Puss Kills the Ogre," from *Puss in Boots* [London: George Routledge and Sons, 1873]. Pen, black ink, and watercolor over graphite on paper; 8-5/8 x 6-9/16". Gift of Mrs. John L. Gardner, Courtesy, Museum of Fine Arts, Boston.

184. Marcia Brown (born 1918). American. "Puss Blowing Trumpet," Frontispiece from *Puss in Boots* [New York: Charles Scribner's Sons, 1952]. Pen, ink, and gouache on paper; 14-1/2 x 11". de Grummond Children's Literature Collection, University of Southern Mississippi. ©1952 by Marcia Brown. Reprinted with the permission of Atheneum Books for Young Readers, an imprint of Simon & Schuster Children's Publishing Division.

185. W. W. Denslow (1856-1915). American. "Little Red Riding Hood meets the Wolf," from *Denslow's Little Red Riding Hood* [New York: G. W. Dillingham, 1903]. Pen and ink on paper; 10-1/2 x 8". de Grummond Children's Literature Collection, University of Southern Mississippi.

186. Edward Gorey (born 1925). American. "And the wicked wolf, without more ado, ate Red Riding Hood and the little cake, too," from *Red Riding Hood.* By Beatrice Schenk de Regniers [New York: Atheneum Books, 1972]. Pen and ink on paper; 5 x 5". Collection of Edward Gorey, Courtesy of Gotham Book Mart Gallery, New York City. ©1972 by Edward Gorey. Reprinted with the permission of Atheneum Books for Young Readers, an imprint of Simon & Schuster Children's Publishing Division.

187. Trina Schart Hyman (born 1939). American. "Little Red Riding Approaching Wolf in Bed," from *Little Red Riding Hood* [New York: Holiday House, 1983]. Pen, india ink, and acrylic on paper; 9-3/8 x 17". Collection of Trina Schart Hyman.

©1983 by Trina Schart Hyman. Reprinted with the permission of Holiday House.

188. Ed Young (born 1931). Born in Tianjin, China; Came to the U.S. in 1951. "Shang and Sisters in Tree Looking Down at Wolf," from *Lon Po Po, A Red-Riding Hood Story from China* [New York: Philomel Books, 1989]. Oil pastel on paper; 16-1/2 x 10-1/2". Collection of Ed Young. ©1989 by Ed Young. Reprinted with permission of Philomel Books, an imprint of the Putnam & Grosset Group; McIntosh and Otis, Inc.; and Ed Young.

189. Kay Nielsen (1886-1957). Born in Copenhagen, Denmark, came to America in 1936. "Snow Drop," from *Hansel and Gretel and Other Stories. By the Brothers Grimm* [London: Hodder & Stoughton, 1925]. Watercolor and gold paint on paper; 13-1/4 x 9-3/4". Courtesy of The Boston Public Library Print Department, John D. Merriam Collection. Used by permission of Hodder & Stoughton.

190a. Nancy Ekholm Burkert (born 1933). American. ". . . in the evening they came back . . . ," from *Snow White and the Seven Dwarfs; A Tale from the Brothers Grimm.* Translated by Randall Jarrell [New York: Farrar, Straus & Giroux, Inc., 1972]. Colored inks and watercolor on paper; 12 x 18". Lent by the Artist. ©1972 by Nancy Ekholm Burkert. Reprinted by permission of Farrar, Straus & Giroux, Inc.

190b. Nancy Ekholm Burkert (born 1933). American. "...a poisoned apple...," from *Snow White and the Seven Dwarfs: A Tale from The Brothers Grimm.* Translated by Randall Jarrell [New York: Farrar, Straus & Giroux, Inc. 1972]. Dry brush, watercolor, and ink on paper; 12 x 17-3/4". Collection of the Brandywine River Museum, Museum Volunteers' Purchase Fund, 1982. ©1972 by Nancy Ekholm Burkert. Reprinted by permission of Farrar, Straus & Giroux, Inc.

191. Maurice Sendak (born 1928). American. "Snow White and the Seven Dwarfs," from *The Juniper Tree and Other Tales from Grimm*, selected by Lore Segal and Maurice Sendak. Translated by Randall Jarrell [New York: Farrar, Straus & Giroux, Inc., 1973]. Pen and ink on paper; 4-3/4 x 4". ©1973 by Maurice Sendak. Courtesy, Maurice Sendak and The Rosenbach Museum & Library. Reprinted by permission of Farrar, Straus & Giroux, Inc.

192. Gustaf Tenggren (1896-1970). Born in Magra, Sweden; Came to the U.S. in 1920. "Jack Stealing Gold," 1930, from *Jack and the Beanstalk* [unpublished] . Tempera on board; 13-1/4 x 11-15/16". The Kerlan Collection, University of Minnesota.

193. Gustaf Tenggren (1896-1970). Born in Magra, Sweden; Came to the U.S. in 1920 "Rapunzel in the Tower," from "Rapunzel," in *The Tenggren Tell-It-Again Book* [Boston: Little, Brown and Company, 1942] . Tempera on paper, mounted on board; 12-5/8 x 10-3/16". The Kerlan Collection, University of Minnesota. By permission of Little, Brown and Company.

194. Tasha Tudor (born 1915). American. "The Real Princess," from *Fairy Tales from Hans Christian Andersen* [New York: Henry Z. Walck, Incorporated, 1945]. Pen, ink, watercolor, and gouache on paper; 9-1/4 x 6-3/8". The Kerlan Collection, University of Minnesota.

195. Margot Tomes (1917-1991). American. "The boy was almost beside himself with curiosity," from *Wanda Gág's The Sorcerer's Apprentice* [New York: Coward-McCann & Geoghegan, Inc., 1979]. Pen and ink on paper; 4-1/2 x 3-1/2". The Kerlan Collection, University of Minnesota. ©1979 by Margot Tomes. Reprinted with permission of Coward-McCann, an imprint of The Putnam & Grosset Group.

196. Leo Dillon (born 1933) and Diane Dillon (born 1933). American. Cover from *The Porcelain Cat. By Michael Patrick Hearn* [Boston: Little, Brown and Company, 1987] . Airbrushed watercolor on paper; 11-3/16 x 15-3/16". Private Collection. ©1987 by Leo and Diane Dillon. By permission of Little, Brown and Company.

197. Margot Zemach (1931-1989). American. "Between times, she scratched a Tune on a fiddle," from *Duffy and the Devil.* Retold by Harve Zemach [New York: Farrar, Straus & Giroux, Inc., 1973]. Pen, ink, and watercolor on paper; 11 x 9-1/2". Collection of Kaephe Zemach-Bersin. ©1973 by Margot Zemach. Reprinted by permission of Farrar, Straus & Giroux, Inc.

198. Paul O. Zelinsky (born 1953). American. "Rumpelstiltskin spinning," from *Rumpelstiltskin* [New York: Dutton Children's Books, 1986]. Watercolor and oil on paper; 14-3/4 x 10-7/8". Collection of Paul O. Zelinsky. ©1986 by Paul O. Zelinksy. Used by permission of Dutton Children's Books, a division of Penguin Books USA Inc.

199a. Tomi Ungerer (born 1931). Born in Strasbourg, France; Came to the U.S. in 1957. "Such was her pity for the hungry giant that she used up half of her market supplies," from *Zeralda's Ogre* [New York: Delacorte Press, 1967]. Chinese ink on tracing paper; 13-13/16 x 11". Donation Tomi Ungerer, Musées de la Ville de Strasbourg. ©1967 by Tomi Ungerer.

199b. Tomi Ungerer (born 1931). Born in Strasbourg, France; Came to the U.S. in 1957 "Such was her pity for the hungry giant that she used up half of her market supplies," from *Zeralda's Ogre* [New York: Delacorte Press, 1967]. Wash drawing of colored inks on paper; 14-7/16 x 11-7/16". Donation Tomi Ungerer, Musées de la Ville de Strasbourg. ©1967 by Tomi Ungerer.

200. Kay Nielsen (1886-1957). Born in Copenhagen, Denmark; Came to the U.S. in 1936. "The Lad in Battle," from *East of the Sun and West of Moon; Old Tales from the North*. By Peter Christian Asbjornsen [London: Hodder & Stoughton, 1914]. Pen and ink, brush and ink with watercolor heightened with gilt on whatman board; 13-15/16 x 10-1/4". Collection of Kendra Krienke and Allan Daniel, New York City.

201. Edmund Dulac (1882-1953). Born in France, settled in England in 1904. "As soon as he came in, she began to jeer at him," from *Stories from the Arabian Nights* [London: Hodder & Stoughton, 1907]. Pen, ink, and watercolor on paper; 11-7/8 x 9-9/16". Collection of Ann Conolly Hughey.

202. Boris Artzybasheff (1899-1965). Born in Kharkov, Ukraine; Came to the U.S. in 1919. "King Douda and Princess Helena at their Wedding Banquet," from *Seven Simeons: A Russian Tale Retold.* [New York: The Viking Press, 1937]. Pen, ink, and gouache on illustration board; 10-7/16 x 7/8". May Massee Collection, William Allen White Library, Emporia State University. ©1937 by Boris Avtzybasheff, renewed ©1964 by Boris Avtzyasheff. Used by permission of Viking Penguin, a division of Penguin Books USA Inc.

203a. Uri Shulevitz (born 1935). Born in Warsaw, Poland; Came to the U.S. in 1959. "They flew over the faggot gatherer," from *The Fool of the World and the Flying Ship*. Retold by Arthur Ransome [New York: Farrar, Straus & Giroux, Inc. 1968]. Pen, ink, and watercolor on paper; 11-1/2 x 23-3/16". Collection of Uri Shulevitz. ©1968 by Uri Shulevitz. Reprinted by permission of Farrar, Straus & Giroux, Inc.

203b. Uri Shulevitz (born 1935). Born in Warsaw, Poland; Came to the U.S. in 1959. "They flew over the faggot gatherer," 1968, from *The Fool of the World and the Flying Ship*. Retold by Arthur Ransome [New York: Farrar, Straus & Giroux, Inc., 1968]. Pen and ink on paper; 6 x 11-1/16". Collection of Uri Shulevitz. [not illus.].

204. Uri Shulevitz (born 1935). Born in Warsaw, Poland; Came to the U.S. in 1959. "Feitel's Reign," from *Fools of Chelm and Their History*. By Isaac Bashevis Singer [New York: Farrar, Straus & Giroux, Inc., 1973] . Pen and ink on paper; 7-1/4 x 6". Collection of Uri Shulevitz. ©1973 by Uri Shulevitz. Reprinted by permission of Farrar, Straus & Giroux, Inc.

205. Uri Shulevitz (born 1935). Born in Warsaw, Poland; Came to the U.S. in 1959. "Moving a Mountain" from *The Diamond Tree: Jewish Tales from Around the World*, selected and retold by Howard Schwartz and Barbara Rush [New York: HarperCollins Publishers, 1991]. Pen, ink, and watercolor on paper; 11-1/8 x 8-3/4". Collection of Uri Shulevitz. ©1991 by Uri Shulevitz. Used by permission of HarperCollins Publishers.

206. Charles Mikolaycak (1937-1993). American. Cover from *Orpheus* [San Diego: Harcourt Brace Johanovich, Publishers, 1992]. Colored pencil, watercolor, and acrylic on paper; 9-1/2 x 7". From the Collection of Mr. and Mrs. Edward E. Wilson. ©1995 by Carole Kismaric Mikolaycak. Reprinted with permission of Harcourt Brace & Company.

207. Gennady Spirin (born 1948). Born in Russia; Came to the U.S. in 1991. Cover from *Sorotchintzy Fair*. By Nikolai Gogol [Esslingen: Esslinger Verlag J. F. Schreiber GmbH, 1990]. Watercolor on paper; 13 x 18-1/2". From the Collection of Rose Sarkisian. ©1990 by Gennady Spirin. Reprinted by permission of Esslinger Verlag J. F. Schreiber Gmbh.

208. Arthur Burdett Frost (1851-1928). American. "Uncle Remus Telling Stories," Frontispiece from *Uncle Remus: His Songs and His Sayings*. By Joel Chandler Harris [New York: D. Appleton & Co., 1895]. Gouache on paper; 18 x 11". Collection of Mr. and Mrs. Henry M. Reed.

209. Arthur Burdett Frost (1851-1928). American. "He Laffed en laffed," from "The Wonderful Tar-Baby Story," from *Uncle Remus: His Songs and His Sayings*. By Joel Chandler Harris [New York: D. Appleton & Co., 1895] . Pen and ink on paper; 10-3/8 x 12-1/2". Print Collection, The Miriam and Ira D. Wallach Division of Art, Prints and Photographs, The New York Public Library, Astor, Lenox and Tilden Foundations.

210a. Edward Gorey (born 1925). American. "The Tar Baby," from *Brer Rabbit and His Tricks*. Retold by Ennis Rees [New York: Young Scott Books, 1967]. Pen and ink on paper; 6-1/4 x 7-3/4". Collection of Edward Gorey, courtesy of Gotham Book Mart Gallery, New York City. ©1967 by Edward Gorey. Published with permission of Edward Gorey.

210b. Edward Gorey (born 1925). American. "The Tar Baby," from *Brer Rabbit and His Tricks*. Retold by Ennis Rees [New York: Young Scott Books, 1967]. Pen and ink on paper ; 6-1/4 x 7-3/4".

Collection of Edward Gorey, courtesy of Gotham Book Mart Gallery, New York City. ©1967 by Edward Gorey. Published with permission of Edward Gorey.

211. Jerry Pinkney (born 1939). American. "The Tar Baby," from *The Tales of Uncle Remus*. Retold by Julius Lester [New York: Dial Books, 1987]. Graphite and watercolor on paper; 12-1/2 x 17". Collection of Jerry Pinkney. ©1987 by Jerry Pinkney, illustrations. Used by permission of Dial Books for Young Readers, a division of Penguin Books USA Inc.

212. Barry Moser (born 1940). American. "Brer Rabbit," from *Jump! The Adventures of Brer Rabbit*. By Joel Chandler Harris [San Diego: Harcourt, Brace and Johanovich, 1986]. Watercolor over pencil with ink highlights on paper; 12-1/2 x 10". Justin G. Schiller (Personal Collection). ©1986 by Pennyroyal Press, Inc., reproduced by permission of Harcourt Brace & Company.

213. Robert Lawson (1892-1957). American. "Two Stories Above the Potato Face Blind Man," ca. 1922, from *The Rootabaga Stories*, from *The Designer*. By Carl Sandburg [*The Designer*, 1922-23]. Pen and ink on paper; 21-1/2 x 15". May Massee Collection, William Allen White Library, Emporia State University.

214. Maud Petersham (1890-1971) American, and Miska Petersham (1888-1960) Born in Hungary; Came to the U.S. in 1912. "There on a high stool in a high tower, on a high hill sits the Head spotter of the Weather Makers," from *The Rootabaga Stories*. By Carl Sandburg [New York: Harcourt Brace & Company, 1922]. Pen and ink on poster-board; 12 x 9-1/16". de Grummond Children's Literature Collection, University of Southern Mississippi. Reproduced by permission of Harcourt, Brace and Company.

215a. Peggy Bacon (1895-1987). American. "How the Animals Lost Their Tails and Got Them Back Traveling from Philadelphia to Medicine Hat," from Rootabaga Country: Selections from *Rootabaga Stories and Rootabaga Pigeons*. By Carl Sandburg [New York: Harcourt Brace and Company, 1922; 1929 edition]. Pen, ink, and graphite on paper; 7-1/2 x 7-1/2". Courtesy of Kraushaar Galleries. ©1922, 1923, 1929 by Harcourt Brace and Company, Inc.

215b. Peggy Bacon (1895-1987). American. "Hot Balloons Used to Open the Window in the Morning," from *Rootabaga Country: Selections from Rootabaga Stories and Rootabaga Pigeons*. By Carl Sandburg [New York: Harcourt Brace and Company, 1922; 1929 edition]. Pen and ink on paper; 10-5/8 x 7-3/8". Private Collection. ©1929

by Harcourt Brace & Company and renewed 1957 by Peggy Bacon, reproduced by permission of the publisher.

216. Dorothy Pulls Lathrop (1891-1980). American. Frontispiece from *Hitty: Her First Hundred Years*. By Rachel Field [New York: Macmillan Publishing Company, 1929]. Pen, ink, and watercolor over graphite; 4-1/2 x 5-3/4". The New York Public Library, Central Children's Room, Donnell Library Center. ©1929 by Macmillan Publishing Company, a division of Macmillan, Inc. ©1957 renewed by Arthur S. Pederson.

217. Leo Dillon (born 1933) and Diane Dillon (born 1933). American. "Mosquito Buzzing in Ear," from *Why Mosquitoes Buzz in People's Ears*. By Verna Aardema [New York: Dial Books for Young Readers, 1975]. Airbrushed watercolor on paper; 10-1/4 x 20-1/4". Collection of Leo and Diane Dillon. ©1975 by Leo and Diane Dillon, illustrations. Used by permission of Dial Books for Young Readers, a division of Penguin Books USA Inc.

218. Ashley Bryan (born 1923). American. "The husband Who counted spoonfuls," from *Beat the Story Drum, Pum-Pum* [New York: Atheneum, 1980]. Tempera on paper; 8-1/16 x 5-3/4". Collection of Ashley Bryan. ©1980 by Ashley Bryan. Reprinted with the permission of Atheneum Books for Young Readers, an imprint of Simon & Schuster Children's Publishing Division.

219. Ashley Bryan (born 1923). American. "The Foolish Boy," from *The Lion and the Ostrich Chicks* [New York: Atheneum, 1986]. Tempera on illustration board; 8 x 5-5/8". Collection of Ashley Bryan. ©1986 by Ashley Bryan. Reprinted with the permission of Atheneum Books for Young Readers, an imprint of Simon & Schuster Children's Publishing Division.

220. Jerry Pinkney (born 1939). American. Cover from *The Talking Eggs*. Retold by Robert D. San Souci [New York: Dial Books for Young Readers, 1989]. Graphite and watercolor on paper; 11-3/8 x 22". Collection of Jerry Pinkney. ©1989 by Jerry Pinkney, illustrations. Used by permission of Dial Books for Young Readers, a division of Penguin Books USA Inc.

221. Brian Pinkney (born 1961). American. "Sukey Meets the Mermaid on the Beach," from *Sukey and the Mermaid*. Retold by Robert D. San Souci [New York: Four Winds Press, 1992]. Scratchboard and oil; 10 x 18". Collection of Brian Pinkney. ©1992 by Brian Pinkney. Reprinted with the permission of Simon & Schuster Books for Young Readers, an imprint of Simon & Schuster Children's Publishing Division.

222. Frederick Richardson (1862-1937). American. "The Griffin and the Minor Canon," from *The Queen's Museum and Other Fanciful Tales*. By Frank R. Stockton [New York: Charles Scribner's Sons, 1906]. Pen, ink, and watercolor on paper; 20-3/4 x 14-5/16". Private Collection. Reprinted with the permission of Scribner, an imprint of Simon & Schuster.

223. Leonard Baskin (born 1922). American. "Gargoyle," from *Did You Say Ghosts?* By Richard Michelson [New York: Macmillan Publishing Company, 1994]. Watercolor on paper; 10 x 8". Courtesy of R. Michelson Galleries, Northampton and Amherst, Massachusetts. ©1994 by Leonard Baskin. Reprinted with the permission of Simon & Schuster Books for Young Readers, an imprint of Simon & Schuster Children's Publishing Division.

224. Marcia Brown (born 1918). American. "Mouse Running from Crow," from *Once A Mouse* [New York: Charles Scribner's Sons, 1961]. Colored woodcut; 12-5/8 x 18-7/8". de Grummond Children's Literature Collection, University of Southern Mississippi. ©1961 by Marcia Brown. Reprinted with the permission of Atheneum Books for Young Readers, an imprint of Simon & Schuster Children's Publishing Division.

225. Ed Young (born 1931). Born in Tianjin, China; Came to the U.S. in 1951. "On Monday, Red Mouse went first to find out," from *Seven Blind Mice*. [New York: Philomel Books, 1992]. Mixed media and collage; 15 x 27". Collection of Ed Young. ©1989 by Ed Young. Reprinted with permission of Philomel Books, an imprint of the Putnam & Grosset Group; McIntosh and Otis, Inc.; and Ed Young.

226. Eric Carle (born 1929). American. "Turtle and Rabbit," 1980, from *Eric Carle's Treasury of Classic Stories* [New York: Orchard Books, 1988]. Mixed media collage on paper; 30 x 20". Collection of the Artist. Loan arranged courtesy of R. Michelson Galleries, Northampton and Amherst, Massachusetts. ©1992 by Eric Carle. Published with the permission of Eric Carle.

227. Charles Santore (born 1935). American. "The Hare and the Tortoise," from *Aesop's Fables* [New York: JellyBean Press, 1988]. Watercolor and ink on paper; 15-3/4 x 23-1/2". Collection of Olenka and Charles Santore. ©1988 by Charles Santore. Published with the permission of Charles Santore.

228. Leo Lionni (born 1910). Born in Amsterdam, The Netherlands; Came to the U.S. in 1939. "Alexander and the Wind-up Mouse," from *Alexander and the Wind-up Mouse* [New York: Pantheon Books, 1969]. Watercolor and collage on illustration board; 11 x 18-3/8". Collection of Leo Lionni. ©1969 by Leo Lionni. Reprinted with permission of Random House, Inc.

229. Leo Lionni (born 1910). Born in Amsterdam, The Netherlands; Came to the U.S. in 1939. "The fish lay there dreaming," from *Fish is Fish* [New York: Pantheon Books, 1970]. Graphite and colored pencil on illustration board; 10-3/8 x 18-1/2". Collection of Leo Lionni. ©1970 by Leo Lionni. Reprinted with permission of Random House, Inc.

230. Arnold Lobel (1933-1987). American. "The Elephant and his Son," from *Fables* [New York: Harper & Row, 1980]. Pen, ink, and watercolor on paper; 11 x 7". The Estate of Arnold Lobel. ©1980 by Arnold Lobel. Used by permission of HarperCollins Publishers.

231. Jerry Pinkney (born 1939). American. Cover from *John Henry*. Retold by Julius Lester [New York: Dial Books for Young Readers, 1994]. Graphite and watercolor on paper; 14-1/2 x 22-1/2". Collection of Jerry Pinkney. ©1994 by Jerry Pinkney, illustrations. Used by permission of Dial Books for Young Readers, a division of Penguin Books USA Inc.

232. Paul O. Zelinsky (born 1953). American. "Angel Wrestled Tarnation," from *Swamp Angel*. By Anne Isaacs [New York: Dutton Signet, 1994]. Oil on cherry veneer; 17 x 24-3/4". Collection of Paul O. Zelinsky. ©1994 by Paul O. Zelinsky. Used by permission of Dutton Signet, a division of Penguin Books USA Inc.

INDEX

Note: Citations followed by letter "r" denote
reproduced illustrations.